# THE AUTHORS

Pamela Castle is Partner and Head of the Environmental Law Group of McKenna & Co, a specialised group within the Firm monitoring the development of environmental and health and safety legislation on a global basis with a particular emphasis on the United Kingdom, the European Union and Eastern Europe. She holds an honours degree in chemistry and before qualifying as a solicitor worked for a number of years in the petrochemical and pharmaceutical industries. She has been responsible for advising numerous United Kingdom and multi-national industrial clients on all aspects of pollution control legislation in both contentious and non-contentious matters, particularly in relation to waste disposal and contaminated land.

Helen Harrison is the Environmental Information Officer attached to the Environmental Law Group of McKenna & Co. She holds an honours degree in Biology and an MSc in Information Science. Before joining the Firm, she worked for a number of years in the pharmaceutical and chemical industries. Her work at McKenna & Co includes the monitoring and provision of information on United Kingdom, European Union and international legislation for clients and McKenna & Co personnel.

# INTEGRATED POLLUTION CONTROL

## CONTROL

*by*

*Pamela Castle & Helen Harrison*

CAMERON
MAY
*L O N D O N*

Published 1996 by Cameron May Ltd.

ISBN 1 874698 80 5

Printed by Watkiss Studios Ltd

*The authors assert their moral right to be identified as the authors of this work.*

### Acknowledgement

*We would like to thank the HMSO for permission to reproduce sections of the Environmental Protection Act that appear in the appendices.*

# CONTENTS

## Chapter 1 Introduction to IPC

## Chapter 2  Legal and Administrative Framework for IPC

## Chapter 3  Regulation of Prescribed Processes

## Chapter 5  Enforcement of IPC

## Chapter 6  Access to Information Relating to IPC

## Chapter 7 Relationship between IPC and Other Regulatory Systems

## Chapter 8 Developments in IPC at International Level

# INTEGRATED POLLUTION

# CONTROL

# PREFACE

This book describes the legislative and administrative aspects of integrated pollution control ("IPC") in England and Wales as it stands at 30th September 1995. Environmental regulation is changing at a rapid pace and IPC is no exception to this. All environmental regulatory systems must evolve to reflect changes in scientific and technical progress and the emergence of new pollution problems. As a relatively innovative system regulating the most complex industrial processes, IPC will be particularly subject to change and already there have been numerous amendments to this regime. Developments in progress will have an even more significant impact on the legislative and administrative aspects of IPC over the next few years.

The new Environment Agency to be established on 1st April 1996 will combine the functions of Her Majesty's Inspectorate of Pollution, the body responsible for IPC, with the National Rivers Authority and the waste regulation authorities. This will obviously have some implications for the practical application of IPC, for example in relation to the consultation and cooperation procedures currently in existence between these separate bodies and the geographical location of Agency offices. It is understood, however, that the majority of changes will be purely internal management ones and the existing IPC system as it appears to the industrial operator is unlikely to alter to any great extent.

The European Commission's proposal for a Directive on Integrated Pollution Prevention and Control, whilst having strong similarities to the existing IPC system in England and Wales, is likely to require some amendments to domestic legislation to extend the system to additional industry sectors or introduce procedural changes. A Common Position on the proposal has been agreed by the Council of Ministers and a final decision on the Directive should be made soon. The final provisions of the Directive will be very close to those set out in the Common Position in view of the delicate nature of the agreement reached by the Council. If adopted, the Directive must be implemented into national law within three years. Any additional obligations will be immediately applicable to new plant and existing plant will be required to comply within eight years.

Although this book has had to be written to reflect the situation as it exists at the present time, we have endeavoured to look forward and to predict the major changes that are likely to be made in the near future. This has been achieved in two ways. Firstly, where we are aware of potential amendments to specific requirements or procedures, these are highlighted at the appropriate section of the text. Secondly, we have devoted several sections to explaining the broad form that the changes are likely to take and predicting the way in which IPC is likely to be modified to incorporate these.

It is essential that industrial decision makers have sufficient information to enable them to incorporate the practical requirements of forthcoming legislative and administrative changes into their future plans. In view of the considerable resources already expended by industry in implementing IPC, any developments in this area should be monitored closely as they are likely to require at least some action on the part of industry.

Chapter 1

# INTRODUCTION TO IPC

## INTRODUCTION

Integrated Pollution Control ("IPC") was introduced under Part I of the Environmental Protection Act 1990 ("EPA 1990") to regulate what were deemed to be the most potentially polluting or technologically complex industrial processes. It represents a new initiative for environmental protection in the UK. It has had significant financial and operational implications for industry and will continue to require the allocation of considerable resources in the future as and when the system is refined and pollution standards are tightened.

IPC is the simultaneous control of industrial emissions to all three environmental media: air, water and land. Releases to these media are covered by a single authorisation which must be obtained before an industrial process can operate. This approach is intended to have two main benefits: a simpler regulatory system and more effective environmental protection.

This book will focus on the implementation of IPC in England and Wales. The separate IPC regime in Scotland is very similar and shares the same legislative framework, although there are important variations in the areas of administration and enforcement as a result of differences between the regulatory authorities and legal systems in the two jurisdictions. At present, there is no system of IPC in Northern Ireland and industrial emissions are regulated separately by a number of legislative provisions and regulatory authorities. The Government intends to introduce an IPC system which broadly parallels that already in place in Great Britain.

IPC has been implemented progressively in England and Wales since 1st April 1991 and will apply to all the relevant industry sectors by 1st November 1995. It is administered and enforced by Her Majesty's Inspectorate of Pollution ("HMIP") in England and

Wales. In Scotland, the counterparts to HMIP are Her Majesty's Industrial Pollution Inspectorate and the river purification authorities. IPC was introduced in Scotland on 1st April 1992. Responsibilities for IPC will pass to the Environment Agency for England and Wales and the Scottish Environment Protection Agency on their creation in April 1996.

## DEVELOPMENT OF IPC

In England and Wales, IPC has developed in two main stages:

(i) the formation of a single authority (HMIP) with responsibility for emissions to air, water and land; followed by

(ii) the establishment of a regulatory system controlling pollution of these environmental media.

This development will be taken a step further in 1996 when HMIP, the National Rivers Authority ("NRA") and the waste regulation authorities, the bodies administering IPC, water pollution and waste disposal respectively, are amalgamated into a single Environment Agency. Although the regulatory systems themselves will continue to operate separately, the formation of the new organisation may simplify some of the administrative aspects of IPC.

The legislation establishing IPC implemented a number of European Union ("EU") directives: the Air Framework Directive (84/360/EEC); the Large Combustion Plants Directive (38/609/EEC); and the Dangerous Substances into Water Directive (76/464/EEC). These directives contain some important provisions which have been incorporated into the IPC system. In particular, the Air Framework Directive requires the use of Best Available Technology, provided that the application of such measures does not entail excessive costs. This has been reflected in the Best Available Techniques Not Entailing Excessive Cost ("BATNEEC") concept (see later in this Chapter).

EU legislation will continue to have an important impact on IPC in the future. The proposal for a Integrated Pollution Prevention and Control ("IPPC") Directive is likely to result in a number of changes to the existing IPC system to harmonise it with pollution regimes in existence in other EU member states. The provisions of the IPPC proposal and its likely effects on national law are discussed in greater detail in Chapter 8.

Prior to the introduction of IPC in England and Wales, discharges to the different environmental media were regulated independently on a sectoral basis under a variety of legislation and by a number of authorities.

Emissions to air from industrial processes were controlled by the Industrial Air Pollution Inspectorate and, latterly, by HMIP under the Alkali Etc. Works Regulation Act 1906 ("AWRA 1906") and the Health and Safety at Work etc. Act 1974 ("HSWA 1974"). Operators of specific industrial processes were required to register with the regulatory authority and there was a general duty to use "Best Practicable Means" ("BPM") to prevent emissions of noxious or offensive substances and to render any residual emissions harmless and inoffensive. This system was supported by a series of guidance notes setting out the technology considered to be BPM for specific processes and a number of presumptive emission limits, which, if exceeded, indicated that BPM was not being used.

Industrial discharges to controlled waters and sewers were regulated under Part II of the Control of Pollution Act 1974 ("COPA 1974"). This was the responsibility of the regional water authorities and then transferred to the NRA and the sewerage undertakers (that is, the privatised water companies) in 1989. The Water Resources Act 1991 and the Water Industry Act 1991 now control discharges to controlled waters and sewers respectively. The disposal of controlled waste to land was regulated by local waste disposal authorities under Part I of the COPA 1974 until the new waste management provisions of Part II of the EPA 1990 came into effect on 1st May 1994.

However, this sectoral approach was not wholly satisfactory, as it had become increasingly apparent that each environmental medium is not self-contained and that there can be significant movement of pollutants between air, water and land. As dramatically demonstrated by acid rain, pollution of one environmental medium can have serious implications for another, in this case, emissions of acidic gases into air resulting in severe pollution of water and soil. The abatement of emissions into one medium was frequently at the expense of an increase in the release of pollution to another. Where a number of pollution abatement options existed the most straightforward or cheapest method could be selected, regardless of the effect on other sections of the environment.

The existing sectoral controls were thus perceived to be an unsatisfactory and ineffective method of regulating polluting processes and protecting the environment. The relatively large number of regulatory authorities involved also led to inefficiency, an inconsistent and fragmented approach, overlap between the different systems and potential confusion for the industrial companies subject to this regulation.

The introduction of IPC therefore represents a significant shift in the approach taken to pollution control. There have been two main conceptual changes. Firstly, to improve environmental protection, IPC applies a concept (see Section 7 of the EPA 1990) known as "Best Practicable Environmental Option" ("BPEO") to consider the overall effect of polluting emissions on the environment and to determine the optimum method of pollution abatement (see later in this Chapter). Further, BATNEEC is to be used for minimising pollution of the environment taken as a whole having regard to the BPEO. BATNEEC is discussed in more detail in Chapter 3. Secondly, to increase the effectiveness of the administration and enforcement of IPC, a single authority has responsibility for regulating the entire system. These two components have been some time in development and were only recently combined to create the existing IPC system.

BPEO and BATNEEC are an expansion of the BPM concept which has been the basis for the regulation of industrial emissions since the mid 19th Century. BPM balances the benefits of protecting human health and the environment against the costs associated with pollution control measures. In BPM, the term "practicable" takes into account a number of factors, including local conditions and circumstances, financial implications and the current state of knowledge concerning technological solutions and the effects of the substances released. Many aspects of BPM have been incorporated into the BPEO and BATNEEC concepts, but in combination with a requirement to consider the impact of pollution on the environment as a whole. BPEO and BATNEEC therefore have a wider application and are a more powerful tool for environmental protection.

In the UK, the term BPEO first appeared in the Fifth Report of the Royal Commission on Environmental Pollution ("RCEP") "Air Pollution Control - An Integrated Approach". This Report was produced in response to a request from the Secretary of State for the

Environment to examine the effectiveness of air pollution controls and the relationship between the different regulatory authorities involved. It highlighted the problems associated with the movement of pollution between the different environmental media and concluded that a single unified authority with wider responsibilities for pollution control should be created, with the primary aim of ensuring an integrated approach to industrial pollution problems at source to minimise damage to the environment as a whole. The RCEP recommended that this authority should seek the optimum environmental improvement by expanding the BPM concept into BPEO.

The Government did not respond to these recommendations until the publication of Department of the Environment Pollution Paper No. 18 "Air Pollution Control". This was supportive of the BPEO concept, although the recommendation for a unified authority was rejected. However, in 1986 a Cabinet Office Efficiency Unit Scrutiny Report "Inspecting Industry - Pollution and Safety" endorsed the RCEP's recommendation for a single unified authority and an integrated regulatory system. As a result, HMIP was created in April 1987 to combine the three existing pollution inspectorates with responsibility for industrial air emissions, radioactive materials and hazardous waste, together with a new inspectorate regulating discharges to water made by the water authorities.

BPEO was discussed again in the RCEP's Tenth and Eleventh Reports. In 1988, the RCEP produced its Twelfth Report "Best Practicable Environmental Option" which sought to advance the argument for BPEO a stage further and to demonstrate its practical application in preventing and abating industrial pollution. The role of HMIP in achieving this was also discussed and the RCEP recommended that the authority's powers should be extended in cases of industrial processes releasing pollutants to several environmental media and that it should be allowed to impose technology based controls to achieve the BPEO for a specific process or waste.

The RCEP considers that the procedure used to select the BPEO should adhere to the following principles:

· environmental considerations should be introduced into project planning at the earliest possible stage;

· alternative options should be sought diligently and imaginatively in order to identify as complete a set as is possible;

· the identification of potential damage to the environment should be done in such a way as to uncover the unusual and improbable as well as the familiar and likely;

· the context within which the principles above are considered should be sufficiently extensive to cover all the significant aspects of the project, whether local or remote, short or long term, and having regard to the people affected;

· the documentation associated with each project should be structured to make it possible to trace decisions back to the supporting evidence and arguments, so providing an "audit trail";

· the documentation should identify the origins of data used with any relevant information concerning their reliability. It should state the procedures used for evaluation of risks and the reasons for the decisions based on those evaluations;

· in order to assist in taking decisions having social and political implications, scientific evidence must be presented objectively;

· the determination of acceptable cost should take full account of any damage to the environment in addition to monetary costs. Financial considerations should not be overriding;

· there must be appropriate and timely consultation with people and organisations directly affected. The circle of those involved in the taking of the decisions should be appropriately wide; and

· the procedure should be adaptable to incorporate innovations in methods of analysis and decision making.

In practice, the RCEP suggests a BPEO selection and implementation procedure consisting of a number of essential steps. Some steps follow in a logical progression, others may be carried out in parallel or repeated.

**Step 1 : Define the Objective**

State the objective of the project or proposal at the outset, in terms which do not prejudge the means by which that objective is to be achieved.

**Step 2 : Generate Options**

Identify all feasible options for achieving the objective: the aim is to find those which are both practicable and environmentally acceptable. When generating alternative options, the following should always be considered:

· low pollution technology;

· recycling rather than disposal;

· risk of cross-media transfer of pollutants; and

· alternative disposal routes.

**Step 3 : Evaluate the Options**

Analyse these options, particularly to expose advantages and disadvantages for the environment. Use quantitative methods when these are appropriate. Qualitative evaluation will also be needed.

**Step 4 : Summarise and Present the Evaluation**

Present the results of the evaluation concisely and objectively, and in a format which can highlight the advantages and disadvantages of each option. Do not combine the results of different measurements and forecasts if this would obscure information which is important to the decision.

**Step 5 : Select the Preferred Option**

Select the BPEO from the feasible options. The choice will depend on the weight given to the environmental impacts and associated risks, and to the costs involved. Decision makers should be able to demonstrate that the preferred option does not involve unacceptable consequences for the environment.

## Step 6 : Review the Preferred Option

Scrutinise closely the proposed detailed design and the operating procedures to ensure that no pollution risks or hazards have been overlooked. It is good practice to have the scrutiny done by individuals who are independent of the original team.

## Step 7 : Implement and Monitor

Monitor the achieved performance against the desired targets especially those for environmental quality. Do this to establish whether the assumptions in the design are correct and to provide feedback for future development of proposals and designs.

## Throughout Steps 1-7 : Maintain an Audit Trail

Record the basis for any choices or decisions through all of these stages, i.e. the assumptions used, details of evaluation procedures, the reliability and origins of the data, the affiliations of those involved in the analytical work and a record of those taking the decisions.

The RCEP believes that any BPEO developed using this procedure will be likely to have certain characteristics:

· it will have been selected after evaluating all feasible courses of action, each one having been assessed for its effects in all environmental media;

· it will represent that option best for the environment as a whole, which does not incur excessive costs;

· it will observe the imposed standards and limits for emissions to air, discharges to water, and the handling and treatment of wastes for disposal to land;

· it will improve upon the relevant environmental standards, if that is practicable;

· it will incorporate a precautionary element to overcome uncertainty about environmental impacts or their scale, and to reduce the possibility of an inadvertent pollution transfer between different environmental media;

- it will envisage the potential for accidental damage to the environment and how it might be mitigated;

· it will include specification of control equipment and operating procedures (technology based controls) when these provide an effective means of achieving the environmental objectives laid down in the brief for the BPEO;

· it will seldom remain the best option forever and therefore it will include provision for monitoring and review.

The existing system of IPC developed from a consultation paper "Integrated Pollution Control" published by the Department of the Environment in July 1988. This proposed that HMIP should regulate a number of industrial processes using the BPEO concept. These fell into three main categories: processes previously regulated by the Industrial Air Pollution Inspectorate; processes releasing specific dangerous substances ("red list" substances) to water and sewers in significant quantities; and processes generating large quantities of hazardous ("special") waste.

Following a lengthy consultation exercise and the production of several more discussion papers dealing with specific aspects of the system, e.g. public registers, the proposals for the legal framework for the new regulatory system were formally published as Part I of the Environmental Protection Bill. This received Royal Assent on 1st November 1990 and the EPA 1990 came into existence. The first industrial processes came under the new IPC system on 1st April 1991 and its introduction will be complete on 1st November 1995.

Having initiated the move towards an integrated regulatory system in the UK, the RCEP now intends to consider the BPEO concept further and examine whether IPC is allowing the full realisation of this concept in practice.

There is particular concern that environmental quality standards are not set in a consistent manner and that, therefore, compliance with them cannot be directly compared. Some standards are based on risk assessments, others incorporate a margin of safety or are based on the "precautionary principle". This is potentially a serious problem, bearing in mind HMIP's intention to introduce a standard method for assessing the BPEO which places a strong emphasis on a quantitative comparison of whether emissions meet applicable environmental quality standards. If standards could be derived using a more consistent approach, the results of the BPEO assessment would be far more valuable (see Chapter 3).

The RCEP also believes that HMIP is restricted from applying the BPEO concept in full by the extent of its pollution control responsibilities. Although effects of emissions to air, water and land are taken into account in IPC, HMIP is not able to consider the impact of some factors, e.g. the environmental effects of "offsite" issues, including raw material and energy production, and waste disposal. In such circumstances, the RCEP considers that it may be misleading to use the term BPEO and that to overcome this, HMIP's and subsequently the Environment Agency's obligations should be broadened.

## OVERVIEW OF IPC

The legal framework for IPC is set out in Part I of the EPA 1990 and subordinate legislation prescribes more specific details, including those processes and substances subject to IPC and administrative aspects of the system.

The main objectives of IPC are broadly:

· to prevent or minimise the release of prescribed substances and to render harmless any such substances which are released; and

· to develop an approach to pollution control that considers releases from industrial processes to all media in the context of the effect on the environment as a whole.

In addition, IPC aims to:

· improve the efficiency and effectiveness of industrial pollution controls;

· streamline and strengthen the regulatory system and clarify the roles and responsibilities of the regulators (HMIP and other authorities) and industry;

· contain the regulatory burden on industry through the provision of a "one-stop shop" for the most potentially polluting processes;

· provide a framework to encourage the use of clean technologies and waste minimisation techniques;

· maintain public confidence in the regulatory system by ensuring that it is clear, transparent, accessible, understandable and simple in operation;

· provide a flexible framework which can respond to developments in pollution abatement technology and new knowledge concerning the effects of pollutants; and

· provide a mechanism to fulfil international obligations on environmental protection.

IPC applies to number of specific "prescribed processes" operated within the fuel and power, metal, minerals, chemical and waste industries and a number of other miscellaneous industries. Operations involving these prescribed processes will require prior authorisation from HMIP. This requirement extends to both new and existing processes. New processes have been subject to IPC since it came into effect in 1991 and the system has been phased in gradually for existing processes. Existing processes undergoing substantial change will come within IPC when that change takes place. The authorisation for a process will be granted subject to conditions intended to achieve certain objectives (see Section 7 of the EPA 1990). BATNEEC must be used to prevent, minimise and render harmless releases of specific "prescribed substances" and to render harmless any other substances which might cause harm if released. Where releases are made into more than one environmental medium, BATNEEC must be used to achieve the BPEO for those releases. HMIP issues guidance on what constitutes BATNEEC for each prescribed process. Finally, conditions will be imposed to ensure compliance with any direction given by the Secretary of State to implement EU or international obligations, or statutory environmental quality standards or objectives, or other statutory limits, plans or requirements. HMIP is developing a range of tools and methodologies to assist industry and HMIP inspectors in implementing IPC (Chapter 3).

Applications for IPC authorisations are determined by HMIP. The determination process includes consultation with relevant statutory bodies and, through the advertisement of applications, with the general public. An application must be refused if HMIP considers that the applicant will not be able to operate the process in compliance with the conditions of the authorisation. Once a process has been authorised, any changes proposed by the operator must be notified to HMIP and, if necessary, an application to vary the conditions of the authorisation made. Alternatively, HMIP can serve a variation notice on the operator to require changes to be made in order to incorporate advances in abatement technology etc.. Where a process is transferred between operators as a result of a sale or purchase, the authorisation must also be transferred and HMIP notified of this. HMIP is obliged to recoup the costs that it incurs in administering and enforcing the IPC system. Application and substantial variation fees are levied and a yearly subsistence charge is also made (Chapter 4).

HMIP has a variety of enforcement powers. If it considers that an operator is contravening any condition of an authorisation or is likely to do so, an enforcement notice may be served. Alternatively, a prohibition notice may be served if a process is being operated in a manner which involves an imminent risk of serious pollution. Authorisations may also be revoked and, in certain circumstances, HMIP has the power to clean up any pollution and recoup reasonable costs from the operator of the process involved. There are a number of criminal offences associated with IPC which are punishable by a variety of penalties, including heavy fines and prison sentences (Chapter 5). It is possible to appeal to the Secretary of State against decisions made by HMIP and notices served on operators (Chapter 4).

The IPC system makes provision for interested parties to take part in the decision making process. This includes advertising applications for authorisations and variations of authorisations, and consultation procedures (Chapter 4). Details of prescribed processes and HMIP's activities are placed on a public register maintained by HMIP although information can be excluded on the grounds of commercial confidentiality or in the interests of national security. HMIP has recently launched a Chemical Release Inventory containing details of releases from prescribed processes and information on IPC can also be obtained using other powers designed to provide public access to environmental information (Chapter 6).

There are some areas of overlap between IPC and other regulatory systems, including those relating to water pollution, waste disposal, statutory nuisances, radioactive substances, air pollution, health and safety, and planning. A variety of mechanisms exist to prevent duplication and conflict (Chapter 7).

The IPC system is continually evolving to reflect developments in pollution control technology and newly perceived pollution problems. In particular, the development of the Directive on IPPC may require amendments to the IPC system (Chapter 8). The incorporation of HMIP into the new Environment Agency in 1996 may also result in some changes (Chapter 2).

Chapter 2

# LEGAL AND ADMINISTRATIVE FRAMEWORK FOR IPC

## LEGAL FRAMEWORK

In common with many other regulatory systems, the legal frame work for IPC is established by an Act of Parliament and specific details are set out in statutory instruments. Information on the practical operation of the system is provided in the non-statutory guidance produced by HMIP which gives advice on legislative, administrative and technical issues. Other guidance may be provided in Department of the Environment Circulars, Planning Policy Guidance Notes, Waste Management Papers etc.. It should be noted that in general, such guidance is not legally binding and is, in theory, open to challenge.

The legislative framework for IPC is contained in Part I and Schedule 1 of the EPA 1990 and two statutory instruments made under the EPA 1990, namely, The Environmental Protection (Prescribed Processes and Substances) Regulations 1991 ("the Prescribed Processes and Substances Regulations") and The Environmental Protection (Applications, Appeals and Registers) Regulations 1991 ("the Applications, Appeals and Registers Regulations"). All of this legislation has been amended since it first came into effect. Appendix I contains the current version of Part I of the EPA 1990. Details of the amendments made to the two statutory instruments can be found in Tables 1 and 2.

Legislation also exists which is applicable to specific aspects of IPC, for example, legislation which sets out the length of the period permitted for the determination of IPC applications. Such legislation will be discussed in the relevant sections of this book.

### The Environmental Protection Act 1990

Part I of the EPA 1990 provides the framework for IPC and also for the separate Air Pollution Control ("APC") system administered by local authorities. This is also the case for the statutory instruments made under Part I. Many aspects of these two regulatory systems are similar as their details are prescribed by the same pieces of legislation. However, IPC regulates emissions to all environmental media from the most polluting processes whilst APC is only concerned with emissions to air.

The scope of the IPC system is established by the EPA 1990 using a number of definitions as set out in Section 1.

IPC is primarily concerned with regulating pollution at a process level. For the purposes of IPC, "process" means any activity carried out in Great Britain (including certain territorial waters) which is capable of causing pollution of the environment. Activities may be industrial, commercial or of any other nature and include the keeping of substances, with or without another activity. IPC covers both processes conducted on premises and processes operated using mobile plant (plant designed to move or be moved). "Prescribed processes" are those prescribed by the "Secretary of State" (that is, either or both of the Secretary of State for the Environment (for England) and the Secretary of State for Wales) as requiring an IPC authorisation prior to their operation (see later in this Chapter).

The terms "pollution of the environment" and "harm", so crucial to determining the scope of IPC and the powers of HMIP, are poorly defined and, ultimately, meaningless. "Pollution of the environment" is defined as pollution of the environment due to the release from any process of substances capable of causing harm to man or any other living organisms supported by the "environment" (consisting of all or any of air, water and land). "Harm" and "harmless" are defined in terms of harm to the health of living organisms or other interference with the ecosystems of which they form a part. Harm to humans extends to cover offence to any of the senses or harm to property. Such definitions beg the question of what is "pollution of the environment" and "harm" in the first place. However, it is interesting to note that, in this context, pollution is caused by releases of substances which are capable of causing harm and is not restricted to substances which cause actual harm.

"Substances" are defined broadly and include electricity or heat. Specific substances which are particularly harmful are subject to special controls under IPC and are prescribed by the Secretary of State. These "prescribed substances" are designated specifically for air, water or land.

"Releases" of substances include emissions into air, discharges into water and the deposit, keeping or disposal of substances in or on land. The EPA 1990 sets out rules for determining the medium into which a substance will be deemed to be released. This is particularly important in the case of releases of prescribed substances which are specific to each environmental medium.

Releases of substances into air are the most straightforward to categorise. Air includes the air within buildings or other natural or man made structures, either above or below ground.

It is more difficult to distinguish between releases to water and to land, for example, in the case of pollutants entering groundwater.

Releases of substances into water are releases into:

· the sea or the surface of the sea bed;

· rivers, watercourses, lakes, lochs, ponds or reservoirs, or the surface of river beds or the surface of other land supporting such waters;

· groundwater (water contained in underground strata, wells or boreholes etc. sunk into underground strata, or excavations into underground strata); or

· sewers.

Releases of substances into land are releases into:

· land covered by waters other than those specified above for releases into water, or the water covering such land; or

· land beneath the surface of the sea bed or beneath the surface of other land supporting rivers, watercourses, lakes, lochs, ponds or reservoirs.

The specific processes subject to IPC are designated by including a description of those processes in the Prescribed Processes and Substances Regulations. Such processes are termed "prescribed processes" and require authorisation before they can be operated.

In addition, a prescribed process may be described in regulations by reference to:

· any characteristic of the process;

· the area or other circumstances in which it is operated; or

· the person operating the process (see Section 2 of the EPA 1990)

but regulations pursuant to this provision have not been made.

In addition to prescribed processes, releases of certain substances can also be prescribed by the Secretary of State for control under IPC by including a description of them in the Prescribed Processes and Substances Regulations. "Prescribed substances" may be designated separately for each environmental medium: air, water or land. In some cases, whether the release of a prescribed substance comes under IPC may depend upon the quantity of that substance discharged over a period of time, its concentration or any other circumstance.

Releases from prescribed processes or releases of prescribed substances will be controlled by means of standards, objectives or requirements set out by the Secretary of State in regulations. These regulations may:

· set standard limits for the concentration, the quantity released (either the total quantity or quantity released over a period of time) or any other characteristic of any substance released from a prescribed process into any environmental medium;

· set standard requirements for measuring or analysing substances or releases of substances for which such standard limits have been set; or

· set standards or requirements for any aspect of a prescribed process.

The standards and requirements set may vary depending the process, operator, locality or other circumstances. The aim of these provisions is to allow for uniform standard setting, whilst allowing some local flexibility.

Regulations may also set out quality objectives or quality standards for any environmental medium in relation to substances which may be released from any process.

Plans which take account of the cumulative effect of emissions from individual processes can be made and revised by the Secretary of State. Under such plans, limits may be set for the total quantity or total quantity in any period of time of a substance released within the UK or any area of the UK. Release quotas for that substance may be allocated to operators of processes subject to such limits. The limits should be established so as to progressively reduce pollution of the environment. Similarly, the plan should allow for progressive tightening of environmental quality objectives and quality standards. The making or revision of these plans must be notified in the London, Edinburgh and Belfast Gazettes and their details made available to the public. In 1990, a National Plan to control emissions of sulphur dioxide and nitrogen oxides from power stations and other combustion plants was made in order to implement the Large Combustion Plants Directive (88/609/EEC). The National Plan sets out increasingly more stringent annual emission targets for different industry sectors in England and Wales, Scotland and Northern Ireland. In Great Britain, these targets will be achieved through the conditions attached to IPC authorisations e.g. both National Power and Powergen are required by the terms of their IPC authorisations to meet an overall company "bubble" for emissions, although some site specific limits are also set.

The ceiling on emissions for a particular sector as represented by the "bubble" of emissions might well form the basis of a system of "tradeable permits", much favoured by the current Government. Where the operator of a prescribed process is willing and able to reduce the level of emissions from that process, a tradeable permit would enable that operator to sell the excess quota of emissions allowed for in his IPC authorisation to an operator of another process. One of the reasons that such a system finds favour with the Government is that the operator of the first process will be able to recoup the costs of reducing his emissions by selling or trading the excess quota. This system has not yet arrived in the UK, but is currently being employed in the United States, especially in the electricity industry.

A number of amendments will be made to the EPA 1990 by sections of the Environment Act 1995 which are not yet in force.

These are mainly concerned with the transfer of HMIP's functions to the new Environment Agency (see later in this Chapter).

## The Prescribed Processes and Substances Regulations

As described above, the processes and substances subject to IPC are set out in Prescribed Processes and Substances Regulations. The Regulations have been amended a number of times to take account of changes made to the IPC system (see Table 1). In particular, following a thorough review of this legislation in 1993, a large number of amendments were made in 1994 to remove processes from IPC, add new processes and transfer processes between IPC and APC. This review formed part of the Government's deregulation initiative which aimed to reduce unnecessary regulatory burdens on industry. A "consolidated" version of the Regulations which incorporates the amendments made during the period 1991-1994 has been published by Her Majesty's Stationery Office to facilitate the interpretation of this legislation. However, it is stressed that the consolidated version is only a tool and has no legal status.

Schedule 1 of the Prescribed Processes and Substances Regulations describes the processes prescribed for IPC. It is divided into six chapters corresponding to different industry sectors, namely: fuel production processes, combustion processes (including power generation) and associated processes; metal production and processing; mineral industries; the chemical industry; waste disposal and recycling; and other industries. Each chapter consists of a number of sections relating to different types of processes which are then further divided into specific process descriptions. The process descriptions are separated into Part A and Part B processes. Part A processes are those with the greatest potential to cause pollution and are subject to IPC; Part B processes relate only to releases to air and are regulated under APC. In addition to prescribed processes, the Prescribed Processes and Substances Regulations set out the prescribed substances for air (Schedule 4), water (Schedule 5), and land (Schedule 6). The Prescribed Processes and Substances Regulations are reproduced in Appendix II.

The Prescribed Processes and Substances Regulations set out details of the application of this legislation, including those circumstances in which a process which appears in Schedule 1 may be exempted from IPC. Schedule 2 provides guidance on interpreting the process descriptions listed in Schedule 1. The Regulations also prescribe the timetable by which processes will become subject to this legislation.

## TABLE 1

## AMENDMENTS TO THE PRESCRIBED PROCESSES AND SUBSTANCES REGULATIONS

### (SI 1991/472)

| STATUTORY INSTRUMENT | EFFECT |
|---|---|
| The Environmental Protection (Amendment of Regulations) Regulations 1991 (SI 1991/836) | Correct an inconsistency between SI 1991/472 and the EPA 1990 concerning the date on which authorisation is required for a prescribed process. |
| The Environmental Protection (Prescribed Processes and Substances) (Amendment) Regulations 1992 (SI 1992/614) | Correct minor errors and clarify some provisions concerning exemptions from IPC and a number of process descriptions. |
| The Environmental Protection (Prescribed Processes and Substances) (Amendment) Regulations 1993 (SI 1993/1749) | Extend the application period for IPC authorisation for certain chemical processes. |
| The Environmental Protection (Prescribed Processes and Substances) (Amendment) (No.2) Regulations 1993 (SI 1993/2405) | Transfer some processes from Section 4.5 of Schedule 1 (inorganic chemical processes) to Section 2.2 (non-ferrous metals). Make amendments to Schedule 2 specifically relating to the interpretation of process descriptions for chemical processes. Postpone the application period for IPC authorisation for prescribed processes involving the conversion of chemical fertilisers into granules (Section 4.6 (b)) and the storage of chemicals in bulk (Section 4.9). |
| The Environmental Protection (Prescribed Processes and Substances Etc.) (Amendment) Regulations 1994 (SI 1994/1271) | Make amendments to process descriptions to transfer some processes between IPC and APC and add or remove some processes from control. Amend Schedule 5 to add threshold quantities for substances prescribed for water. Make a number of other minor amendments relating to exemptions and the interpretation of process descriptions. |

| | |
|---|---|
| The Environmental Protection (Prescribed Processes and Substances Etc.) (Amendment) (No.2) Regulations 1994 (SI 1994/1329) | Correct errors in the amendments made by SI 1994/1271 relating to transitional provisions for processes becoming or ceasing to be subject to IPC or transferring between IPC and APC. |

The Department of the Environment has produced proposals for more amendments to the Prescribed Processes and Substances Regulations. These will address a number of issues which have come to light in the period since the last amendments were made, including changes to some process definitions in Schedule 1 and the Schedule 2 rules for interpreting process descriptions.

### The Applications, Appeals and Registers Regulations

Although the EPA 1990 sets out much of the administrative framework for IPC, more specific details are given in the Applications, Appeals and Registers Regulations. These Regulations describe the procedures for applying for IPC authorisations, applying for variations of the conditions attached to authorisations and appealing against decisions made by HMIP or notices served by HMIP. This includes details of the information to be provided in such circumstances and the arrangements for advertising applications and consulting with interested parties. The Regulations also set out the information to be placed on the public register and procedures for applying for exemptions for reasons of commercial confidentiality or national security.

The Applications, Appeals and Registers Regulations have been amended several times (see Table 2).

## TABLE 2

## AMENDMENTS TO THE APPLICATIONS, APPEALS AND REGISTERS REGULATIONS

## (SI 1991/507)

| STATUTORY INSTRUMENT | EFFECT |
|---|---|
| The Environmental Protection (Amendment of Regulations) Regulations 1991 (SI 1991/836) | Correct minor errors. |
| The Environmental Protection (Prescribed Processes and Substances Etc.) | Amend to require consultation with Scottish islands or district councils in |

| (Amendment) Regulations 1994 | connection with authorisations etc. for |
|---|---|
| (SI 1994/1271) | certain types of prescribed processes. |

The Applications, Appeals and Registers Regulations are to be amended further in the near future. A consultation paper issued by the Department of the Environment in 1994 sets out the amendments proposed which are intended to address a number of anomalies, inconsistencies and problems of interpretation that have arisen during the implementation of IPC. The amendments include changes to the information required in an application for IPC, the list of statutory consultees, the advertising and appeals procedures, the information to be placed on public registers and the procedures for substantial changes to processes which result in an environmental gain or a reduction in environmental impact. These amendments are discussed in greater detail in Chapter 4.

## ADMINISTRATIVE FRAMEWORK: THE ROLE OF HMIP

HMIP is part of the Department of the Environment. It was formed in April 1987 to create a unified regulatory authority by combining:

· the Industrial Air Pollution Inspectorate, which had responsibility for industrial air emissions;

· the Radiochemical Inspectorate, which had responsibility for the use, storage and disposal of radioactive materials and waste under the Radioactive Substances Act 1960;

· the Hazardous Waste Inspectorate, which was responsible for ensuring a consistent approach to the regulation of such waste by the waste disposal authorities (now local authority waste disposal companies, "LAWDCs"); and

· the Water Pollution Inspectorate, which was formed when HMIP was created to control discharges to water made by the regional water authorities, responsibility for which has now been transferred to the NRA.

HMIP itself will be combined with the NRA and the waste regulation authorities on 1st April 1996 to form the Environment Agency. This new authority will have responsibility for the regulation of pollution in England and Wales. The structure, organisation and functions of the new Environment Agency are discussed in greater detail later in this Chapter.

HMIP has responsibility for the regulation of the most potentially polluting industrial processes and high-risk substances. In addition to IPC, it regulates premises where radioactive materials or radioactive waste are present, controls discharges of special category trade effluent into sewers (i.e. trade effluent containing specific dangerous substances), administers the system controlling air emissions from industrial processes not subject to IPC or APC and enforces legislation relating to the use of sewage sludge on agricultural land.

## HMIP Functions

HMIP has a range of administrative and enforcement functions in relation to IPC. An HMIP Advisory Committee has recently been established to review the efficiency and effectiveness of HMIP's performance in discharging these functions.

### · Regulation of Processes Prescribed for IPC

HMIP is responsible for determining applications for the authorisation of prescribed processes and the variation of granted authorisations. Once a process has been authorised, HMIP will ensure that it is operated in compliance with the conditions attached to that authorisation. This is achieved through HMIP inspections and monitoring programmes conducted by process operators, the results of which are then passed to HMIP for analysis. In addition, HMIP organises independent check monitoring programmes to validate the results provided by operators. The information gathered on releases from prescribed processes is used to produce the Chemical Release Inventory ("CRI").

Where non-compliance is detected and this cannot be resolved with the cooperation of the operator, HMIP can make use of a wide range of enforcement powers, including serving enforcement and prohibition notices, revoking authorisations and prosecuting companies for violations of legal requirements. HMIP also has powers to allow it to investigate incidents of suspected non-compliance.

### · Development of Policy and Research

HMIP has a statutory duty to follow developments in pollution abatement technology and techniques. It initiates, commissions and conducts research in relation to all areas of its responsibilities with the aim of providing advice within HMIP and to other Government departments. The results of these activities are disseminated in the form of HMIP research reports. Several "national centres of excellence" have been established to conduct research and develop techniques for use by the regulatory section of HMIP. HMIP formulates and develops policy and practice on all aspects of IPC.

### · Provision of Expert Advice

HMIP provides advice and support to other Government departments on pollution issues. Giving general advice and guidance to industry is also important. This is achieved through the publication of various guidance notes which provide information on BATNEEC, pollution abatement techniques and the general requirements of IPC etc..

### · Representation at International Level

HMIP represents the Government on international bodies and working groups involved in the development of new policy and legislation in the areas for which it has responsibility.

### · Dissemination of Information and Public Consultation

HMIP must ensure that the information produced in connection with the carrying out of its functions is accessible to the public. This is available through the public register and the CRI (see Chapter 6) and includes both information on the performance of individual operators and HMIP's own performance in regulating IPC. HMIP also conducts consultation procedures which allow the views of other official bodies and the general public to be taken into account when decisions are made in relation to IPC.

### HMIP Organisation and Structure

HMIP's internal organisation reflects these different functions. The Inspectorate is headed by a Chief Executive/Chief Inspector, Dr Allan Duncan. Dr David Slater, the previous Chief Inspector, has recently been appointed as Director of Pollution Prevention and Control for the new Environment Agency. Reporting to the Chief Inspector are a number of directors with specific areas of responsibility: operations, regulatory systems, pollution policy, business strategy and information, corporate affairs, finance and personnel. Each of these divisions has a different role. Operations Division is concerned with administering and enforcing IPC at regional level. Regulatory Systems Division has responsibility for developing regulatory standards and monitoring procedures, and providing technical advice to the rest of HMIP. Pollution Policy Division formulates, reviews and develops policy and practical arrangements for IPC, provides advice to Government, liaises with other regulatory authorities and interested parties, and represents HMIP or the Government at meetings, working parties etc.. Business Strategy and Information Division develops environmental assessment methods and the information systems required for HMIP's operations.

HMIP's headquarters are based in London. This office is concerned with planning and policy issues. All regulatory work is carried out in the regional offices. There are seven HMIP regions: North West, North East, Wales, Midlands, Anglian, South West and Southern. Each region has one or a number of regional offices. The addresses of HMIP's headquarters and the regional offices can be found in Appendix IV.

HMIP has developed close links with other regulatory authorities in the UK and in the EU. Memoranda of Understanding exist to facilitate cooperation between HMIP and the different regulatory authorities, e.g. the NRA and local authorities. In 1992, a European Union Network for the Implementation and Enforcement of Environmental Law was established to provide a forum for the exchange of information and experience between such bodies. HMIP also has close links with the European Environment Agency.

## ADMINISTRATIVE FRAMEWORK: THE ENVIRONMENT AGENCY

The notion of an environment agency for England and Wales with wide responsibility for environmental protection has been in development for some time. In 1991, the Prime Minister announced that the Government intended to create a new, independent environment agency which would bring together the pollution control authorities responsible for air, water and land. After a period on the legislative "back burner", a paving bill for the Environment Agency was announced in the Queen's Speech in 1993, but was squeezed out of the 1993-1994 Parliamentary Session. The precursor to the Environment Act 1995 ("EA 1995"), the Environment Bill, had its first reading in the House of Lords on 1st December 1994 and received Royal Assent on 19th July 1995.

The EA 1995 provides for the establishment of an Environment Agency for England and Wales and sets out its objectives, functions, duties and powers. It also makes a number of amendments to the statutes from which the powers of the Environment Agency's constituent pollution control authorities are derived, in order that these powers may be aligned. In addition to the provisions relating to the Environment Agency, the EA 1995 covers many other environmental issues including the establishment of a separate Scottish Environment Protection Agency, new powers relating to contaminated land, national parks, producer responsibility for waste, water pollution from abandoned mines, a national waste strategy and new air quality powers for local authorities. The various sections of the EA 1995 will be brought into effect by commencement orders.

The Environment Agency is established by Part I of the EA 1995. This sets out the functions which are to be transferred to the Environment Agency from the existing regulatory authorities on 1st April 1996.

· All the functions of the NRA (including water resources management, water pollution control, flood defence/land drainage, fisheries and navigation).

· All the functions of the waste regulation authorities.

· All the functions of HMIP (including IPC, regulation of radioactive substances and waste, and the control of air emissions under the AWRA 1906 and the HSWA 1974).

· Certain functions of the Secretary of State (including powers relating to the disposal of radioactive waste, the release of special category trade effluent to sewers, the registration of works under the AWRA 1906 and HSWA 1974 and the regulation of the use of sludge in agriculture (in practice, these functions are carried out by HMIP and other sections of the Department of the Environment)).

There are some notable exclusions, including the APC and statutory nuisance control functions of the local authorities, the regulation of discharges to sewers, the functions of the Drinking Water Inspectorate and the environmental responsibilities of the Ministry of Agriculture, Fisheries and Food.

## Environment Agency Functions

The EA 1995 provides for the functions of the existing regulatory authorities to be transferred to the Environment Agency. These will be combined with a number of new responsibilities, including new powers to deal with contaminated land, producer responsibility for waste and the provision of advice on a national waste strategy. The principal aim of the Environment Agency is the protection or enhancement of the environment, taken as a whole, so as to make a contribution towards the objective of achieving sustainable development, whilst taking into account any statutory requirements or likely costs. The Environment Agency must have regard to any guidance provided by ministers on the objectives considered appropriate for it to pursue in the discharge of its functions. In particular, guidance will be provided in relation to its contribution towards the goal of sustainable development.

The EA 1995 sets out the functions of the Environment Agency. These can be divided broadly into pollution control functions and water management functions. The Environment Agency should use its pollution control powers to prevent, minimise, remedy or mitigate the effects of pollution of the environment. These powers include HMIP's functions under Part I of the EPA 1990, together with other pollution control powers relating to industrial air pollution (under the AWRA 1906 and the HSWA 1974), waste management, special category trade effluent, contaminated land, radioactive substances and waste, and water pollution. To assist the Environment Agency in the exercise of its pollution control powers and to form an opinion of the general state of pollution of the environment, it should compile information relating to such pollution. It may also be required to carry out assessments of the effects on the environment of existing or potential levels of pollution and the available options for pollution control. It must monitor developments in technology and techniques for preventing and controlling pollution and remedying existing pollution.

The Environment Agency's functions in relation to water management include promoting the conservation and enhancement of the natural beauty and amenity of inland and coastal waters and associated land, promoting the recreational use of such areas, promoting the conservation of fauna and flora dependant on the water environment, water conservation and management, flood defence and fisheries.

The Environment Agency must have a regard to its general environmental and recreational duties when formulating or considering any proposals relating to its functions. These general duties relate to the conservation and enhancement of natural beauty and the conservation of flora, fauna and geological or physiographical features of special interest; the protection and conservation of buildings, sites and objects of archaeological, architectural, engineering or historic interest; and the consideration of the effects of proposals on the beauty or amenity of any rural or urban area or on any flora, fauna, features, buildings, sites or objects, or on the economic and social well being of local communities in rural areas. Freedom of access to certain areas of natural beauty and sites of archaeological, architectural, engineering or historical interest is also to be considered. In some cases, the extent of these duties depends on whether a proposal concerns a water management or pollution control function. The Environment Agency will be obliged to consult with the Nature Conservancy Council for England, the Countryside Council for Wales, the National Park authorities or the Broads Authority before carrying out or authorising any activities which may adversely affect sites of special interest or sites of particular importance to these bodies.

The Environment Agency must, when considering whether or not to exercise any of its powers or the manner in which these should be exercised, take into account the likely costs and benefits of its actions. Only if it is unreasonable in the particular circumstances or in view of the nature or purpose of the power will the Environment Agency be excused this consideration, although this will not affect its obligation to discharge any duties or comply with any requirements or pursue any of the objectives imposed upon it. This cost/benefit requirement was the subject of great discussion during the passage of the Environment Bill. It is popular with industry because the Environment Agency would be forced to consider the cost of any action and, therefore, disproportionately large costs incurred by industry for little environmental gain would be avoided. However, environmental groups are concerned that the Environment Agency could be weakened by the necessity to conduct such assessments and have questioned how it is possible to value damage to the environment. The regulatory authorities comprising the new Environment Agency have expressed concern about how this power would be applied in practice as there is no guidance in the EA 1995 as to what should be considered as "unreasonable".

## Environment Agency Organisation and Structure

The Environment Agency will be the largest environmental authority in Europe. It became a legal entity in August 1995 and will be launched on 1st April 1996. On this date, the existing regulatory authorities will be transferred to become part of the new body. A great deal of effort has been expended in determining the organisation and structure for the Environment Agency.

The Environment Agency will be overseen by a Chairman, Lord De Ramsey, and an Environment Agency Board comprising of members with a range of experience. It will be headed by a Chief Executive, Ed Gallagher, who was formerly Chief Executive of the NRA. Reporting to the Chief Executive will be eight directors, each with responsibility for an Environment Agency department, namely: pollution prevention and control, environmental strategy, water management, operations, personnel, finance, legal services and corporate affairs. HMIP's functions in relation to IPC will come within the pollution prevention and control department. Dr David Slater, formerly the Chief Inspector of HMIP, has been appointed as Director of Pollution Prevention and Control.

The Environment Agency will be organised into three tiers. The Chief Executive and directors will be based at a Head Office, together with other staff responsible for the formulation of policy, the setting of consistent national standards and financial controls. The Environment Agency will be divided into eight regions headed by a regional general manager and each region will consist of a number of smaller areas. Operational activities will be conducted at regional or area level. The Environment Agency's operational activities will be divided into pollution prevention and control functions and water management functions, although these will be closely linked. There will also be functional links between specialists at regional or area levels and their counterparts at Head Office. There will be a clear separation between the formulation of policy and operational activities.

The determination of its geographical structure and the positioning of the regional boundaries for the Environment Agency have been given a high priority. It has been emphasised that the new body is not merely a combination of HMIP, the NRA and the waste regulation authorities with the addition of a layer of management. The functions of these authorities will be completely integrated, requiring the adoption of a single set of regional boundaries. The determination of these boundaries has required careful consideration because all the constituent authorities already have a geographical organisation designed to meet their own specific needs, e.g. the NRA is organised on the basis of river catchment areas, whilst the boundaries of the waste regulation authorities follow those of local authorities. However, in order to avoid confusion for the Environment Agency's users, a single set of boundaries is necessary.

The regional organisation determined for the Environment Agency is a compromise which meets all of these requirements. For external users, a single point of contact will be provided, whatever their business, which will depend on their location. The borders of the eight regions will follow the existing NRA water management boundaries, modified to fit the nearest county or district council boundary. Wales will comprise a single region. For internal management purposes, however, there will be boundaries for each of the Environment Agency's two sets of operational functions. The boundaries for the pollution prevention and control functions are the same as those for external users, i.e. they follow county or district council borders. For the water management functions, the boundaries will be exactly the same as those of the existing eight NRA regions which are based on river catchment basins. In practice, the two sets of boundaries are very closely correlated. Special inter-regional arrangements will exist to cover those small areas where there are discrepancies.

The location of the Environment Agency Head Office and the organisation of regional and area offices will be determined in the near future.

A number of advisory committees are to be created to support the work of the Environment Agency, including an advisory committee for Wales, flood defence committees, fisheries advisory committees and environmental protection advisory committees.

Chapter 3

# REGULATION OF PRESCRIBED PROCESSES

## PRESCRIBED PROCESSES

The processes which come within IPC are described in Schedule 1 to the Prescribed Processes and Substances Regulations. These Regulations are reproduced in Appendix II.

A process which appears in Schedule 1 may be exempted from IPC if prescribed substances are not released or only released in very small quantities which cannot cause harm to the environment. However, if the process gives rise to an offensive smell noticeable outside the premises where it is operated, it will not be exempted and will require authorisation. Specifically, a process will be exempted if:

· it cannot result in the release into air of any prescribed substance listed in Schedule 4 to the Regulations or there is no likelihood that it will result in the release of a prescribed substance except in a trivial quantity incapable of causing harm or with an insignificant capacity to cause harm; and

· it cannot result in the release into water of any prescribed substance listed in Schedule 5 to the Regulations except in a concentration no greater than the background concentration or, in any twelve month period, in a quantity which does not exceed the background quantity by more than the amount specified for that prescribed substance in Schedule 5; and

· it cannot result in the release into land of any prescribed substance listed in Schedule 6 to the Regulations or there is no likelihood that it will result in a release of a prescribed substance except in a trivial quantity incapable of causing harm or with an insignificant capacity to cause harm.

It is important to note that because of the presence of the word "and", all these criteria must be fulfilled.

The background quantity of a substance is that amount present in the water supplied to the premises where the process is operated, the water abstracted for use in that process or precipitation onto the premises where the process is operated. The background concentration of a substance is that which would be present in the release irrespective of the effect of the process on the composition of the release and includes the concentration of that substance in the water supply, in water abstracted for process use or in precipitation.

The case *Tandridge District Council v. P&S Civil Engineering Ltd and Others* involved an appeal by the Council against the dismissal of four informations preferred. The company had been found to be operating a roadstone coating plant without, in the opinion of the Council, an APC authorisation. The defence relied on by the respondents was that the Council had failed to show that the exemptions for "triviality" under regulation 4 of the Prescribed Processes and Substances Regulations were not applicable. The High Court held that the burden of proof is upon the defendant to an information to prove any exemption and that because the respondents here called no evidence they could not establish that any of the exemptions applied. Accordingly, the case was remitted to the justices with directions to convict.

A number of other exemptions from IPC exist for:

· processes operated in working museums which demonstrate industrial processes of historical interest;

· processes operated for educational purposes in schools;

· the operation of engines which propel or provide electricity for aircraft, hovercraft, mechanically propelled road vehicles, railway locomotives, ships and other vessels;

· the operation of engines for testing purposes before installation or during development;

· the operation of fume cupboards used for laboratory research or testing, although this exemption does not apply to fume cupboards which are industrial and continuous production process enclosures or those in which substances or materials are manufactured; and

· processes operated as domestic activities in connection with private dwellings.

Schedule 1 to the Prescribed Processes and Substances Regulations lists descriptions of processes operated in the energy, metal, mineral, chemical and waste industries and a number of other miscellaneous industries. Only those processes included under Part A of Schedule 1 are subject to IPC. The other processes listed under Part B are regulated by local authorities under the separate APC system. The processes prescribed for control are listed in Table 3 together with details of the implementation schedule for existing processes.

## TABLE 3
## PRESCRIBED PROCESSES AND IMPLEMENTATION TIMETABLE FOR EXISTING PROCESSES

| SCHEDULE 1 PROCESS DESCRIPTIONS | WITHIN IPC | APPLICATION PERIOD |
|---|---|---|
| Fuel Production Processes, Combustion Processes (Including Power Generation) and Associated Processes | | |
| Section 1.1 Gasification and Associated Processes | 1.4.92 | 1.4.92 - 30.6.92 |
| Section 1.2 Carbonisation and Associated Processes | 1.4.92 | 1.4.92 - 30.6.92 |
| Section 1.3 Combustion Processes (Boilers and Furnaces ›50MWth) (Remainder) | 1.4.91 1.4.92 | 1.4.91 - 30.4.91 1.4.92 - 30.6.92 |
| Section 1.4 Petroleum Processes | 1.4.92 | 1.4.92 - 30.6.92 |
| Metal Production and Processing | | |
| Section 2.1 Iron and Steel | 1.1.95 | 1.1.95 - 31.3.95 |
| Section 2.2 Non-ferrous Metals | 1.5.95 | 1.5.95 - 31.7.95 |
| Mineral Industries | | |
| Section 3.1 Cement and Lime Manufacture and Associated Processes | 1.12.92 | 1.12.92 - 28.2.93 |
| Section 3.2 Processes Involving Asbestos | 1.12.92 | 1.12.92 - 28.2.93 |
| Section 3.3 Other Mineral Fibres | 1.12.92 | 1.12.92 - 28.2.93 |
| Section 3.4 (Only APC Processes) | | |
| Section 3.5 Glass Manufacture and Production | 1.12.92 | 1.12.92 - 28.2.93 |
| Section 3.6 Ceramic Production | 1.12.92 | 1.12.92 - 28.2.93 |
| The Chemical Industry | | |
| Section 4.1 Petrochemical Processes | 1.5.93 | 1.5.93 - 31.10.93 |
| Section 4.2 The Manufacture and Use of Organic Chemicals | 1.5.93 | 1.5.93 - 31.10.93 |
| Section 4.3 Acid Processes | 1.11.93 | 1.11.93 - 31.1.94 |
| Section 4.4 Processing Involving Halogens | 1.11.93 | 1.11.93 - 31.1. |

| Section 4.5 | Inorganic Chemical Processes | 1.5.94 | 1.5.94 - 31.7.94 |
|---|---|---|---|
| Section 4.6 | Chemical Fertiliser Production | | |
| | (Manufacture of Fertilisers) | 1.11.93 | 1.11.93 - 31.1.94 |
| | (Conversion into Granules) | 1.5.94 | 1.5.94 - 31.7.94 |
| Section 4.7 | Pesticide Production | 1.5.93 | 1.5.93 - 31.10.93 |
| Section 4.8 | Pharmaceutical Production | 1.5.93 | 1.5.93 - 31.10.93 |
| Section 4.9 | (Only APC Processes) | | |
| **Waste Disposal and Recycling** | | | |
| Section 5.1 | Incineration | 1.8.92 | 1.8.92 - 31.10.92 |
| Section 5.2 | Recovery Processes | 1.8.92 | 1.8.92 - 31.10.92 |
| Section 5.3 | The Production of Fuel from Waste | 1.8.92 | 1.8.92 - 31.10.92 |
| **Other Industries** | | | |
| Section 6.1 | Paper and Pulp Manufacturing Processes | 1.11.95 | 1.11.95 - 31.1.96 |
| Section 6.2 | Di-isocyanate Processes | 1.11.95 | 1.11.95 - 31.1.96 |
| Section 6.3 | Tar and Bitumen Processes | 1.11.95 | 1.11.95 - 31.1.96 |
| Section 6.4 | (No Prescribed Processes) | | |
| Section 6.5 | Coating Processes and Printing | 1.11.95 | 1.11.95 - 31.1.96 |
| Section 6.6 | The Manufacture of Dyestuffs, Printing Ink and Coating Materials | 1.11.95 | 1.11.95 - 31.1.96 |
| Section 6.7 | Timber Processes | 1.11.95 | 1.11.95 - 31.1.96 |
| Section 6.8 | (Only APC Processes) | | |
| Section 6.9 | The Treatment and Processing of Animal or Vegetable Matter | 1.11.95 | 1.11.95 - 31.1.96 |

Schedule 2 to the Prescribed Processes and Substances Regulations provides guidance on the interpretation of the process descriptions set out in Schedule 1. The majority of sections in Schedule 1 represent manufacturing processes with practical industrial significance. In some circumstances, however, the nature of a process can make the identification of the appropriate process description(s) difficult. Three main types of problem arise when applying Schedule 1 in practice:

· the boundaries of a process may be difficult to determine;

· a process could be described by several of the process descriptions in Schedule 1; or

· a process involves two or more process descriptions appearing in Schedule 1.

To overcome such difficulties, Schedule 2 sets out a number of rules for determining the relevant section of Schedule 1. There are a number of exemptions to these general rules relating to situations involving complex processes or where there is particularly wide overlap between process descriptions. In particular, the application of the chemical industry process descriptions in Chapter 4 of Schedule 1 created problems when that industry became subject to IPC. In comparison to the organisation of the majority of Schedule 1 which is classified into relatively discrete industrial processes, Chapter 4 is divided on the basis of process chemistry. This classification gave rise to a number of problems, e.g. in relation to chemical processes involving a number of different stages equivalent to several process descriptions falling within different sections of Chapter 4. In such cases, several authorisations could have been required for a single process. It was anticipated that this would cause problems for both the applicant and HMIP in relation to the environmental standards to be set for a process, particularly where, due to the phased implementation of IPC, some parts of the process would be subject to regulation before others. There were also serious cost implications for applicants because of the increased number of authorisations required. Problems also existed for pilot plants and fine chemical production plants in which many operations are carried out on a small scale. In view of these difficulties, the Prescribed Processes and Substances Regulations were amended in 1993 to include special interpretation rules specifically for the chemical industry processes in Chapter 4 of Schedule 1. More guidance is given in the relevant Chief Inspector's Guidance Notes ("CIGNs").

To assist in the determination of process boundaries, Schedule 2 provides that a process description will include any other process carried on as part of that process by the same operator at the same location. This will not apply however to two or more processes which are described in different sections of Schedule 1 and these will require separate authorisations. Specific rules for determining process boundaries exist for chemical industry processes. Two or more chemical processes described in different sections of Chapter 4 will be treated as if they come within the same section although if they produce different products and are operated separately, they may require separate authorisations.

Specific interpretation rules exist for a number of situations where one prescribed process is an integral part of another. Where a combustion process (Section 1.3) is carried out as an inherent part of and primarily for the purpose of a process described in Sections 1.1, 1.4, 6.3 or any section of Chapter 4 of Schedule 1, that combustion process will be treated as part of the other process and not as a separate combustion process. This is also the case for boilers, furnaces or other combustion appliances which form part of a combustion process. The other processes in this case are gasification processes (Section 1.1), petroleum processes (Section 1.4), tar and bitumen processes (Section 6.3) and all the chemical industry processes (Chapter 4). Similarly, when the reforming of natural gas (Section 1.1(a)) is carried out as an inherent part of and primarily for the purpose of producing a feedstock for any of the chemical industry processes described in Chapter 4, the reforming process will be treated as part of that chemical process.

Where coal, lignite, coke or any other coal product, or iron ore or burnt pyrites for use in a prescribed process is unloaded by a person other than the operator of the prescribed process at the place where that process is operated, the unloading operation will be treated as part of that process.

Processes of different descriptions may be carried out using the same plant or machinery as a result of the use of different fuels or materials or the disposal of different wastes at different times. In such cases, where one or more of the process descriptions comes within Part A of Schedule 1, any other processes will be treated as coming within the description of the IPC process.

Special rules apply where in the course of or as an ancillary process to a prescribed process waste is used, treated or disposed of (whether as fuel or otherwise) at the same location as the prescribed process. These waste operations will be treated as part of the prescribed process, whether or not the waste was produced by the operator of the process or acquired by him for such use, treatment or disposal.

Where an operator carries on a process which could be described by two or more process descriptions listed in Schedule 1 it should be regarded as coming within only that description which fits it most aptly. Where a chemical process would appear to fit into several of the chemical process descriptions in Chapter 4 of Schedule 1 and these definitions are equally apt, the appropriate process description will be determined with reference to a ranking sequence for the different sections within Chapter 4 (see Table 4). The appropriate section will be that which appears first in the ranking sequence.

# TABLE 4

# CHEMICAL INDUSTRY PROCESSES RANKING SEQUENCE

| SECTION OF CHAPTER 4 | PROCESS DESCRIPTION |
|---|---|
| 4.5 | Inorganic Chemical Processes |
| 4.2 | The Manufacture and Use of Organic Chemicals |
| 4.1 | Petrochemical Processes |
| 4.4 | Processes Involving Halogens |
| 4.3 | Acid Processes |
| 4.6 | Chemical Fertiliser Production |
| 4.7 | Pesticide Production |
| 4.8 | Pharmaceutical Production |

Where an operator carries on a process involving two or more processes described in the same section of Schedule 1 they will be treated as a single process and covered by one authorisation. Conversely, a process involving several processes described in different sections of Schedule 1 will require a separate authorisation for each process. If an operator carries on a process involving several processes which come within both Part A (i.e. subject to IPC) and Part B (i.e. subject to APC) of the same section of Schedule 1, all the processes will be regarded as part of the Part A process and regulated by IPC. If the Part A and Part B processes fall into different sections of Schedule 1, each process will be subject to the requirements of that regulatory system.

For chemical processes, Schedule 2 provides that a single authorisation may be issued where a process comprises of two or more process descriptions falling within different sections of Chapter 4. Pilot plants, small scale batch processes and, on a larger scale, activities which are mutually dependent or interrelated can be authorised as a single process. The process description to be used will be determined with reference to the ranking sequence set out in Table 4. There are special rules for small scale chemical operations. Where an operator carries out, at the same location, a number of processes described by any section of Chapter 4, these processes will be treated as a single process requiring only one authorisation if they are not likely to produce more than 250 tonnes of product in total in any twelve month period. Solid, liquid or gaseous wastes, by-products with an insignificant total value in comparison to the total value of the output of the processes and additives such as diluents, stabilisers, preservatives etc. which are included in the final product formulation will not be taken into account when calculating the quantity of product produced by the processes. The process description to be used by the operator in these circumstances will be that appearing first in the ranking sequence in Table 4. This rule was specifically included to take account of the problems experienced by chemical companies producing a range of fine chemicals on a small scale. Such operations use a variety of processes and, without this rule, would have required numerous authorisations.

## PRESCRIBED SUBSTANCES

In addition to regulating specific prescribed processes, IPC controls releases of certain dangerous chemicals, termed "prescribed substances". The Prescribed Processes and Substances Regulations set out three lists of substances prescribed for air, water and land (see Table 5). Operators are required to use BATNEEC to prevent, or where this is not practicable, to minimise releases of prescribed substances and, if any prescribed substances are released, to render these harmless. This requirement is more stringent than that for non-prescribed substances under which BATNEEC need only be used to render harmless any other substances that might cause harm if released, i.e. the operator is not obliged to prevent or minimise such releases. Thus, there is a general presumption that operators will aim to prevent, rather than control, releases of prescribed substances through waste minimisation and the use of clean technologies.

The list of substances prescribed for air in Schedule 4 includes those substances controlled under the Air Framework Directive (84/360/EEC), with a few additions. The prescribed substances for water (Schedule 5) are those appearing on the "red list" and are also similar to those listed in Schedule 1 to The Trade Effluents (Prescribed Processes and Substances) Regulations 1989 which set out the emissions to sewers containing special category trade effluent (again, containing red list substances) or emissions from specific processes that are to be controlled by HMIP under the Water

Industry Act 1991. The "red list" is a list of substances identified by the Government for strict control because of their toxicity, persistence and capacity for bioaccumulation. The list of prescribed substances for land is derived from The Control of Pollution (Special Waste) Regulations 1980 which set out controls for the handling and disposal of the most dangerous types of waste. However, the scope of Schedule 6 is narrower than the 1980 Regulations and only covers those substances likely to be hazardous if landfilled.

# TABLE 5

# PRESCRIBED SUBSTANCES

| SCHEDULE 4 |
| --- |
| **RELEASE INTO THE AIR: PRESCRIBED SUBSTANCES** |
| Oxides of sulphur and other sulphur compounds |
| Oxides of nitrogen and other nitrogen compounds |
| Oxides of carbon |
| Organic compounds and partial oxidation products |
| Metals, metalloids and their compounds |
| Asbestos (suspended particulate matter and fibres), glass fibres and mineral fibres |
| Halogens and their compounds |
| Phosphorus and its compounds |
| Particulate matter |

## SCHEDULE 5

## RELEASE INTO WATER: PRESCRIBED SUBSTANCES

| (1)   Substance | (2)   Amount in excess of back ground quantity released in any 12 month period (grammes) |
|---|---|
| Mercury and its compounds | 200 (expressed as metal) |
| Cadmium and its compounds | 1000 (expressed as metal) |
| All isomers of hexachlorocyclohexane | 20 |
| All isomers of DDT | 5 |
| Pentachlorophenol and its compounds | 350 |
| Hexachlorobenzene | 5 |
| Hexachlorobutadiene | 20 |
| Aldrin | 2 |
| Dieldrin | 2 |
| Endrin | 1 |
| Polychlorinated biphenyls | 1 |
| Dichlorvos | 0.2 |
| 1,2-Dichloroethane | 2000 |
| All isomers of trichlorobenzene | 75· |
| Atrazine | 350* |
| Simazine | 350* |
| Tributyltin compounds | 4 |
| Triphenyltin compounds | 4 |
| Trifluralin | 20 |
| Fenitrothion | 2 |
| Azinphos-methyl | 2 |
| Malathion | 2 |
| Endosulfan | 0.5 |
| | * Where both Atrazine and Simazine are released, the figure in aggregate is 350 grammes. |

| SCHEDULE 6 |
| --- |
| **RELEASE INTO LAND: PRESCRIBED SUBSTANCES** |

Organic solvents

Azides

Halogens and their covalent compounds

Metal carbonyls

Organo-metallic compounds

Oxidising agents

Polychlorinated dibenzofuran and any congener thereof

Polychlorinated dibenzo-p-dioxin and any congener thereof

Polyhalogenated biphenyls, terphenyls and naphthalenes

Phosphorus

Pesticides, that is to say, any chemical substance or preparation prepared or used for destroying any pest, including those used for protecting plants or wood or other plant products from harmful organisms; regulating the growth of plants; giving protection against harmful creatures; rendering such creatures harmless; controlling organisms with harmful or unwanted effects on water systems, buildings or other structures, or on manufactured products; or protecting animals against ectoparasites

Alkali metals and their oxides and alkaline earth metals and their oxides

## AUTHORISATION FOR PRESCRIBED PROCESSES

Schedule 3 to the Prescribed Processes and Substances Regulations sets out the dates from which IPC authorisation is required for different types of processes. The IPC system came into effect from 1st April 1991 for new processes and has a phased application for existing processes. Existing processes are those that were operated at some time in the 12 months immediately before 1st April 1991. Existing processes that are "substantially changed" will become subject to IPC when the change is made. "Substantial change" is defined in Section 10(7) of the EPA 1990 and relates to the quantity and character of the substances released from the process. The Secretary of State is able to give directions to HMIP on what constitutes a substantial change, either in general terms or for a specific process description or a single process.

It is quite clear that in some cases HMIP inspectors have interpreted any change to a process as being a substantial change. The result of this is that not only is the process deemed to be a "new process" and therefore immediately subject to the IPC system (instead of being phased into the system, according to the timetable applicable to existing processes), it is also subject to the potentially more stringent emission levels which are applicable to new processes. In connection with this it should be noted that in the publication "IPC - A Practical Guide", HMIP inspectors should only regard a change to be "substantial" where the concentration of emissions has been <u>increased</u>. Where the levels of emissions have been decreased it would appear that on no account should HMIP regard this as a substantial change. This is reflected in the definition of "substantial change" as set out in the proposed IPPC Directive (see Chapter 8), that is, a change with significant negative effects on humans or the environment. This is at odds with the Department of the Environment's proposal for a "fast track" procedure for applications for variations of authorisations in respect of substantial changes resulting in environmental gains or a reduction in environmental impact.

All unchanged existing prescribed processes will come within the IPC system by 1st November 1995, according to the implementation timetable (see Table 3). Operators must apply for IPC authorisation within the three month period specified in Schedule 3 to the Prescribed Processes and Substances Regulations. The first processes coming within control were combustion processes involving boilers or furnaces with a capacity of over 50MW (th), in order to comply with the Large Combustion Plants Directive (88/609/EEC). The last prescribed processes to be brought under IPC are those in the Other Industries sector (Chapter 6 of Schedule 1).

It is an offence to operate a prescribed process without authorisation or in contravention of the conditions of an authorisation. Applications should be made in accordance with Schedule 1 to the EPA 1990 and procedures for applications for authorisations, applications for variations of authorisations, appeals and information requirements are set out in the Applications, Appeals and Registers Regulations. Further details can be found in Chapters 4 and 6.

For new processes, applications should be made when formal plans are drawn up, but prior to the commencement of construction. For particularly novel or complex processes, a staged procedure is possible where the application for authorisation is submitted over a period of time as the plans develop, to allow a greater degree of flexibility.

On receiving an application for authorisation, HMIP can either refuse to grant the authorisation or will grant it subject to conditions. These conditions can be divided into express conditions and a general implied condition. The express conditions fall into three categories: conditions which HMIP considers appropriate to achieve the statutory objectives set out in Section 7(2) of the EPA 1990; conditions specified by the Secretary of State under Section 7(3); and any other conditions which appear to HMIP to be appropriate. HMIP may not grant an authorisation if it considers that the applicant will not be able to operate the process in compliance with the conditions that would be attached to the authorisation. The conditions of an authorisation should be reviewed by HMIP at least once every four years. It is possible to appeal against the conditions attached to an authorisation (see Chapter 4).

HMIP will include express conditions designed to achieve all of the following statutory objectives (Section 7(2) of the EPA 1990):

· to ensure that in operating the prescribed process BATNEEC is used to prevent or, where this is not practicable, to minimise the release of prescribed substances and to render harmless any prescribed substances which are released;

· to ensure that in operating the prescribed process BATNEEC is used to render harmless any other substances which might cause harm if released into any environmental medium;

· to comply with directions given by the Secretary of State to implement the UK's obligations under EU or international laws relating to environmental protection;

· to comply with any limits or requirements, and to achieve any quality standards or quality objectives set by the Secretary of State;

· to comply with any requirements associated with a plan made by the Secretary of State;

· to ensure that, where the process authorised is likely to result in the release of substances into more than one environmental medium, in addition to the above objectives, BATNEEC will be used to minimise pollution of the whole environment, having regard to the BPEO for those releases.

Where any of these standards or requirements give rise to conflict, the more stringent condition will apply. Thus, in some circumstances, conditions requiring the use of more than BATNEEC
may be required in order to achieve a statutory objective.

For those aspects of processes not subject to specific conditions
there is also a general condition implied in every authorisation
that the operator of a prescribed process will use BATNEEC to
prevent or, where this is not practicable, to minimise the release of
prescribed substances and to render harmless any prescribed substances released, or any other substances which might cause harm
if released into any environmental medium.

The Secretary of State may issue directions specifying the conditions
which are or are not to be included in all authorisations, authorisations of
a particular description or a particular authorisation. HMIP may also
impose any other conditions which it believes are appropriate. The scope
of conditions can be wide ranging. An authorisation may include conditions setting limits on the quantity or composition of the substances used
or produced by the process at any time. HMIP may also require advance
notice of any proposed change in the operation of the process. It is not
possible however for HMIP to impose conditions solely for the purpose of
protecting the health of workers, to prevent duplication of the controls
administered by the Health and Safety Executive ("HSE") under the
HSWA 1974.

### BATNEEC

The application of BATNEEC is central to the operation of the IPC
system and it is essential to appreciate the extent and practical significance of this concept. However, it must be emphasised that the use of
BATNEEC is only one of the statutory objectives under Section 7 and
that, if necessary, more stringent techniques may be required.

Although new to UK legislation, a concept similar to BATNEEC has
been used in EU legislation for nearly a decade. The Air Framework
Directive (84/360/EEC), which regulates polluting air emissions from
industrial plants, requires that all appropriate preventative measures
against air pollution are taken, including the use of Best Available Technology, provided that this does not involve excessive costs. The proposal
for an IPPC Directive which is currently under discussion (see Chapter 8)
also uses this term although in this case, as under IPC, reference is made
to Best Available Techniques rather than Best Available Technology.

"Techniques" has a wider meaning than "technology" and includes the management of operations, not just the equipment used at the facility.

Although the term BATNEEC is not defined in any detail in the EPA 1990, it would appear that it is intended to be quite wide in its scope. General guidance on the interpretation of this term is given in the Department of the Environment publication "IPC - A Practical Guide". This guidance provides an explanation of BATNEEC by interpreting the meaning of the phrases which make up this concept: "Best Available Techniques" and "Not Entailing Excessive Cost". The phrase "BAT" is further broken down into its component words. Each of these elements should be considered alone and also in combination when considering the meaning of "Best Available Techniques".

"Best" means the most effective technique for achieving the objectives of preventing, minimising or rendering harmless polluting releases from the process. It is not necessary to identify a single "best" technique as there may be several procedures with equal efficacy.

"Available" means that the technique is generally accessible to the operator of the process. It need not be in widespread use but the operator should be able to use it if he so wishes. This would encompass a technique which exists outside the UK or a technique which has been developed and proved as commercially feasible at pilot scale. The technique need not be available on the open market: a procedure only available under licence from a patent holder or from a monopoly supplier will be available, provided that all operators wishing to use it can freely do so.

"Techniques" refers to both the technology used to operate the process and the manner of that operation. This is defined in Section 7(10) of the EPA 1990 which states that references to BATNEEC should include, in addition to details of the technical means and technology to be used, information on those operating the process (their qualifications, training, supervision and the numbers employed) and the premises in which the authorised process is operated (its design, construction, layout and maintenance).

The "NEEC" phrase is extremely important as a qualifier to the BAT concept. There has been criticism from some quarters that the introduction of an economic element amounts to a "watering down" of environmental protection measures and that only BAT should be considered. However, HMIP considers that BAT:

"can properly be modified by economic considerations where the costs of applying best available techniques would be excessive in relation to the nature of the industry and the environmental protection to be achieved" ("IPC - A Practical Guide").

The assessment of what is excessive should be an objective view of the nature of the industry in general and not of the economic constraints acting upon any individual operator.

The precise meaning of NEEC will depend upon whether the process to which BATNEEC is to be applied is a new or an existing process.

For new processes, it is likely that BAT and BATNEEC will be the same and will be applied from the commencement of the operation of the plant. The potential of the process to cause pollution will be an important factor in determining when the NEEC qualifier should enter the equation and on the relative weight given to the cost element. For a particularly polluting process, HMIP would require the expense associated with BAT to be correspondingly high before any cost could be deemed to be "excessive". NEEC should be balanced against the environmental benefit associated with the use of a particular technique. A small environmental gain achieved at very great extra cost in comparison to the next best technique may not be justified. It is also important to recognise that the objective is to prevent or minimise polluting releases as far as possible without imposing excessive cost. If it is not possible to achieve this using BATNEEC, HMIP can refuse an application for IPC authorisation.

For existing processes, the use of BATNEEC will be phased in over a period of time. This will be achieved through the upgrading of existing plant to meet the standards applicable to new plant or to approach these as closely as possible. Alternatively, processes which cannot meet the new plant standards, either due to technical reasons or because it is not economically feasible, will be closed down. Upgrading processes in this way is having a significant effect on some areas of industry. For example, many existing municipal waste incinerators cannot be upgraded to meet the new standards without incurring excessive expenditure and will become obsolete and therefore closed down. The construction of a new generation of incinerators able to meet the requirements for BATNEEC and more stringent release limits is now under way.

As they are phased into IPC, according to the timetable set out in Table 3, existing processes will become subject to the new process standards as indicated in the conditions attached to their authorisations and in the CIGNs. It should be noted that, at least in theory (and in most cases, this is difficult to challenge in practice), the CIGNs are just that - "guidance" to which HMIP should "have regard" (see Section 7(11) of the EPA 1990). The timescale for upgrading and the standards set for an existing process will take into account a range of factors, including:

· the equipment already used in the process;

· the level of operation of the process;

· the remaining working lifespan of the process;

· the nature and volume of the polluting emissions produced by the process; and

· the general economic situation of the industry sector (so as not to entail excessive upgrading costs).

HMIP will prescribe what is BATNEEC for a particular process. This could either be in terms of the technology to be used or through the setting of pollutant release standards. In general, HMIP will express BATNEEC in terms of a performance standard, set to result in pollution equal to or less than a specified level. This is judged to be more satisfactory than specifying a particular technique or technology as it gives a wider range of choice to operators and permits companies to develop abatement technologies meeting standards more stringent than those set out in the legislation and guidance.

BATNEEC will be specified for individual processes by HMIP inspectors when each application for authorisation is determined. The decision as to the appropriate BATNEEC for a process will be given by way of the conditions attached to the authorisation.

What constitutes BATNEEC for a particular process is often an area of contention between HMIP and an IPC applicant. As mentioned above, the CIGNs are guidance to which the HMIP inspectors should have regard but in practice most inspectors regard such guidance as mandatory. It is difficult for an applicant to challenge the guidance in that any such challenge will require detailed technical backup and in any event where the applicant is anxious to obtain an IPC authorisation, it is not often felt to be in their best interest to challenge HMIP. One area which does not seem to have been explored in any detail by either HMIP or applicants is that in some circumstances it may be possible to achieve the prescribed emission limits by the use of techniques which do not involve the installation of new abatement technology. An example of this may be an environmental management system where the use of skilled personnel may be equivalent to or better than the installation of expensive computerised technology. In other words, it should be remembered that the "T" in BATNEEC stands for techniques and not for technology.

## CHIEF INSPECTOR'S GUIDANCE NOTES

It is important that there is consistency between decisions on BATNEEC for similar processes. One way in which this is achieved is by following the general guidance on the meaning of the BATNEEC concept discussed above. More specifically, guidance on BATNEEC for prescribed processes is set out in the CIGNs. These provide advice to HMIP inspectors on the assessment of applications for IPC authorisations and applications for variations of authorisations. They can also be used by applicants and other interested parties (e.g. members of the public wishing to make representations in relation to an application) to identify the criteria against which applications will be assessed and the conditions which may be imposed. Several guidance notes may have been published for each section within Schedule 1 of the Prescribed Processes and Substances Regulations. Conversely, some guidance notes contain information of relevance to several sections. A list of CIGNs grouped under the appropriate Schedule 1 section headings is provided in Appendix III. At the beginning of each process guidance note is a statement which indicates those process descriptions to which the CIGN is applicable.

CIGNs have now been produced for all the processes described in Schedule 1 of the Prescribed Processes and Substances Regulations. These were published between 1991 and 1995, in parallel with the progressive implementation of the IPC system. HMIP has aimed to publish the relevant CIGN at least three months before the commencement of the application period for a particular prescribed process. Before all the process-specific CIGNs were published, guidance was provided to operators applying for authorisations for new or substantially changed existing processes in a series of five industry sector guidance notes covering the fuel and power, metal, mineral, chemical and waste industries. These provided information on prescribed processes, relevant legal obligations, likely releases, release levels, available abatement techniques and monitoring requirements. The industry sector notes have now been largely superseded by the more specific information contained in the process-specific CIGNs.

CIGNs set out information on the prescribed processes, the substances which may be released and the techniques available for preventing, minimising and rendering harmless releases of such substances. Although they have no statutory force, the CIGNs represent HMIP's views on the appropriate techniques to be used in connection with the operation of a specific prescribed process. They will therefore be a material consideration to be taken account of in every case. Where HMIP departs from the guidance, it must be prepared to state the reasoning for this. The release levels set out in CIGNs are those considered to be achievable by applying techniques appropriate to the specific process or industry sector. However, it is important to stress that the existence of a CIGN will not prejudice the final decision taken by the HMIP inspector in relation to the actual release levels and conditions to be attached to an authorisation, as this must take into account the specific environmental and economic circumstances of that application and the outcome of any representations made during the consultation exercise.

The information contained in all CIGNs is essentially the same, although their focus and the format in which the information is presented has changed slightly over the period of their publication. The most recent CIGNs are generally organised as follows.

· **Introduction**

A general introduction to the role of CIGNs.

## · Process Definitions

The process definition(s) in Schedule 1 to the Prescribed Processes and Substances Regulations to which the CIGN applies, details of related processes and the criteria to be used when determining process boundaries.

## · General Provisions

Details of the requirement to use BATNEEC in the operation of the process and a note that the operator should be aware of BAT relevant to that process at the time of the application and keep informed of relevant developments in the future. The CIGN cannot be used as a reason to delay the introduction of improved best techniques.

## · General Requirements

General requirements (release limits and techniques to be used) for new and existing processes. New processes must comply with these requirements immediately. For existing processes, details are provided of the issues to be taken into account when upgrading plant and the timescale within which the new process standards should be achieved. This timetable will be used as a general guideline by inspectors, whilst also taking into account plant-specific factors. In some cases, the CIGNs state that where upgrading by a specific date will result in a major change in plant or process configuration, that deadline may be extended subject to the approval of the Chief Inspector, where this is necessary to satisfy the requirements of BATNEEC/ BPEO. The requirement to move towards new plant standards is emphasised. Details of release monitoring and notification requirements are also given.

## · Releases into Air

Achievable levels of release for air. It is important to note that the achievable levels of release indicate what is achievable, using the best combination of techniques to limit the environmental effects of a process. These levels should not be confused with the release limits included in authorisations which are based on the use of BATNEEC and site-specific factors.

· **Releases into Water**

Achievable levels of release for water.

· **Releases into Land**

Achievable levels of release for land.

· **Process Changes**

Details of what constitutes a substantial change and non-substantial change for that process.

· **Processes**

An overview of the processes covered by the CIGN including environmental impacts and potential release routes.

· **Techniques for Minimising/Controlling Releases**

Techniques to be used to control releases to air, water and land.

· **Compliance Monitoring**

Monitoring requirements for air, water and land, together with details of record keeping and reporting procedures.

· **References and Other HMIP Publications**

Details of other relevant documents, including legislation, other CIGNs and official guidance notes, and publications issued by non-governmental bodies, e.g. industry associations.

There are some anomalies between the release levels set in different CIGNs for processes which, although similar, come within different industry sectors and different Chapters of Schedule 1 of the Prescribed Processes and Substances Regulations.

One example of this is the difference between the emission levels set for waste to energy schemes which fall within Section 1.3 of Schedule 1 of the Prescribed Processes and Substances Regulations (as set out in Table 3) and waste incineration processes as set out in Section 5.1 of Schedule 1.

HMIP has a statutory duty to follow developments in pollution abatement technology and techniques applicable for preventing and controlling releases from prescribed processes. To fulfil this obligation, HMIP commissions studies on best practice covering all aspects of the operation of processes, from raw material selection to the generation of products and wastes. The results are published in the form of BAT review reports and this information is used during the preparation of CIGNs.

CIGNs are the final product of a lengthy review procedure, involving not only HMIP staff, but also representatives from industry, Government departments and other interested parties. Prior to the drafting of a CIGN, a comprehensive review is conducted of the current "best available techniques" for pollution abatement used throughout the world in order to identify suitable techniques which are commercially viable and applicable to UK industry. This includes the use of BAT review reports. Consultation with industry on the issues to be covered in the CIGN is carried out at an early stage before the guidance is prepared, at the draft stage and when a final draft version has been produced. Through this process, the views of a wide range of interested parties from industry, Government etc. are taken into account. The CIGNs are published by Her Majesty's Stationery Office.

HMIP is to review and update the CIGNs at least once every four years. A revised series of CIGNs is in preparation and some second editions e.g. IPR 1/2 on Gas Turbines have already been published. The emphasis of the CIGNs in the new series will be slightly different from that in the original series. In particular, the new CIGNs will concentrate on those features of processes with the most potential to impact on the environment and the techniques for their control. Advice on the financial, economic and market factors to be taken into account in the assessment of BATNEEC for each process type is to be included.

## TECHNICAL GUIDANCE NOTES

In addition to CIGNs, HMIP produces Technical Guidance Notes in three series: Monitoring, Dispersion and Abatement. These are applicable to a range of processes and provide information on the technology to be used when implementing the requirements of environmental legislation. The Technical Guidance Notes published to date are listed in Table 6.

# TABLE 6

## HMIP TECHNICAL GUIDANCE NOTES

| MONITORING SERIES | |
|---|---|
| M1 | Sampling Facility Requirements for the Monitoring of Particulates in Gaseous Releases to Atmosphere |
| M2 | Monitoring Emissions of Pollutants at Source |
| M3 | Standards for IPC Monitoring : Part 1 - Standards Organisations and the Measurement Infrastructure |
| M4 | Standards for IPC Monitoring : Part 2 - Standards in Support of IPC Monitoring |
| M5 | Routine Measurement of Gamma Ray Air Kerma Rate in the Environment |
| **DISPERSION SERIES** | |
| D1 | Guidelines on Discharge Stack Heights for Polluting Emissions |
| **ABATEMENT SERIES** | |
| A1 | Guidance on Effective Flaring in the Gas, Petroleum, Petrochemical and Associated Industries |
| A2 | Abatement Technology for the Reduction of Solvent Vapour Emissions |
| A3 | Pollution Abatement Technology for Particulate and Trace Gas Removal |

## MONITORING

Monitoring of releases from prescribed processes forms an important part of IPC. This has a dual purpose: it provides evidence to HMIP that operators are complying with regulatory standards, and the information collated on releases is made available through the public register and the CRI.

Monitoring activities carried out in connection with IPC fall into two categories. Firstly, the conditions of an authorisation will require the operator of a prescribed process to monitor releases produced by that process. The results of such tests are reported to HMIP for analysis. Secondly, HMIP operates a number of check monitoring programmes which are conducted by independent contractors to confirm the results of the monitoring carried out by the operators of prescribed processes.

There are three types of check monitoring.

### · Routine Monitoring

Long term monitoring programmes are conducted for specific types of process, e.g. incinerators and power stations. This type of monitoring activity is to be expanded in relation to IPC and it is intended that processes in the fuel and power, waste, chemical and mineral industry sectors will be subject to routine monitoring programmes by April 1996.

### · Reactive Monitoring

Monitoring is also carried out to support inspection programmes, to follow up on unusual results produced from routine monitoring activities or as part of enforcement action.

### · Investigative Site Surveys

More detailed studies of particular facilities or the environment surrounding them are carried out to supplement routine and reactive monitoring programmes. Site surveys will frequently include an assessment of the impact of releases on the environment and their comparison with published standards. Such programmes can be conducted on HMIP's initiative or in response to public complaints.

Finally, HMIP commissions and conducts research to support these monitoring activities and to improve monitoring standards and assessment methods.

## INSPECTIONS

Processes are inspected regularly by HMIP to ensure that all the conditions attached to authorisations are being met. HMIP inspectors will also visit a site following a complaint or report of a polluting incident.

Plans have been announced for a series of large scale audit inspections of major industrial sites. They are intended as a trial to develop a method for regular use. If effective, these audits would be carried out routinely by the Environment Agency from April 1996. The audits will go beyond the normal site visits conducted by HMIP inspectors and provide an overall assessment of the site which is carried out over several days. A report summarising each audit will be published, a move aimed at increasing pressure on operators to improve their performance.

### Operator and Pollution Risk Appraisal

To assist HMIP in targeting its regulatory effort, an Operator and Pollution Risk Appraisal system ("OPRA") has been developed to assess operator performance and the pollution risks of processes prescribed for IPC. This formalises HMIP's existing approach to risk assessment and is being piloted by inspectors on site visits. A review will be conducted in 1996.

The OPRA system comprises of two elements: an assessment of the operator's performance to provide an indication of the probability of a pollution incident occurring and an assessment of the process to determine the potential pollution hazard. These factors are combined to give an indication of comparative risk. The first element is termed the Operator Performance Appraisal, the second element is the Pollution Hazard Appraisal.

The Operator Performance Appraisal uses seven key indicators:

· compliance with release limits and adequacy of record keeping;

· knowledge of authorisation requirements and their implemen tation;

· plant maintenance and operation;

· management and training;

· procedures and instructions;

· frequency of incidents and justified complaints; and

· existence of auditable environmental management systems.

Each of these indicators will be awarded a score which will be multiplied by a factor reflecting HMIP's view of its relative importance.

The Pollution Hazard Appraisal considers seven process attributes:

· hazardous substances;

· techniques for prevention and minimisation;

· techniques for abatement;

· scale of process;

· location;

· frequency of operation; and

· use of offensive substances in the process.

Again, each process attribute is rated, awarded a value and multiplied by a factor to reflect its relative importance.

The OPRA system is seen as having a number of advantages, allowing HMIP to improve its effectiveness and efficiency in regulating IPC.

· **Pollution Prevention**

Identifying areas where improvements are necessary or desirable and stimulating discussion between HMIP and the operator.

· **Regulatory Oversight**

Allowing HMIP to link the frequency of inspection with the operator's performance, e.g. reducing inspections for operators with good environmental practices.

### · Provision of Strategic Information

Allowing trends in performance and regulation to be identified.

### · Scheme of Fees and Charges

The OPRA scheme may be used as the basis for a revised Scheme of Fees and Charges for IPC (see Chapter 4).

### · Incentive Effect

An award scheme may be introduced to provide an incentive for good environmental practice whereby companies receive star ratings.

## ENVIRONMENTAL ASSESSMENTS

One of the major problems encountered by IPC applicants has been the requirement to assess the environmental impact of releases and to demonstrate the use of BATNEEC and that the preferred option is the BPEO. In response to this, HMIP is providing guidance on determining site specific BPEO and BATNEEC. There are three main approaches:

· increasing the amount of economic information on industry sectors and cost information on process and abatement options in the new series of CIGNs (see earlier in this Chapter);

· developing a "toolkit" for environmental analysis for use by industry; and

· developing principles and procedures for carrying out environmental, economic and BPEO assessments.

### Environmental Analysis Toolkit

The "toolkit" for environmental analysis aims to provide the means for improving the quality and consistency of IPC applications. A group consisting of industrial companies, trade associations and representatives from the regulatory authorities has been set up to develop the tools needed when conducting the assessments required by IPC applications. The first step has been to draw up an environmental analysis framework manual setting out best practice for industry which should be produced in early 1996. Other tools proposed include:

· an environmental screening tool for identifying and evaluating potentially significant releases to the environment;

· an ambient quality database providing access to quality assured data on background environmental concentrations;

· a set of emission tools providing assistance in compiling site inventories of process emissions;

· a model benchmarking procedure providing a systematic basis for selecting appropriate models for use in specific environmental analysis applications, e.g. models for the dispersion and fate of emissions.

### Environmental, Economic and BPEO Assessments

HMIP is also developing procedures which will help to ensure that sufficient information is provided by operators to allow the environmental effects of releases to be assessed adequately and that the option chosen uses BATNEEC and represents the site specific BPEO. A draft guidance note was produced in 1993 and a formal consultation document issued in 1994. A three volume draft guidance note has now been produced and a programme of case studies has been undertaken to test the methodology in practice. It is envisaged that these procedures will be used when applications for authorisations are made and also when operators conduct environmental assessments under improvement programmes as a requirement of the conditions of granted authorisations.

The draft guidance note sets out procedures for assessing harm and comparing options for specific industry processes to determine the BPEO. Advice is also given on the economic information required to determine the practicality of the process options identified. HMIP has aimed to strike a balance between a procedure which is applicable to all operators, but which takes into account the complexities of representing the effects of environmental releases. The procedure consists of four stages.

### · Preliminary Assessment

Identifying and quantifying releases and their environmental effects to determine significant releases. The selection of priority releases for control, involving a consideration of CIGNs, chimney heights and comparison with environmental assessment levels (against which releases are assessed).

### · Option Generation

Identifying and screening control techniques, combining into control options and selecting those appropriate for further assessment.

### · Environmental Assessment to Determine the Best Environmental Option

Assessing the effects of all the options put forward, including short and long term effects, global warming, ozone creation potential, waste arisings etc.. Comparing and ranking these options and then determining the Best Environmental Option.

### · Determination of the Best Practicable Environmental Option

Where the Best Environmental Option is not the preferred option, the economic assessment of the preferred option.

The draft guidance note provides technical data to be used in this methodology, including environmental quality standards and environmental assessment levels for releases to air, water and land; sources of information on ambient environmental quality; and environmental assessment of different effects. A worked example is also included.

### "3 E'S" PROJECT

In March 1995, HMIP and Allied Colloids Ltd launched a joint initiative to review site practices at its Low Moor plant considering particularly the "3Es": Emissions, Efficiencies and Economics. The aim was to improve the environmental performance at the site taking into account IPC principles. The study involved staff working with HMIP on a check list of questions provoking consideration of various scenarios and their costs and benefits. In addition, a study of all material inputs and outputs of the processes and vital equipment was carried out. HMIP hope that through such initiatives other companies will be encouraged to have a positive approach to pollution control. The initiative with Allied Colloids proved a success with major cost savings being found. The initiative has now been extended to other firms in association with Business in the Environment.

Chapter 4

# ADMINISTRATION OF IPC

## APPLYING FOR AUTHORISATION

Applications for the authorisation of prescribed processes are made to HMIP. The applicant is required to provide details of the design and operation of the process involved, to assess the environmental effects of any releases from that process and to specify the means to be used to ensure compliance with the conditions attached to the authorisation. HMIP is responsible for determining the application for authorisation, including ensuring that the correct information is supplied by the applicant, liaising with other regulatory authorities and official bodies, making information available to the public and assessing whether the conditions to be attached to the authorisation can be achieved by the applicant. Some aspects of the application procedure for authorisations also apply to applications for the variation of the conditions of granted authorisations.

### When to Apply

The stage at which the application for authorisation should be made varies, depending on whether the process is a new or existing one. HMIP recommends that applicants consult with its inspectors prior to the preparation of the application, to discuss how the IPC requirements are to be satisfied. Applications for existing processes which have remained unchanged since the introduction of IPC should be made at the appropriate point in the implementation timetable for IPC (see Table 3). The introduction of IPC is virtually complete and the remaining existing processes will come within IPC in November 1995. Applications for such processes must be made by the end of January 1996.

Applications for existing processes undergoing "substantial change" should be made when that change takes place.

IPC applied immediately to new processes, i.e. from April 1991.

Applications for the authorisation of new processes should normally be made prior to the construction of the facility, once the full design plans have been completed. This is the optimum stage for applications to be considered: there is sufficient concrete information available for a satisfactory and complete application to be submitted to HMIP, for the consultation exercise to proceed and for the determination of the application. However, should HMIP's determination impose conditions requiring alterations to the plant design or operation, it would not be too late to incorporate these relatively easily and without too much inconvenience. It should be stressed that if the applicant makes any changes to the process design, HMIP must be informed as it may be necessary to vary the conditions attached to the granted authorisation.

## Special Cases

### Staged Applications

Where a new plant is particularly complex or the process is novel, the design and construction of the facility may take a longer period of time. In such cases, it will be difficult for HMIP to determine an application for authorisation in the normal manner because the required information may not all be available and the design may change in the future. A staged application procedure may be followed in which agreement is reached with HMIP that the application and any supporting information will be provided in tranches during the development of the facility design. This allows HMIP to be consulted at an earlier stage in the design process to provide advice on the pollution control techniques that may be required. It also enables representations by interested parties concerning the proposed process to be made at an early stage to avoid unnecessary expenditure by the applicant on facilities which are unsuitable or unnecessary in some way.

The application can be submitted either when an outline of the design is finalised or at the earlier stage of primary process selection. As much information as possible should be provided as early as possible. The applicant will submit the remaining information required for HMIP to determine the application during the design, construction and commissioning phases of the project. Although a longer period for the determination of the application will be agreed between HMIP and the applicant, the other procedural requirements relating to advertising, public consultation, notification to statutory consultees and placement on the public register will continue to apply. As the additional information is submitted, this will be added to the public register and will be subject to the standard consultation procedure.

Finally, once all the necessary information is provided, HMIP will determine the application. It is important to note that, in the case of staged applications, the normal charging scheme will not apply. Instead, a fee based on the time spent and expenses incurred by HMIP during the application and determination process will be levied (see later in this Chapter).

## · Envelope Authorisations

In cases where chemical products are manufactured on a batch wise basis using multi-purpose plant, an application may be made for an envelope authorisation. This will cover a range of processes and products and is granted instead of separate authorisations for each single process. Relatively minor modifications are permitted within the envelope, although if there is a major change to the process, the normal variation procedures will apply. Details of the products to be manufactured within the envelope are provided to HMIP, together with information on the processes involved, expected releases, the equipment and abatement techniques to be used, and the product schedule. Similarly, for pilot plants, where products are manufactured on a small scale and work may be investigative, a pilot plant envelope authorisation can be granted. Details of the individual investigations to be undertaken are not required for such authorisations.

## Information to be Provided in the Application

The application for authorisation should be made in writing, preferably using a form obtainable from HMIP (see Appendix IV for the addresses of HMIP offices). This form is also used for applications for substantial changes to authorised prescribed processes (although reference is only made here to the information required in connection with applications for authorisation; details of the specific information required in relation to applications for variations of authorisations can be found later in this Chapter). Supporting technical information should be provided as a separate document.

Copies of applications will be placed on the public register and it is therefore important that they are completed in a way which will facilitate public understanding of the regulated processes at a particular location. The information provided should be clear, comprehensive and accurate. Nine copies of the application form and supporting technical information should be provided together with the originals to assist with the administration of the application and to allow the determination process to proceed as rapidly as possible.

In addition to the application form and supporting technical information, the applicant must submit the appropriate application fee. The level of fee is dependant upon the number of defined components in the process, although a special charging scheme exists for staged applications. A new Scheme of Fees and Charges is introduced on 1st April each year. If the fee is not paid or the incorrect fee is paid, HMIP can refuse to proceed with the application (see later in this Chapter).

The completed application and fee should be sent to the HMIP office with responsibility for the county in which the process is located: Bristol or Bedford (see Appendix IV).

Certain particulars which must be included in an application for authorisation are given in the Applications, Appeals and Registers Regulations. In addition to the information specified in these Regulations, other details may be required to facilitate the determination of the application. If any of this information is omitted the application will be invalid and will not be determined. The supporting technical information should be provided in the structured format outlined below to facilitate the determination procedure.

The information to be included in an application for authorisation is listed below. The details required by the Applications, Appeals and Registers Regulations are listed first, followed by any other information required by HMIP on the application form or in the supporting technical information, and any guidance given by HMIP on this information.

## 1. Applicant Details and Administrative Information

Name, address and telephone number of the applicant, correspondence address if different from the applicant's address and, for corporate applicants, the address of the registered office or principal office.

In addition, HMIP requires the following information to be included on the application form.

· Companies House Registration Number, where appropriate (this should be the number of the company operating the process, not a parent company).

· Type of organisation operating the process.

· A contact to discuss the contents of the application form.

· Payment details, including details of an invoice contact, the fee submitted, the process type (the reference of the process description from Schedule 1 to the Prescribed Processes and Substances Regulations) and the number and type of components contained within the process.

The names and addresses of all trading partners and the name of the trading partnership should be provided where appropriate. The Department of the Environment has proposed that the name of the applicant's ultimate holding company be supplied. This information would also be placed on the public register.

## 2. **Location of Prescribed Process - Stationary Plant**

The local authority for the area in which the prescribed process is operated, the address of the premises where the prescribed process is operated, the location of those premises shown on a map or plan and, if not all the premises, that part of the premises to be used for the operation of the prescribed process (shown on a plan or other means of identification).

In addition, HMIP requires the following information to be included on the application form.

· National Grid Reference of the process location.

· A principal contact on the operation of the process.

· The waste regulation authority for the area in which the process is operated.

The local authority identified should be the district or borough council rather than the county council. Any plans provided to identify the location of the premises on which the process is to be operated must identify clearly the location of that process and its relationship with the surrounding area. Any on-site drainage arrangements, discharge points from the site into sewers or controlled waters, and on-site collection points for effluent from prescribed processes and non-prescribed processes should be identified on a plan where releases to water are made.

### 3. Location of Prescribed Process - Mobile Plant

The local authority for the area in which the applicant's principal place of business is located and the address of the principal place of business.

### 4. Prescribed Process

A description of the prescribed process to be operated.

In addition, HMIP requires that the supporting technical information should include details of the following.

· Process operation under normal conditions and other conditions, e.g. start up, shut down.

· The purpose of the process, the products manufactured and production rate.

· Process operation represented as a process flow diagram (main and ancillary processes).

· If appropriate, the chemistry of the process, including details of the generation and minimisation of wastes and by-products.

· All potential sources of releases.

· Maximum release rates and the location of all release points.

· Results of a mass balance exercise for the materials used within the process to identify where releases occur (including process losses and fugitive releases).

· Raw material specifications and level of usage (during both normal operation and at maximum continual operation of the process).

· Storage and handling of raw materials, intermediates, by-products and wastes prior to their use, disposal or re-use (including delivery).

· Abatement plant.

· Surface drainage and facilities for trade effluent drainage (including plans).

· Measures for minimising the effect of malfunctions with the potential to impact on the environment and the testing and maintenance of any stand-by facilities.

## 5. Prescribed Substances

A list of prescribed substances and any other substances which might cause harm to the environment if released which will be used in connection with or which will result from the operation of the prescribed process.

In addition, HMIP requires that the supporting technical information should include details of the following.

· List of all raw materials used (trade name and chemical composition), by-products generated, products manufactured, with details of all associated releases.

· Any prescribed substances or any other substances that may cause harm to the environment which are present in the raw materials used.

· All releases to the environment from the process (including final product and uncontrolled releases).

The assessment of potential releases should extend to fugitive releases or the potential for fugitive releases resulting from the handling and storage of raw materials, by-products, wastes and releases from process malfunctions.

## 6. Pollution Abatement Techniques

Details of the techniques which will be used to prevent and minimise the release of substances into the environment and to render harmless any which are released.

In addition, HMIP requires that the supporting technical information should include details of the following.

· Aspects of the process which impact particularly heavily on the environment and their management.

· Techniques to be used to minimise the release of prescribed substances to the environment and their design, operation etc.

· Techniques to be used to render harmless any releases to the environment and their design, operation etc.

The emphasis must be placed on preventing, rather than controlling releases of prescribed substances. This should be considered at all stages of the design process. Waste containing prescribed substances should only be produced when no other option exists.

## 7. Releases of Substances

Details of any proposed releases into air, water or land, and an assessment of their environmental effects.

In addition, HMIP requires the following information to be included on the application form.

· The relevant sewerage undertaker, NRA region or harbour authority, where releases are made from the process to sewers, directly to controlled waters or into harbours.

· Sites of Special Scientific Interest within two kilometres of the process or likely to be affected by it.

In addition, HMIP requires that the supporting technical information should include details of the following.

· Release rates of substances to air, water  and land and where substances are released in combination with others, the concentrations of the substances involved.

· Indication of whether releases are continuous or intermittent and the maximum hourly and yearly mass releases for each substance.

· Maximum release rates and quantities.

· Release rates under normal operating conditions.

· Any uncontrolled releases.

· Time periods during which releases to controlled waters are likely to occur.

· Assessment of the effects of the releases on the environment (including details of their transportation in the environment, local and remote effects, the background environmental concentrations of substances in the media into which they are released, any increases in background levels resulting from the releases, the status of organisms likely to be particularly affected by the substances released, and the effects of such releases on any other organisms likely to be adversely affected).

Where discharges are made to controlled waters or sewers, it is advisable to consult with the NRA and the relevant sewerage undertaker prior to making the application for authorisation.

Similarly, where there are likely to be other significant environmental impacts from a process, it may be advisable to contact other statutory consultees prior to making the application.

## 8. Monitoring of Releases

Details of the methodology to be used to monitor releases of substances and their environmental effects, and the operation of the pollution abatement techniques.

In addition, HMIP requires that the supporting technical information should include details of the following.

· Sampling and analysis techniques to be used when demonstrating compliance with the conditions of the authorisation relating to releases to the environment.

· Measures used to monitor the effectiveness of techniques used to prevent and minimise or render harmless substances released into the environment (this should include details of equipment, staff management and training).

· Monitoring programme to assess the environmental consequences of all releases from the process.

### 9. Compliance

Details of the matters on which the applicant will rely to achieve the objectives of Section 7 of the EPA 1990.

Throughout the application, the applicant must fully justify the techniques etc. chosen. Where alternative techniques exist, the applicant must have considered all options and justify this as the BPEO. Justification for existing plant not reaching new plant standards immediately must be given. Details of the methodologies developed to assist HMIP inspectors and applicants in this regard are given in Chapter 3.

### 10. Additional Information

Details of other information not listed elsewhere which the applicant wishes HMIP to consider during the determination of the application.

It is important that non-relevant information is not provided as this can obscure the information that is required and the determination by HMIP may then take longer.

### 11. Existing Permissions

Details of other current permissions or applications held or made by the applicant to HMIP should also be included on the application form. These are those made or held under Part I of the EPA 1990, the Radioactive Substances Acts 1960 and 1993, The Control of Industrial Air Pollution (Registration of Works) Regulations 1989 (made under the HSWA 1974) and any referral made to the Secretary of State under the Water Industry Act 1991. Where an application is to vary an existing IPC authorisation, details of that authorisation should be included.

## 12. Exclusion from the Public Register

HMIP requires that any information considered by the applicant to be commercially confidential or which should be excluded on the grounds of national security is specified on the application form.

Further details of the information required to be supplied in an application for authorisation or variation of an authorisation is given in the IPC application form and "Guidance to Applicants" which will be supplied by HMIP on request.

HMIP may request any further information from the applicant which it requires in order to determine the application. This request must be made in writing and state the specific information required and the timescale within which it should be provided. If the applicant does not supply any of the additional information within the time period set, HMIP can refuse to proceed with the application.

## EXCLUSION OF INFORMATION FROM THE PUBLIC REGISTER

Information provided to HMIP with an application, together with details of the authorisation, notices served by HMIP, revocations of authorisations, appeals and connected convictions will be placed on the public register. This is open to public inspection and is held at HMIP regional offices, the offices of the relevant local authority and, where discharges to water are involved, at the regional NRA office. Applications can be made for commercially confidential information or information which would affect national security to be withheld. In such circumstances, the period permitted for HMIP to determine the application may be extended. Further details are given in Chapter 6.

The applicant should specify the information contained in the application which is believed to be commercially confidential and give precise reasons for this. HMIP recommends that discussions are held before an application is made and that the applicant considers whether the information can be presented in a way which makes commercial confidentiality unnecessary. To facilitate the exclusion of commercially confidential information it should be submitted on separate pages, wherever possible. HMIP has 14 days to determine whether such information is to be excluded. Where information is not deemed to be commercially confidential, it will not be placed on the public register for 21 days. Where the applicant does not agree with HMIP's determination, an appeal may be made to the Secretary of State or the application may be withdrawn before it is made public. An appeal will suspend the application process. Where agreement is reached between HMIP and the applicant that certain information is commercially confidential, HMIP suggests that another copy of the application is submitted which does not contain that information to ensure that confidential information is properly removed before the consultation procedures begin. No information which is the subject of an application or appeal will be placed on the public register until these issues are resolved.

If the applicant believes that certain information is contrary to the interests of national security, or a direction from the Secretary of State is in existence to this effect, it should be made clear on the application. At the HMIP office there will be an inspector to whom such information may be sent. Before making the application, the applicant should identify this person and the application should be placed in an envelope and addressed to that inspector. The first few pages of the application form, which will not contain any sensitive information, should be photocopied and provided in a separate envelope, together with the application fee, to allow general processing to continue.

## CONSULTATION PROCEDURES

The decision on whether or not to grant an authorisation does not rest solely with HMIP. Other regulatory authorities and official bodies, termed "statutory consultees", and the general public are entitled to give their opinion on the application and the Secretary of State may also make a direction to this effect.

### Statutory Consultees

The Applications, Appeals and Registers Regulations identify a number of statutory consultees to which HMIP must send notification of an application for authorisation or an application for the variation of an authorisation (see later in this Chapter). The list of statutory consultees is wide ranging. Some bodies must be consulted in all instances, others only when the prescribed process is carried out in a geographical area in which they have an interest, releases pollution into an environmental medium regulated by them or impacts on property over which they have control. The statutory consultees and the circumstances in which they are notified by HMIP are listed in Table 7.

# TABLE 7
## STATUTORY CONSULTEES

| STATUTORY CONSULTEE | CIRCUMSTANCES OF NOTIFICATION BY HMIP |
|---|---|
| Health and Safety Executive | All prescribed processes |
| Ministry of Agriculture,Fisheries and Food | Where a prescribed process is operated in England |
| Secretary of State for Wales | Where a prescribed process is operated in Wales |
| National Rivers Authority | Where the operation of a prescribed process in England or Wales may result in the release into controlled waters of any substance |
| Sewerage Undertaker | Where the operation of a prescribed process in England or Wales may involve the release into a sewer vested in the Undertaker of any substance |
| Nature Conservancy Council for England (English Nature) | Where the operation of a prescribed process may involve the release of any substance which may affect a Site of Special Scientific Interest in England |
| Countryside Council for Wales | Where the operation of a prescribed process may involve the release of any substance which may affect a Site of Special Scientific Interest in Wales |
| Harbour Authority | Where the operation of a prescribed process may involve the release of any substance into a harbour managed by that Authority |

In addition to the statutory consultees set out in the Applications, Appeals and Registers Regulations, HMIP may also be directed by the Secretary of State to notify a specific consultee in relation to a particular application for authorisation. It is also proposed that local authorities and sea fisheries committees should become statutory consultees for applications for processes to be operated in areas for which they have responsibility.

HMIP must notify a statutory consultee of an application for authorisation or the variation of an authorisation of interest to it within 14 days of the receipt of that application. Where HMIP has served a variation notice and the action proposed by the operator constitutes a substantial change, HMIP must notify the statutory consultees within 14 days of the date on which the holder is notified of the substantial change (see later in this Chapter). A copy of the application is sent to the statutory consultee and any representations made by it must be considered by HMIP during the determination of the application. Such representations must be made within 28 days of the notification of the application, unless the Secretary of State specifies otherwise. Representations must be made in writing.

If an applicant has requested that information be excluded from the public register for reasons of commercial confidentiality or in the interests of national security, HMIP will notify the statutory consultee of the application for authorisation not less than 14 days and not more than 28 days after the date on which a final decision on the exclusion of that information has been reached. Sewerage undertakers, the Nature Conservancy Council for England, the Countryside Council for Wales and harbour authorities will not be consulted on commercially confidential information or information affecting national security unless it is directly relevant to them.

## Advertising of Applications and Public Consultation

An important objective of the IPC system is to promote public accountability and access to information. This is discussed further in Chapter 6. To this end, there are a number of publicity requirements, one aim of which is to bring the application for authorisation or variation of an authorisation to the attention of the general public and to facilitate public consultation.

The applicant must publish an advertisement in one or more local newspapers circulating in the neighbourhood of the premises where the prescribed process will operate (this does not apply to prescribed processes operated using mobile plant).

The advertisement should include the following information:

· the name of the applicant or holder of the authorisation;

· the address of the premises where the prescribed process will operate;

· a brief description of the prescribed process;

· the location of the public register where details of the application can be inspected, including a statement that this inspection is free of charge;

· the procedure for making representations in connection with the application, including the information that any person may make a representation in writing to HMIP within 28 days of the date of the advertisement; and

· the address of the relevant HMIP office.

The advertisement should be published not less than 14 days and not more than 42 days after the date on which the application for authorisation or variation of an authorisation was made, or where a variation notice has been served, the date on which the operator is informed by HMIP that the variation proposed will constitute a substantial change (see later in this Chapter). Where an applicant has requested that certain information is excluded from the public register on the grounds of commercial confidentiality or national security, the application should be advertised not less than 14 days and not more than 42 days after the date on which a final decision is reached on the exclusion of that information.

Representations made by any person as a result of this procedure should be considered by HMIP when determining the application. As for statutory consultees, any representations must be in writing and oral representations will not be accepted.

The Department of the Environment has proposed that applications relating to IPC processes should be advertised in the London or Edinburgh Gazettes to allow parties outside the immediate locality the opportunity to make representations. Local advertising requirements may also be extended.

## TRANSMISSION TO THE SECRETARY OF STATE

The Secretary of State may direct HMIP that a specific application or class of applications for authorisation are sent to him for determination. In such circumstances, HMIP must inform the applicant that the application has been "called in" by the Secretary of State.

The Secretary of State can either require that a local inquiry is held in relation to the application or allow the applicant and HMIP an informal hearing before a person appointed by him. The applicant or HMIP may make a request concerning the mode of hearing by giving notice to the Secretary of State within 21 days of the date on which the applicant is informed of the calling in of the application. Following these procedures, the Secretary of State will direct HMIP on whether he considers the application should be granted and on any conditions that should be attached to the granted authorisation.

The Secretary of State may also direct HMIP not to determine or proceed with a specific application or particular class of applications for authorisation, either for a specified time period or until directed to do otherwise.

## PERIOD PERMITTED FOR DETERMINING THE APPLICATION

HMIP must usually determine an application for authorisation within four months of its receipt. There are a number of exemptions to this general rule. The applicant and HMIP may agree on a longer determination period, for example in cases where a staged application is made. In circumstances where an application is referred to the Secretary of State, the determination period may also be longer than four months. The Secretary of State is able to substitute alternative determination periods by order. The Environmental Protection (Authorisation of Processes) (Determination Periods) Order 1991 extends the period available to HMIP for the determination of applications for authorisations in cases where an application may involve commercially confidential information or information affecting national security and a decision must be made whether to exclude that information from the public register.

In circumstances where:

· the Secretary of State is to determine whether to exclude information affecting national security;

· an application is made to HMIP for the exclusion of information on the grounds that it is commercially confidential; or

· an objection is made to the inclusion of commercially confidential information on the public register;

the determination period will be extended to four months from the date on which the decision on the exclusion or inclusion of the information is made or, in cases where an appeal against that decision is brought, on the date on which the Secretary of States finally determines the appeal, on which the appellant withdraws the appeal, or on the date on which the period for bringing an appeal expires. Alternatively, agreement may be reached between HMIP and the applicant on a longer determination period.

If HMIP does not determine the application for authorisation within the agreed time scale, the application shall be deemed to be refused if the applicant notifies HMIP in writing that he treats it as such. He may then appeal to the Secretary of State against the refusal of the grant of the authorisation.

## DETERMINING THE APPLICATION FOR AUTHORISATION

HMIP's assessment and determination of an application can be divided into three stages.

· Stage 1 - Preliminary Administration

· Stage 2 - Technical Assessment

· Stage 3 - Determination of Authorisation Conditions

## Stage 1 - Preliminary Administration

Before the technical assessment of the application commences, it will be reviewed to ensure that it is complete and fulfils all the relevant legal requirements.

The administrative checks and procedures include the following.

· Entering the application into HMIP's computerised Corporate Information System which logs and tracks the application.

· Checking the validity of the application, i.e. whether it complies with legal requirements, but not whether the information included is complete or accurate (if found to be invalid, the application will not progress any further).

· Dealing with an invalid application, either by returning it to the applicant or requesting further information in writing if only minor details are missing.

· Checking that the correct fee has been submitted with the application, i.e. whether the applicant has calculated the number of components in the process correctly.

· Notifying the relevant statutory consultees.

· Requesting the applicant to advertise the application.

· Placing the application on the public register.

· Checking for commercial confidentiality.

These procedures are generally carried out by HMIP administrative staff, although HMIP inspectors may provide advice in relation to the charging scheme, the consultation process and any commercially confidential information.

## Stage 2 - Technical Assessment

Once the administrative stage is complete, the technical assessment of the application will be carried out by an HMIP inspector.

The technical assessment will include the following considerations.

· Whether the applicant provides full justification for the techniques etc. selected and demonstrates compliance with the statutory objectives of the EPA 1990.

· Whether a reasonable range of options has been considered and whether there are any other options which should be examined, based on information provided in the relevant CIGNs and the inspector's knowledge.

· Where the applicant has not selected the Best Environmental Option, whether this is sufficiently justified on the basis of excessive cost.

· Whether the application is in compliance with any relevant quality standards or quality objectives, limits, directions or requirements associated with a plan made by the Secretary of State.

If the inspector does not believe that the applicant is correct in his view that the statutory objectives will be met, the applicant may be asked to justify his decision.

When assessing the application, the inspector must have regard to the advice given in any relevant CIGN and any developments since the publication of that advice. If the inspector considers that the application is incomplete and additional information is required, this may be requested from the applicant. In such cases, the determination period will usually be extended.

In determining whether the preferred option set out in the application meets the statutory objectives of the EPA 1990, the inspector will review whether the applicant has considered:

· the prevention and minimisation of wastes;

· the environmental effects of the process;

· release limits;

· the design, construction and operation of the process;

· quality assurance matters.

The inspector will also take into account whether a process is a new or existing one and any representations made by statutory consultees or members of the public.

### Stage 3 - Determination of Authorisation Conditions

Following the technical assessment procedure, the HMIP inspector will consider and make recommendations concerning the conditions to be attached to the authorisation. This should take into consideration the advice set out in the relevant CIGN, the proposals made in the application and any representations received as a result of the consultation procedure.

The conditions specified must only be concerned with the statutory objectives set out in Section 7 of the EPA 1990. They must be clear, practicable and enforceable and must minimise the pollution potential of the process to the environment as a whole. The conditions may address release limits or standards for monitoring and sampling. If the inspector considers that the applicant will not be able to construct or operate the process in compliance with these conditions, the application for authorisation must be refused. Finally, the inspector will complete a summary setting out his conclusions in connection with the application and any specific recommendations that must be addressed in the authorisation.

### HMIP'S DECISION

On determination of an authorisation HMIP has two options. It can grant the authorisation subject to conditions or refuse to grant the authorisation because it does not consider that the applicant can operate the process in compliance with the conditions to be attached to the authorisation. The applicant may appeal to the Secretary of State if an application is refused or if he disagrees with any of the conditions attached to it. The Secretary of State is able to direct HMIP to refuse to grant an authorisation and can specify any conditions which should or should not be attached to it. HMIP may also refuse to proceed with the determination due to lack of information or because the correct application fee has not been paid.

The authorisation granted by HMIP will consist of four parts:

· a certificate setting out the details of the authorisation holder, the location of the process and date of application;

· a schedule setting out requirements for the process operation, release limits, waste treatment etc;

· any other conditions or limitations;

· details of the monitoring and sampling programmes required.

## APPLYING FOR VARIATION OF AN AUTHORISATION

Once granted, the conditions attached to an authorisation may be varied by HMIP or by the operator of the authorised process if a change to that process is required. The procedures involved will depend on the nature of that change. The variation may constitute a "relevant change" or a "substantial change" to the process, depending on the degree of variation. These terms are defined in Sections 10 and 11 of the EPA 1990.

A "relevant change" to a prescribed process is:

"a change in the manner of carrying on the process which is capable of altering the substances released from the process or of affecting the amount or any other characteristic of any substance so released" (Section 11(11)).

This is a broad definition and is therefore likely to cover even relatively minor changes to a process.

A "substantial change" to a prescribed process is:

"a substantial change in the substances released from the process or in the amount or any other characteristic of any substance so released" (Section 10(7)),

i.e. it is of greater magnitude than a relevant change (see Chapter 3 for discussion).

The Secretary of State can issue directions to HMIP to indicate what is or is not a substantial change in relation to prescribed processes generally, a specific process description or an individual process. In practice, a definition of substantial change for each process is included in the relevant CIGN. The Department of the Environment has proposed a "fast track" procedure for applications for substantial change which result in environmental gains or reductions in environmental impact. In such cases, advertising and consultation procedures would not apply.

### Variation by HMIP

The conditions of a granted authorisation may be varied by HMIP at any time and a variation notice served on the operator of the prescribed process. If it appears to HMIP that in order to satisfy the statutory objectives set out in Section 7 of the EPA 1990 the conditions of the authorisation should be supplemented, altered or rescinded, the authorisation may be varied to incorporate these revisions. In any event, HMIP is required to review the conditions of an authorisation at intervals of at least four years. This power is particularly important in relation to the use of BATNEEC. HMIP has a duty to monitor developments in pollution control techniques. Where new, improved techniques become available, HMIP can require operators to make use of them by varying the conditions of authorisations.

HMIP must inform the holder of an authorisation of its intention to vary the authorisation by serving a variation notice on that person. The variation notice will set out the specific changes to be made and the timescale within which they should be achieved.

The holder of the authorisation must respond, within a period specified in the notice, by informing HMIP of the steps he proposes to take to comply with the conditions of the authorisation, as varied. Where such steps are considered by HMIP to be a "substantial change" in the operation of the process, the holder will be informed and an application for the variation of the conditions of the authorisation will then be made on the correct form. If the change is not deemed to be a substantial change, no further action need be taken.

As is the case for the initial application for authorisation, the variation of a granted authorisation will be subject to consultation with statutory consultees and the general public (see earlier in this Chapter). Accordingly, the application for variation will be notified by HMIP to the relevant statutory consultees and the authorisation holder should advertise the changes to be made. Any representations made must be taken into consideration by HMIP when a decision on the variation is made. The Secretary of State may exempt certain variations or types of information from this requirement. As for applications for authorisation, the procedure may alter where information is commercially confidential or might prejudice national security. A fee will be charged for the variation of the authorisation.

**Variation by Operator**

The conditions of an authorisation may be varied by the operator where a change is to be made to a process. A number of different procedures may be used, depending on the nature of the change to be made, whether the process concerned is in operation and whether the authorisation holder is certain that the change will require the variation of the conditions of the authorisation.

**Procedure 1:** If the authorisation holder is not certain of the impact of the change, he may notify HMIP in writing of the proposed relevant change and request a determination of whether that change will breach the conditions of the authorisation, require the variation of any conditions or represent a substantial change. If necessary, he can then apply for the variation of any conditions of the authorisation.

HMIP will determine:

· if the change proposed would involve a breach of any of the conditions attached to the authorisation;

· if, where the change proposed would not breach the conditions, HMIP would be likely to vary those conditions as a result of that change;

· if, where the change proposed would breach the conditions, HMIP would consider varying those conditions to enable that change to be made; or

· if the change proposed would constitute a "substantial change" in the operation of the process.

The authorisation holder will be informed of HMIP's decision. There are three possible outcomes.

(a) Firstly, HMIP may decide that the change will not breach any conditions and therefore will not require their variation. The holder can then make the proposed change, although HMIP can keep the conditions under review and serve a variation notice if it wishes.

(b) Secondly, if HMIP considers that the change proposed will not involve a substantial change but will lead to or require the variation of the conditions attached to the authorisation, the holder will be informed of the variation likely to be considered and the holder can then apply to vary the conditions of the authorisation to enable the proposed change to be made.

(c) Thirdly, if HMIP considers that the change proposed will involve a substantial change to the operation of the process, which will lead to or require the variation of the conditions attached to the authorisation, it will inform the authorisation holder of the variation likely to be considered and the holder can then apply to vary the conditions of the authorisation to enable the proposed change to be made. In such circumstances, both statutory consultees and the general public will have the opportunity to make representations in relation to the proposed change. HMIP will send a copy of the application for variation to the relevant statutory consultees and details of the application for variation will be advertised by the holder in local newspapers circulating in the neighbourhood of the premises (see earlier in this Chapter). As for applications for authorisation, this procedure will be slightly different where an application contains information which is commercially confidential or which could be prejudicial to national security. HMIP will consider any representations made.

**Procedure 2:** The holder of an authorisation need not notify HMIP and request a determination of the impact of the proposed change. Instead, where it is clear that the conditions of the authorisation will need to be varied and the operator knows what changes are to be made, an application for that specific variation may be made to HMIP. The consultation procedure will apply if the variation is a substantial change.

**Procedure 3:** The holder of an authorisation who is not making a relevant change (i.e. a very minor change) or who wishes to vary a process which is not in operation may apply for a variation to HMIP.

When corresponding with HMIP in connection with any application for the variation of an authorisation or for the determination of the impact of the proposed change (Procedure 1) the authorisation holder must provide details of:

· his name, address and telephone number;

· the address of the premises where the prescribed process is operated (if a stationary prescribed process);

· the address of his principal place of business (if the prescribed process is operated using mobile plant);

· details of any change to the information originally supplied in connection with the initial application for authorisation concerning the applicant, the location of the prescribed process or the applicant's principal place of business if the prescribed process is operated using mobile plant.

In addition to this information, other details must be supplied to HMIP, depending on the variation procedure used.

Where a request is made for the determination of the impact of the proposed change (Procedure 1) or an application is made by the holder of an authorisation who is not making a relevant change or who wishes to vary a process not in operation (Procedure 3), the following details are also supplied to HMIP:

· a description of any proposed change in the operation of the prescribed process;

· any alteration to the prescribed substances used in connection with or resulting from the operation of the process, the abatement techniques to be used, the proposed releases of substances into the environment and their environmental effects, the monitoring techniques used, and other matters relied upon to ensure compliance, which would result if the proposed change were made;

· any additional information that HMIP should take into account in considering the application; and

· where the application is made for a non-relevant change or for a process which is not in operation, an indication of the variation that HMIP is to consider.

Where a holder makes an application to HMIP following a determination that either the proposal will not involve a substantial change but will lead to or require the variation of the conditions (Procedure 1(b)) or the proposal constitutes a substantial change requiring the variation of the authorisation (Procedure 1(c)), the holder of the authorisation should also provide HMIP with:

· an indication of the variation that the holder wishes HMIP to make;

· a statement of any changes to any information previously supplied to HMIP relating to the name and address of the holder or the location of the premises;

· any additional information that HMIP should take into account in considering the application.

Finally, where a person makes an application for variation without going through the determination procedure (Procedure 2), HMIP should also be provided with details of:

· an indication of the variation that the holder wishes HMIP to make; and

· any additional information that HMIP should take into account in considering the application.

Applications for variations of authorisations should be made on forms provided by HMIP. A substantial variation fee will be payable to HMIP.

## APPEALS

It is possible to appeal against HMIP's actions in variety of circumstances. An operator may appeal to the Secretary of State against:

· a refusal to grant an authorisation (either within the determination period or deemed refusal where no decision was taken by HMIP within this period);

· the conditions attached to an authorisation;

· a refusal to vary the conditions of an authorisation;

· the revocation of an authorisation;

· the serving of a variation notice, enforcement notice or prohibition notice (see Chapter 5); or

· a refusal to exclude certain information believed to be commercially confidential from the public register (see Chapter 6).

An appeal is not possible if HMIP's decision implements a direction issued by the Secretary of State. Only the authorisation holder or applicant or the person served with a notice can appeal. An aggrieved neighbour, for example, has no right of appeal, although should the operator appeal, an "interested party" may have the right to be notified (see later in this Chapter). The only cause of action open to the aggrieved neighbour et al is judicial review but this may also not be an easy remedy in view of the fact that the Courts have not generally accepted that "environmental rights" in this regard are available to the public. However, what is apparently the first challenge to an IPC authorisation by a third party is to be brought by a Mr Chapman *(R v. Chief Inspector (HMIP), ex parte Chapman)*. Mr Chapman objects to the use of Orimulsion, a bitumen based fuel, which HMIP has authorised to be burnt at National Power's Pembroke Dock power station. He claims that the resulting air pollution will aggravate his cystic fibrosis and that HMIP should not have allowed the use of this fuel. The thrust of Mr Chapman's argument is expected to be that the BAT requirements are not met by the conditions of the authorisation and he has been granted leave to apply for judicial review of HMIP's decision.

Where an appeal is made against a revocation of an authorisation, the authorisation will not be revoked until the appeal is determined or withdrawn by the appellant. In contrast, appeals against authorisation conditions or variation, enforcement or prohibition notices will not have the effect of suspending these conditions or notices. Information believed by the operator to be commercially confidential will not be placed on the public register until the appeal is determined or withdrawn.

The Secretary of State can refer either any matter involved in the appeal or the determination of the appeal to a person appointed by him specifically for that purpose.

**Procedure for Making Appeals**

There is no prescribed form for use in the appeals procedure. No charge is made for an appeal. The appeal is initiated by the authorisation holder or person served with the notice etc. Written notice of the appeal and the following documents should be sent by the appellant to the Secretary of State.

· A statement setting out the grounds for the appeal.

· A statement setting out the appellant's preference for the format of the appeal (i.e. as a hearing or through written representations).

· A copy of any relevant application or authorisation.

· A copy of any relevant correspondence between HMIP and the appellant.

· A copy of the decision or notice about which the appeal is concerned.

The appellant should also send a copy of the notice of appeal to HMIP, together with copies of the statements setting out the grounds for the appeal and the preferred format for the appeal proceedings. If the appellant wishes to withdraw an appeal, the Secretary of State must be notified in writing and a copy of the notice sent to HMIP.

It is important to recognise that an appeal against a decision by HMIP or a notice served by HMIP may only be made within a certain period of time. The grounds for appeal and corresponding time limits are set out in Table 8. Generally, if the appeal is made outside this period, it will not be considered. In very exceptional circumstances, the Secretary of State does have the discretion to allow a notice of appeal to be given after these periods have expired, but this does not apply to appeals in relation to revocations of authorisations or the determination of commercial confidentiality.

# TABLE 8

## TIME LIMIT FOR APPEALS

| GROUNDS FOR APPEAL | TIME LIMIT |
|---|---|
| Refusal to grant an authorisation (where HMIP's decision is made within the permitted determination period). | Before the expiry of six months, beginning with the date on which the decision on the refusal is made. |
| Deemed refusal to grant an authorisation (where HMIP has not determined the authorisation within the permitted time period). | Before the expiry of six months, beginning with the date on which the application is deemed to have been refused. |
| Conditions attached to an authorisation. | Before the expiry of six months, beginning with the date on which the decision on the conditions is made. |
| Refusal of an application for variation of the conditions of an authorisation. | Before the expiry of six months, beginning with the date on which the decision on the application for the variation is made. |
| Revocation of an authorisation. | Before the date on which the revocation takes effect. |
| Serving of a variation notice. | Before the expiry of two months, beginning with the date of the notice. |
| Serving of an enforcement notice. | Before the expiry of two months, beginning with the date of the notice. |
| Serving of a prohibition notice. | Before the expiry of two months, beginning with the date of the notice. |
| Determination that information is not commercially confidential and will not be excluded from the public register. | Before the expiry of twenty one days, beginning with the date of the notice of determination. |

Appeals should be sent to the addresses below.

For processes in England:

The Planning Inspectorate
Environmental Pollution Appeals
Tollgate House
Houlton Street
Bristol BS2 9DJ

For processes in Wales:

Welsh Office Environment Division 3
IPC Appeals
Cathays Park
Cardiff CF1 3NQ

The Secretary of State will coordinate the appeals procedure. During the appeal both the appellant and HMIP will have an opportunity to put forward their case, as will any other interested parties. Before any formal steps are taken, the appellant and HMIP may be allowed time for discussions which may resolve the disagreement without the need for an exchange of written representations or a hearing.

### Notification of Interested Parties

HMIP is responsible for bringing the appeal to the attention of any interested parties. Once HMIP has received from the appellant a copy of the notice of appeal to the Secretary of State, it must notify any interested parties of the appeal within 14 days of the receipt of the copied notice. These persons can make representations to the Secretary of State concerning the appeal and may also attend any hearings associated with the appeal if these are held in public. The Department of the Environment has proposed that such persons should also be informed by HMIP if an appeal is withdrawn. The arrangements for informing interested parties do not apply to appeals against determinations made in relation to commercially confidential information. Such appeals will be held by private hearing or written representations.

The persons deemed to be interested parties vary depending on the subject of the appeal. If the appeal is made against the revocation of an authorisation or the serving of a variation, enforcement or prohibition notice, HMIP must give written notice to any person whom it considers to have a particular interest in the appeal. If the appeal is in connection with a refusal to grant or vary an authorisation or the conditions attached to an authorisation, written notice must be given to the statutory consultees notified of the application for authorisation or the variation of an authorisation. Any other person who has made a representation to HMIP in relation to the grant or variation of an authorisation must also be notified in writing of the appeal.

The written notice sent to these interested parties must contain the following information.

· A statement that an appeal has been lodged.

· The appellant's name, the address of the premises where the prescribed process is operated or the operator's principal place of business if the prescribed process is operated using mobile plant.

· A description of the application or authorisation with which the appeal is concerned.

· A statement that a copy of the representations made to HMIP (either by the statutory consultees or any other person) in relation to the original application will be sent to the Secretary of State and the appellant.

· A statement that these representations will be considered by the Secretary of State during the determination of the appeal unless the person who made the representation requests him to disregard them within 21 days of the date of the written notice.

· A statement that written representations concerning the appeal may be made by any recipient of the notice to the Secretary of State within 21 days of the date of the notice (it is proposed by the Department of the Environment that a statement that such representations will be sent to HMIP and the appellant be inserted here).

· A statement that those persons making representations concerning the appeal and statutory consultees will be notified of the date of the hearing of the appeal where it is to be conducted wholly or partly in public.

Any representations concerning the original application which HMIP had received from statutory consultees or other persons will be copied to the Secretary of State within 14 days of the written notice of the appeal, together with details of to whom the written notice was sent. They will also be copied to the appellant.

The Department of the Environment has proposed that the requirement for HMIP to copy to the Secretary of State representations received from interested parties concerning the original application should be removed. Instead, HMIP would only be required to forward details of the persons to whom written notice was sent and the date on which it was sent. In addition, the requirement for the written notice to contain a statement that copies of such representations are to be sent to the Secretary of State and considered during the determination of the appeal, unless the interested party requests otherwise, would be removed. Instead, interested parties, on receiving the written notice of an appeal, would decide whether their original representation is relevant to the appeal. If so, a copy would be forwarded to the Secretary of State. This amendment would make the determination process quicker and more straightforward, as irrelevant representations would not be considered.

### Consideration of Appeals

An appeal may proceed by way of written representations or in the form of a hearing. The appellant should state the preferred method when making the appeal. If either party requests it, an appeal hearing will be held, part of which may be held in private (if the person conducting the appeal so decides). Alternatively, the Secretary of State may decide that the appeal should be the subject of a hearing, e.g. because he feels that this would be in the public interest. In general, the written representations procedure is quicker as it requires less organisation than a hearing. Written representations may be a more appropriate method of dealing with appeals on commercial confidentiality.

### Written Representations

The appellant must inform the Secretary of State in his written notice of appeal if he wishes the appeal to be determined on the basis of written representations. The Secretary of State will then inform HMIP and the appellant that this procedure will be used.

HMIP will submit any written representations to the Secretary of State no later than 28 days after receiving the copies of the statements setting out the grounds for the appeal and the preferred format for the appeal proceedings from the appellant. The representations must be copied to the appellant. The appellant may make further representations to reply to any representations made by HMIP. These must be made no later than 17 days after the date on which HMIP's representations were submitted. Copies of all representations sent to the Secretary of State by either HMIP or the appellant must also be sent to the other party at the same time. Representations must be dated and sent on the date borne by that document.

Any representations made by interested parties which are received by the Secretary of State will be copied to the appellant and HMIP who may then respond. They will be permitted a period of not less than 14 days in which to respond, although the Secretary of State has discretion to lengthen the time limits set for this procedure. In some circumstances, the Secretary of State can require that HMIP and the appellant exchange additional representations. On completion of the exchange of representations, the person conducting the appeal may make an accompanied site visit and report to the Secretary of State.

### Hearings

Rather than proceed by way of written representations, the appeal may proceed in the form of a hearing at which HMIP and the appellant can make their representations. The person conducting the hearing will decide whether any part or all of the hearing will be conducted in private. A hearing may include a site inspection.

The Secretary of State will give the appellant and HMIP at least 28 days written notice (or a shorter period if they agree) of the date, time and place for the appeal hearing. A copy of the written notice will also be sent to those persons who have made representations concerning the appeal and statutory consultees.

Where all or part of the hearing is to be held in public, the Secretary of State will publish a copy of the written notice of the arrangements for the appeal hearing at least 21 days before the date on which the hearing is to take place. The notice should be published in a local newspaper circulating in the neighbourhood of the prescribed process. If the appeal is against the revocation of an authorisation for a process operated using mobile plant or the serving of a variation, enforcement or prohibition notice for such a process, the written notice of the hearing should be published in a local newspaper circulating in the locality in which the process was operating when the relevant notice was served. Advertisement will not be required when the appeal relates to a decision on commercially confidential information as such appeals are heard in private.

If the Secretary of State wishes to alter the date fixed for the hearing, HMIP, the appellant, persons making representations and statutory consultees must again be informed by written notice and details of the hearing be published. However, if the time or place of the hearing is changed, the Secretary of State need only give such notice as appears to him to be reasonable.

HMIP and the appellant are required to submit details of their case well in advance of the hearing. These will be copied to the other party. At the hearing, the appellant, HMIP and any statutory consultees are all entitled to be heard. However, permission for any other person wishing to be heard should not be unreasonably withheld by the person conducting the appeal. Any written representations made by interested parties may be read out.

Once the hearing is complete, the person appointed to conduct it will send a report to the Secretary of State (or the person appointed to determine the appeal) setting out his conclusions and recommendations, or his reasons for not making any recommendations. A copy of this report will be sent to the appellant once the appeal has been determined.

### Determination of Appeals

The Secretary of State (or the person appointed by him) may, on determination of the appeal:

· affirm HMIP's original decision;

· direct HMIP to grant or vary the authorisation, and may also give a direction as to the conditions to be attached;

· quash any or all of the conditions attached to the authorisation, and may also give a direction as to other conditions to be attached (conditions not subject to the appeal may be added to or changed);

· quash the decision to revoke the authorisation, and may also give a direction as to the conditions to be attached;

· quash the variation, enforcement or prohibition notice;

· affirm the variation, enforcement or prohibition notice, either in its original form or with appropriate modifications.

The appellant will receive written notice of that determination and, where a hearing was conducted, a copy of the report prepared by the person conducting it. These documents will also be copied to HMIP and the statutory consultees required to be notified of the appeal. A copy of the determination will be sent to any person making representations concerning the appeal or any other person making representations at the appeal hearing. A copy of the determination letter and the report of the hearing will be placed on the public register. There is no provision made for the Secretary of State to award the costs incurred during an appeal. No means are specified for challenging the Secretary of State's determination of the appeal, although an application for judicial review could be made.

Where an appeal is made in respect of commercially confidential information, the Secretary of State's decision will balance a number of factors. His main concerns will be:

· "to determine whether inclusion of the information in the register would "prejudice to an unreasonable degree" an appellant's commercial interests;

· in assessing "prejudice", to take into account both the extent of any damage that might be caused and the likelihood of such damage in fact being caused, looking at "the balance of probabilities" rather than demanding "conclusive proof" of prejudice;

· in determining whether any prejudice would be caused "to an unreasonable degree", to balance, against prejudice to an appellant's commercial interests, any benefits to the public interest that would arise from inclusion of the material in question in the register. The assessment of the public interest and the carrying out of the balancing process are matters for the judgement of the Secretary of State;

· in assessing the public interest in having the information in the public register, to assess directly the importance to the public of the information at issue. This might involve establishing, among other things, in what way the information might enable the public to be better informed on the likely environmental impact of the process and the relative importance of this information. There may be instances where the information submitted to an enforcing authority is no more than peripheral to the application and subsequent authorisation, and in such cases the degree of prejudice which would be required to make entry in the register unreasonable might be relatively slight. The nature and significance of the information are therefore relevant considerations." (Department of the Environment Guidance on Appeals under Section 22 of the EPA 1990).

Written notice of the decision will be sent to the appellant and HMIP, together with the hearing report if appropriate. These documents will not be placed on the public register if the appeal is dismissed.

## TRANSFERRING AUTHORISATIONS

Where a company is purchased or sold, or for any other reason, it may be necessary to transfer an authorisation for a prescribed process from the original holder to another person who intends to operate that process.

In such circumstances, the person to whom the authorisation is transferred must write to HMIP to inform it of the transfer within 21 days of the date of the transfer. Failure to do so is an offence. The transferred authorisation will take effect from the date of transfer as if it had been granted to the new operator. All the conditions that applied immediately before the transfer date will continue to apply. It is open to HMIP to vary or revoke an authorisation if it considers that the circumstances of the new operator require this.

## SCHEME OF FEES AND CHARGES

HMIP has a statutory duty to recover the costs it incurs in determining applications for authorisations and variations of authorisations, monitoring compliance, sampling and analysis operations, enforcement and maintaining the public register, together with any associated administration costs. The cost of non-regulatory work such as policy development and research is not recovered.

These costs are recovered by way of charges levied on those applying for authorisations or holding granted authorisations. A Scheme of Fees and Charges first came into effect for the period 1991-1992 and, to date, a revised Scheme has been issued in April each year. Before a new Scheme is finalised HMIP will consult with industry and any other interested parties. The current Scheme took effect on 1st April 1995 and will probably apply until April 1996. The charges levied by HMIP may also contain an element which is then passed on to the NRA where it incurs any expense in connection with IPC.

The Scheme of Fees and Charges is comprised of:

· application fees;

· substantial variation fees; and

· subsistence charges.

In most cases, the level of these fees and charges will be dependant upon the number of defined "components" contained in the process in an attempt to relate the amount paid to the level of regulatory effort involved. It is important to recognised that this division of a process into components does not have any bearing on the technical assessment of the process; it is purely used for the calculation of fees. Definitions for the components for each type of prescribed process are given in the Appendix to the Scheme of Fees and Charges which reproduces the list of prescribed processes given in Schedule 1 to the Prescribed Processes and Substances Regulations. The operator will determine the number of components contained in the process and then multiply this by the appropriate flat rate fee to calculate the final charge. For example, in combustion processes coming within the process descriptions detailed in Section 1.3(a) of Schedule 1, each boiler or furnace between 50-300 MWth capacity will constitute one component, whilst those of over 300 Mwth are worth two components.

The definitions of components are revised annually as the number of processes within IPC increases and HMIP gains experience of administering the system. Any change made to the component definitions will apply when determining the level of subsistence charges during the year of the current Scheme. It will not apply to application fees for applications already received or authorised by HMIP, but will be used to calculate the fees for any new applications received that year.

There are a number of cases in which special rules apply. The component based charging system will not be used for processes which contain no defined component or are subject to IPC only because of the quantity of special waste generated. In such cases, the appropriate flat rate fee will be charged. For application fees, the level of charge will be dependant on whether or not the process was previously regulated by HMIP under other legislation.

Where the Secretary of State directs that a process subject to APC should be transferred to HMIP control, the operator of that process will be charged the appropriate fee or charge prescribed by the separate local authority Scheme of Fees and Charges but this will be paid to HMIP.

### Application Fees

Application fees are charged to cover the costs incurred during the consideration of an application for the authorisation of a process subject to IPC. They cover applications for both new and existing processes received by HMIP on or after the date on which the Scheme came into effect, regardless of the date of the application or the posting date. The correct application fee should be submitted with the application for authorisation and HMIP may refuse to proceed with the determination of the application if any part of the fee is outstanding.

If an application for authorisation is withdrawn by the applicant within 56 calendar days of the date on which it was made, it may be possible to obtain a refund. Fees for applications withdrawn after this date will not be refunded as HMIP reserves the right to retain them in full. However, if an application is received for a process which is subsequently deemed to be trivial or is exempted from IPC or transferred to APC, as long as the process has not been authorised, HMIP will make a full refund of the application fee with a deduction of the appropriate local authority fee if appropriate.

The application fee charged per component is lower for processes previously regulated by HMIP for air emissions, i.e. which are the subject of current certificates of registration under the AWRA 1906.

Where only part of a process has previously been regulated by HMIP, then the lower application fee will apply to the whole process.

If a staged application for authorisation is made (see earlier in this Chapter), in which the information relating to the authorisation is submitted in tranches over a longer period of time, the application fee will not be based on the number of components in the process. Instead, the fee will be calculated according to the actual time and costs incurred by HMIP in determining the staged application. The fees will be charged quarterly in arrears using a standard rate charged per inspector day.

### Substantial Variation Fees

A fee will be payable where a substantial change is to be made to a prescribed process. Such changes may be required because the operator proposes to alter some aspect of the process or because HMIP has exercised its power to amend the conditions of the authorisation and the process must be changed to comply with this. A substantial change to a process will involve the advertisement of the proposed alteration. HMIP will then have to consider any representations made and reassess the authorisation.

Substantial variation fees are approximately one third of the application fee which would normally be applied to the number of components in the process following the variation. Where a variation to a process constitutes a non-substantial change, no variation fee is charged. In such cases, the costs incurred by HMIP will be covered by subsistence charges.

### Subsistence Charges

Subsistence charges are paid each year by the holders of granted authorisations to cover ongoing inspection, monitoring and enforcement activities. If the subsistence charge is not paid, the authorisation may be revoked or other enforcement action initiated by HMIP. The subsistence charge may also cover the costs of check monitoring and HMIP's costs which were not recovered in previous years.

As is the case for application fees and substantial variation fees, subsistence charges are calculated on the basis of the number of components in the process as authorised. The first subsistence charge is payable from the date on which a new authorisation comes into effect. It will be calculated on pro rata basis, depending in how much of the financial year remains. HMIP will determine the level of the charge and inform the operator of this when the authorisation is issued. The following year, the full subsistence charge will be payable from 1st April.

The subsistence charge levied by HMIP also covers the costs incurred by the NRA in regulating IPC processes which involve discharges to controlled waters. HMIP will pass this to the NRA. The subsistence charge for such processes will therefore be higher than that for processes which only involve releases to air and land as it includes that part of the charge payable under the NRA Charging for Discharges Scheme.

If a process is changed in such a way that the number of components alters, this will be reflected in the subsistence charge levied for the following financial year which will then be based on the new number of components in the process. Supplements or refunds for increases or decreases in the number of components respectively are not calculated. The subsistence charge will not be refunded if a process is revoked as the remaining charge will be used to cover the costs associated with the revocation.

In addition to the basic charge and any charge made with regard to NRA activities, the subsistence charge may also contain components which cover the costs of monitoring programmes and any costs unrecovered by HMIP in previous years.

The costs of check monitoring programmes conducted by independent contractors for HMIP will be charged directly to the operator. The amount charged will be forecasted for each year in advance and the monitoring charge for the following year will then be adjusted to take account of the actual expenditure. Where new or unforeseen monitoring activity is required at a site, the actual cost will be added to the subsistence charge for the following year. The operator of a revoked authorisation will still be required to pay the monitoring charges during the remainder of that financial year. Any additional charges or refunds will be paid the following year.

Finally, part of the subsistence charge is levied to enable HMIP to recover costs which were not covered by income in previous years. In the period 1991-1992 HMIP seriously underestimated the amount of regulatory time required to fulfil its responsibilities and the application fees charged were too low to recover these costs. Operators of processes with authorisations granted in respect of applications made during 1991-1992 are therefore required to pay an annual recovery charge to recoup the shortfall during this period. As is the case for application fees, the recovery charge is lower for processes previously regulated by HMIP and is calculated on the number of components in the process. HMIP has levied this type of charge over the last four years and it is included in the 1995-1996 Scheme of Fees and Charges, together with a supplementary charge which is levied on all operators, regardless of when their applications were made. This is to cover the under recovery of costs, including setting up costs, incurred by HMIP in 1991-1992 and 1992-1993.

### Scheme of Fees and Charges for 1995-1996

The current Scheme of Fees and Charges for 1995-1996 took effect on 1st April 1995. It applies to applications for authorisations or variations of authorisations made on or after 1st April 1995, action which is required by a variation notice served on or after 1st April 1995 and subsistence of granted authorisations. A copy of the most recent Scheme of Fees and Charges can be obtained from the Finance Branch of HMIP at its headquarters in Romney House, London (see address in Appendix IV). The levels of fees and charges are given in Table 9.

## TABLE 9

## 1995-1996 SCHEME OF FEES AND CHARGES

| FEE OR CHARGE | LEVEL |
|---|---|
| Application fee (processes not previously regulated by HMIP) | £3,860 per component |
| Application fee (processes previously regulated by HMIP) | £2,570 per component |
| Substantial variation fee | £1,290 per component |
| Subsistence charge (basic charge, i.e. inclusive of supplementary contribution to cover start up and cost recovery of £150 per component, but exclusive of any NRA costs) | £1,805 per component |

| Supplementary charge for applications made in 1991-1992 (processes not previously regulated by HMIP) | £610 per component |
|---|---|
| Supplementary charge for applications made in 1991-1992 (processes previously regulated by HMIP) | £410 per component |
| NRA costs | Dependant on fee payable under NRA Charging for Discharges Scheme |
| Check monitoring charge (per authorisation) | Dependant on actual expenditure incurred during monitoring |
| Charge levied per inspector day (for staged applications) | £924 per inspector day |

The levels of fees and charges levied have increased dramatically since they first came into effect in April 1991. The majority of these increases occurred in the early years of the implementation of IPC. In the 1995-1996 Scheme, only the subsistence charges have been increased from the previous year (by £75 per component, an increase of nearly 5%). HMIP has stated that the increase in subsistence charges was required because of a 10% increase in regulatory activity anticipated in this area. The level of the application and the substantial variation fees remains unchanged (a decrease in real terms).

Application fees and substantial variation fees are sent, together with the application to which they apply, to the Applications Units at HMIP's Bristol or Bedford offices (see Appendix IV).

### Future Structure of the Scheme of Fees and Charges

The Scheme of Fees and Charges has not been well received by operators and has been one of the most contentious areas of the introduction of IPC. In many cases, the component based charging scheme has been deemed to be too inflexible as small companies feel that they pay too much in comparison to larger companies. There is also general consensus that the daily rates for HMIP inspectors are too high.

HMIP has made several efforts to amend the Scheme and has conducted a review of alternatives, focusing particularly on schemes based on direct time charging or the pollution potential of a process. However, industry has been generally unreceptive to these alternatives.

HMIP now intends to conduct a more wide ranging review of the Scheme of Fees and Charges. The HMIP Advisory Committee has suggested that more emphasis should be placed on the "polluter pays" principle, with charges to operators reflecting the amount of time and work spent by HMIP inspectors when dealing with different companies. A method of classifying companies could be developed to apportion fees more fairly and to reward firms which through their own actions, reduce HMIP's workload. HMIP is also considering charging for any pre-application advice given. The creation of the Environment Agency may also require alterations to the Scheme and provisions for making schemes of fees and charges are included in the EA 1995.

HMIP has put forward five main options for a new Scheme of Fees and Charges:

· a direct charging scheme, with fees based on the time and materials used by HMIP;

· an emissions based scheme which would involve the CRI;

· a risk based scheme using the OPRA system;

· a scheme based on company size; or

· the retention of the existing component based scheme.

These options may be introduced individually or a combination of any of these may be used. The advantages and disadvantages of these options are discussed in greater detail below.

· **Direct Charging Scheme**

The level of fees and charges would be based on the amount of time spent by HMIP in administering and enforcing IPC for a process, together with the costs of any materials.

Advantages: It would provide an incentive for operators to increase the quality of applications and improve their performance, as the time spent by HMIP inspectors would be directly related to the charges levied.

Disadvantages: Some companies may limit their interaction with HMIP in an attempt to reduce costs, with potentially damaging effects on the environment. A charging scheme based on the time spent by HMIP staff would raise problems in relation to time utilisation, in-service training and any time spent investigating public complaints. It would also make future budgeting for charges difficult although the fee could be capped to ensure some level of predictability. Finally, companies appealing to the Secretary of State or with applications subject to lengthy determination periods as a result of public opposition may be disadvantaged.

## · Emissions Based Scheme

The level of fees and charges would be based on the emissions produced by a process, as detailed in the CRI maintained by HMIP (see Chapter 6). The information in the CRI is obtained from operators' own monitoring activities.

Advantages: It would be in line with the "polluter pays" principle.

Disadvantages: There have already been criticisms of the validity of data included in the CRI because the monitoring of releases is not comparable between different processes and can have inherent inaccuracies. It may be difficult to compare emissions because of the different volumes and compositions involved.

## · Risk Based Scheme

The level of fees and charges would be based on the OPRA system, which HMIP proposes to use to formalise its risk assessment for IPC processes (see Chapter 3).

Advantages: A system based on the OPRA system would be both equitable and beneficial in that it would reward good environmental performance by companies.

Disadvantages: The scheme may not be wholly representative of the environmental performance of a company as it focuses on selected indicators and process attributes.

### · Company Size Scheme

The level of fees and charges would be based on the size of the company operating the process.

Advantages: This would take account of the problems experienced by small firms under the existing component based system.

Disadvantages: This option has not been popular with industry, although a consideration of company size could be incorporated into the other schemes proposed.

### · Retention of Existing Scheme

The level of fees and charges would be based on the number of components in a process, with a small number of exceptions.

Advantages: The component based scheme is already in place and allows the level of charges to be predicted.

Disadvantages: It is already unpopular although it could be modified to overcome the most serious problems, e.g. to take account of process complexity and the risk posed to the environment. Under this scheme, companies with good environmental performance are effectively subsidising those with poor records which take up more of HMIP's time and resources.

Any changes will be introduced in April 1997. HMIP is particularly keen that the final Scheme should be in line with the "polluter pays" principle, take into account the amount of regulatory effort involved and reward companies reducing pollution or with environmental management systems in place. The Scheme should also take account of different company sizes and be predictable, simple and transparent. However, it may prove difficult for HMIP to develop a Scheme incorporating all of these factors.

Chapter 5

# ENFORCEMENT OF IPC

## INTRODUCTION

H MIP has a range of enforcement powers in relation to IPC. These include powers to prevent pollution and the contravention of the conditions of authorisations, to bring prosecutions if pollution does result and to require the remediation of any environmental damage.

Where non-compliance is identified, a number of enforcement options are available. The action taken will depend on the environmental consequences of that non-compliance, the culpability of the operator and whether the requirement to carry out remedial action will be sufficient to ensure that there is no recurrence of the incident. HMIP publishes general guidelines setting out the issues which should be taken into consideration by its inspectors when considering whether a company should be prosecuted.

Where the decision is taken not to prosecute a company for non-compliance, a number of other options are available to HMIP inspectors including a letter of admonishment or the serving of an enforcement or prohibition notice. If necessary, an authorisation for a prescribed process may be revoked.

Many of the provisions setting out HMIP's enforcement powers and the offences relating to IPC contained in the EPA 1990 are to be replaced by provisions of the EA 1995 which establish the enforcement powers for the new Environment Agency. The existing powers of HMIP, the NRA and the waste regulation authorities vary on some points and the new powers will harmonise these to a greater extent. Powers relating to IPC will not be reduced, but in some circumstances may potentially be extended to include powers which have previously been assigned to other regulatory authorities.

# HMIP INVESTIGATORY AND EXAMINATION POWERS

In order that HMIP can gather information on incidents of potential pollution and non-compliance, its inspectors have a number of investigatory and examination powers. The EPA 1990 provides HMIP inspectors or other authorised persons of HMIP with a number of powers to enable them to discharge their statutory duties in this area.

These are exercisable in relation to:

· premises on which a prescribed process is, or (on reasonable grounds) is believed to be, operating; and

· premises on which a prescribed process has been operated (whether or not the process was a prescribed process when it was operated), the condition of which is believed (on reasonable grounds) to be such as to give rise to a risk of serious pollution of the environment.

## Powers of Entry

HMIP inspectors are empowered to enter premises which they have reason to believe it is necessary for them to enter. They may do so at any reasonable time (which is usually construed to mean within working hours). However, if in the opinion of the inspector there is an immediate risk of serious pollution of the environment, the inspector may enter the premises at any time. The inspector is not required to give notice, nor is he obliged to obtain a warrant. He must, however, produce his authority if required to do so.

## Persons who may Accompany Inspectors

HMIP inspectors may take with them on entering any premises any person who is duly authorised by the Chief Inspector and, if the inspector has reasonable cause to believe that there is likely to be any serious obstruction in the execution of his duty, he may also take with him a police constable.

## Equipment and Materials

HMIP inspectors are also entitled to take with them on entering any premises any equipment or materials required for any purpose for which the power of entry is being exercised.

### Investigatory and Examination Powers

HMIP inspectors have wide powers in relation to the premises they enter.

· To make such examination and investigation as may in any circumstances be necessary.

· To take such measurements and photographs and such recordings as the inspector considers necessary for the purposes of his examination and investigation.

· To take samples of any articles or substances found in or on the premises and of the air, water or land in, on or in the vicinity of the premises.

· To require the production of, or where the information is recorded in computerised form, the furnishing of extracts from, any records which are required to be kept under Part I of the EPA 1990 or which it is necessary for the inspector to see for the purposes of his examination or investigation and to inspect and take copies of such records or entries. It should however be noted that the right to withhold documents on the grounds of legal professional privilege is expressly preserved.

### Powers to Require Information

Any person whom an HMIP inspector has reasonable cause to believe may be able to give information relevant to his examination or investigation may be required to answer such questions as the inspector requires and to sign a declaration of the truth of such answers. This questioning may be carried out in the absence of any persons other than persons whom the inspector may allow to be present or in the presence of a person nominated to be present.

This power is not designed to extract admissions. Consequently, any answer given by a person pursuant to this power is not admissible in evidence against that person in any proceedings. However, this proviso is restricted to that person. Consequently, if a director of a company were to make an admission, this admission could not be employed against that director personally in any proceedings but may be employed against, for instance, the company in any proceedings. The decision of the European Commission of Human Rights in the case of *Saunders v. United Kingdom* may also be relevant in this regard. The Department of Trade and Industry had, during its investigations into the Guinness Affair, secured evidence from Mr Saunders which was later used against him in criminal proceedings. The Commission held that the incriminating evidence which had been obtained under compulsory powers was oppressive and substantially deprived him from facing a fair trial, which was contrary to Article 6 paragraph 1 of the European Convention on Human Rights.

### Important Ancillary Powers

HMIP inspectors have certain important ancillary powers which could, depending on the particular circumstances, have the effect of stopping production or closing a facility, at least temporarily.

The inspector may direct that any premises that he has the power to enter, or any part of those premises, or anything in them, be left undisturbed for so long as is reasonably necessary for him to carry out his examination and investigation. If the inspector finds on any premises which he is entitled to enter any article or substance which appears to him to have caused, or be likely to cause pollution of the environment, he may have that article or substance dismantled or subjected to any process or test (but not so as to damage or destroy it unless this is necessary). Before doing so, the inspector must consult with such persons whom he thinks are appropriate for the purpose of ascertaining what dangers, if any, may occur from the exercise of this power. The person responsible for the premises is entitled to have the dismantling or testing of the article or substance done in his presence.

The inspector is entitled to take possession of any article or substance which has caused or is likely to cause pollution and to detain it for so long as is necessary in order:

· to examine it and to do anything with it which he otherwise has power to do;

· to ensure that it is not tampered with before his examination is completed;

· to ensure that it is available for use as evidence in any proceedings for an offence under Section 23 of the EPA 1990 or other proceedings relating to a variation notice, enforcement notice or prohibition notice.

The inspector when taking possession of such articles or substances must notify the person responsible for the premises or, if this is impractical, leave a notice in a conspicuous position and, if practical to do so, take a sample of the article or substance and give a portion of that sample, sufficiently identified, to the responsible person.

In addition, if in the case of any article or substance which an inspector finds on any premises which he has power to enter, he has reasonable cause to believe that the article or substance is a cause of imminent danger of serious harm, the inspector may seize it and cause it to be rendered harmless as above. Before rendering the article or substance harmless and, if practical to do so, the inspector must take a sample of the article or substance and give a sufficiently identified sample to a person responsible for the premises. As soon as possible, the inspector should prepare and sign a written report on these proceedings and give a signed copy to the person responsible and also to the owner of the article or substance.

The HMIP inspector has the power to require any person to afford to him such facilities and assistance with respect to any matters which are within that person's control or in relation to which that person has responsibilities, as are necessary to enable the inspector to exercise any of his powers in relation to IPC.

Where these investigatory and examination powers are applicable to mobile plant, the inspector will have corresponding powers. It is important to note that it is an offence for any person, without reasonable excuse, to fail to comply with any of the requirements imposed under Section 17 of the EPA 1990 or intentionally to obstruct an HMIP inspector in the exercise or performance of his powers or duties.

## ENFORCEMENT NOTICES

An enforcement notice can be served on the operator of an authorised process if HMIP believes he is contravening any condition attached to that authorisation or is likely to do so. It is an offence to fail to comply with an enforcement notice. An operator may appeal against the service of an enforcement notice.

The enforcement notice must set out:

· HMIP's opinion that the condition is being or is likely to be contravened;

· the nature of the contravention or likely contravention;

· the action that should be taken to remedy the contravention or to prevent it occurring;

· the time scale within which this action must take place.

The Secretary of State has the power to require the service of an enforcement notice and to specify the remedial action to be taken.

## PROHIBITION NOTICES

A prohibition notice will be served by HMIP where there may be a more immediate threat of damage to the environment. If HMIP believes that the continued operation of an authorised process, or its operation in a particular manner, involves an imminent risk of serious pollution of the environment, a prohibition notice will be served on the operator of that process. A prohibition notice is a powerful tool in preventing or mitigating pollution: it may be served regardless of whether the operation of the prescribed process contravenes a condition of its authorisation. Similarly, the notice may relate to any aspect of the process, including those aspects not regulated by the conditions of the authorisation.

The prohibition notice must set out:

· HMIP's opinion;

· the risk involved in the process;

· the action that should be taken to remove that risk;

· the time scale within which this action must take place;

· a direction that, until the notice is withdrawn, the authorisation will cease to have effect to authorise the operation of the process, either wholly or to the extent specified in the notice;

· where the direction only applies to part of the process, any conditions to be observed when operating the remainder of that process.

The Secretary of State can direct HMIP to serve a prohibition notice and to specify any matters to be included in that notice. HMIP can withdraw a prohibition notice by giving written notice to the person on whom it was served that the action required has been taken. It is possible to appeal against the service of a prohibition notice. Failure to comply with the terms of a prohibition notice is an offence.

## REVOCATION OF AUTHORISATIONS

HMIP has the power to revoke an authorisation at any time. This must be done by giving written notice to the holder of the authorisation. A revocation will then take effect from the date specified in the notice: this must be at least 28 days from the date on which the notice was served. The notice may be withdrawn by HMIP before that date or the revocation date may be varied. The Secretary of State also has the power to direct that an authorisation should be revoked. HMIP may serve a revocation notice where it believes that an authorised prescribed process has not been operated for a period of 12 months. The first revocation notice under IPC was served on the company A W Stokes and Sons in November 1994. The authorisation was revoked at the end of December 1994. The company had failed to comply with the requirements of an improvement programme to upgrade its incineration process.

## OFFENCES UNDER IPC

As is the case with all regulatory systems, non-compliance or contravention of some statutory requirement may be an offence. The offences relating to IPC are set out in Section 23 of the EPA 1990. The penalties for these offences will depend on the Court in which the case is heard. Offences such as these are generally "triable either way" meaning that either the Magistrates Court or the Crown Court can be competent to hear them. Section 23(2) and (3) set the maximum penalties for a number of the offences under Section 23, these being triable either way with possible fines on summary conviction and possible imprisonment or fines on conviction on indictment. Under Section 23(4) a number of the offences are only triable in the Magistrates Court, the penalty being a fine up to the statutory maximum.

The prosecution of an offence triable either way begins with the mode of trial hearing before magistrates. The hearing is to decide whether the Magistrates Court or the Crown Court should deal with the matter. The magistrates must take into account:

· the nature of the offence and whether in the circumstances it is serious;

· whether the punishment they can inflict would in the circumstances be adequate;

· other circumstances due to which trial in either Court is more appropriate.

If the magistrates decide that they cannot deal with the matter then it must be heard in the Crown Court. If, however, the magistrates are prepared to try the case then the defendant may still elect to have his case heard in the Crown Court.

The following offences are punishable, on summary conviction, to a fine of not more than £20,000 and, on conviction on indictment, to a fine or to imprisonment for a term not exceeding two years, or to both. There are provisions in the Environment Act 1995 (not yet in force) for the penalty on summary conviction to include an option for a three month prison sentence, and also to remove the offences marked * below.

· Operating a prescribed process without authorisation or in contravention of the conditions attached to that authorisation (Section 6(1)). This is a strict liability offence. Where there is non-compliance with the general condition implied in every authorisation that BATNEEC will be used to prevent, minimise or render harmless releases of prescribed substances and to render harmless releases of other substances, the onus of proof rests with the accused (i.e. the operator) to show that there was no better available technique not entailing excessive cost than was used to satisfy this condition. Where any entry in any record is required to be made as to the observance of a condition of an authorisation, and that entry has not been made, this fact will be admissible as evidence that the condition has not been observed.

· Failing to comply with an enforcement or prohibition notice or contravening any requirement or prohibition imposed by such notices.

· Failing to comply with a Court Order requiring an offence to be remedied (see later in this Chapter).

A person guilty of the following offences will be liable, on summary conviction, to a fine not exceeding the statutory maximum and, on conviction on indictment, to a fine or to imprisonment for a term not exceeding two years, or to both.

· Failing to notify HMIP of the transfer of an authorisation, not later than 21 days after that transfer (Section 9(2)).

· Failing, without reasonable excuse, to comply with any requirement imposed by a notice issued by the Secretary of State or Chief Inspector requesting information (Section 19(2)).

· Making a statement known to be false or misleading in a material particular or recklessly making a statement which is false or misleading in a material particular which is made to comply with any requirements to provide information under Part I of the EPA 1990 or if made in order to obtain the grant or variation of an authorisation.

· Intentionally making a false entry in a record required to be kept under Section 7.

· Forging or using, with intent to deceive, a document issued or required in connection with an authorisation under Section 7.

A person will be liable on summary conviction to a fine not exceeding the statutory maximum where he is found guilty of the following offences.

· Failing without reasonable excuse, to comply with any requirement imposed by an inspector (Section 17).*

· Preventing any other person from appearing before or from answering any question to which an inspector requires an answer (Section 17(3)).*

· Intentionally obstructing an inspector in the excercise or performance of his powers or duties.*

· Falsely pretending to be an inspector.*

Where HMIP believes that criminal proceedings brought before a Magistrates Court for failing to comply with or contravening an enforcement or prohibition notice would result in an ineffectual remedy, proceedings may be brought in the High Court to secure compliance, i.e. in order to seek an injunction.

## HMIP PROSECUTIONS

There has been a marked shift from the mainly advisory role previously taken by pollution authorities towards a more adversarial stance. Details of prosecutions brought by HMIP in connection with IPC are given in Table 10. In the financial year 1994-1995, although the number of successful prosecutions remained fairly constant, the number of enforcement notices issued increased dramatically, partly as a result of the increased number of inspections conducted.

HMIP's policy on prosecutions shows a clear intention to prosecute for non-compliance with a legally issued notice. Where the offence involves breach of a condition of an authorisation or of a regulation or statute the decision to prosecute will depend on the degree of harm and nuisance, the willingness of the company to remedy the breach and comply in the future, and the foreseeability of the incident. Prosecution will also be more likely if there are perceived benefits such as publicity and a deterrent effect.

# TABLE 10

## SUCCESSFUL PROSECUTIONS FOR BREACHES OF IPC

| NAME | OFFENCE | HEARING DATE | FINE/COSTS |
|---|---|---|---|
| Brookridge Timber Ltd | Breach of Section 6(1) and Section 23(1) - use of a toxic substance without authorisation. | March 1993 | Fine: £1,650 Costs: £3,000 |
| National Power plc | Failure to comply with the conditions of an authorisation to prevent a release (of oil) to controlled waters. | Feb 1994 | Fine: £7,500 Costs: £13,248 |
| Aga Gas Ltd | Unauthorised operation of an acetylene plant in contravention of the requirements of the regulations. | May 1994 | Fine: £10,000 Costs: £5,135 |
| Drum Laundry Services Ltd. | Failure to comply with the conditions of an authorisation to prevent a release to controlled waters | June 1994 | Fine: £5,000 Costs: £5,000 |
| Safety-Kleen UK Ltd | Failure to comply with the conditions of an authorisation to prevent a release to controlled waters. | Sept 1994 | Fine: £5,000 Costs: £6,040 |
| Enichem Elastomers Ltd | Failure to use BATNEEC to prevent the unauthorised release of styrene to the atmosphere. | Nov 1994 | Fine: £5,000 Costs: £12,062 |
| Coal Products Ltd | Breach of the conditions of an authorisation in relation to the limits for the discharge of ammonia in the permitted releases to controlled waters. | Nov 1994 | Fine: £22,500 Costs: £10,000 |

| Southern Refining Services Ltd | Failure to comply with the conditions of an authorisation | Dec 1994 | Fine: £12,000 Costs: £6,571.85 |
|---|---|---|---|
| Vinamul Ltd | Breach of the conditions of an authorisation by failure to prevent the release of unauthorised substances and failure to ensure control of process during production | Jan 1995 | Fine: £19,000 Costs: £13,716 |
| ICI Chemicals and Polymers Ltd | Breach of the conditions of an authorisation by failure to prevent the release of an unauthoris-ed substance (degraded organic peroxide) | Feb 1995 | Fine: £10,000 Costs: £10,250 |
| Hickson Fine Chemicals | Failure to comply with the conditions of an authorisation to prevent a release to controlled waters | Feb 1995 | Fine: £5,000 Costs: £10,694.50 |

The first prosecution in relation to IPC was of the company Brookridge Timber Ltd for breach of Section 6(1) (i.e. operating a process without authorisation) of the EPA 1990 between April and September 1992. The company pleaded guilty and was fined £1,650 with costs of £3,000. HMIP expressed a serious view of companies which knowingly operate potentially polluting plant using a hazardous substance (in this case treating timber with tributyltin napthanate) without authorisation.

National Power plc was the first company to be prosecuted for breaching the conditions of an IPC authorisation. The fines and costs of over £20,000 related to two oil discharges from Littlebrook "D" power station in Kent. The fines were £7,000 and £500 with the most serious offence involving a discharge of over 2,000 gallons of oil into the River Thames.

Aga Gas Ltd was fined £10,000 with over £5,000 in costs for running an acetylene plant without authorisation. The company failed to apply for the authorisation and commenced production regardless.

Drum Laundry Services Ltd was charged for breach of a condition of its authorisation prohibiting releases from a storage area to surface waters. Following a guilty plea the Aldershot Magistrates imposed a fine of £5,000 and costs of £5,000. This case shows the ease of prosecuting under the EPA 1990: HMIP merely had to show that a condition of the authorisation had been breached but did not actually have to show that damage had been caused.

HMIP brought a prosecution against Safety-Kleen UK Ltd following a spill of cement kiln fuel produced on its site. The cemfuel escaped from a road tanker which had been parked overnight in an uncontained area of the site and entered the River Ryton. The charge was under Section 23(1) of the EPA 1990 for breach of a condition of the company's IPC authorisation for a solvent recovery process. Safety-Kleen pleaded not guilty but was convicted and fined £5,000 with £6,040 costs. The important point in this case was the scope of the term "process". Safety-Kleen did not dispute the facts of the spillage and its entry into controlled waters but argued that the parking of the tanker containing the product was outside the meaning of process and not subject to the authorisation conditions. The Court found in favour of HMIP which had argued that the keeping of the product of a process in a tanker on the same site is part of the IPC process and subject to the conditions of the authorisation in view of Schedule 2 of The Environmental Protection (Prescribed Processes and Substances) Regulations 1991 which states that an IPC process "includes any other process carried on at the same location by the same person as part of that process", and Sections 1(5) and 1(6) of the EPA 1990 which state that "process" includes any activity capable of causing pollution, including the keeping of a substance.

Enichem Elastomers Ltd was fined for failing to comply with the Section 7(4) requirement to use BATNEEC to prevent an unauthorised release of styrene. The company pleaded guilty and was ordered to pay over £17,000 in fines and costs. In addition, a deadline was set for fitting alarms to the styrene tanks concerned at a cost of £60,000 by a Court Order under Section 26. A blocked drain fortunately prevented a much more serious incident in this case.

An example of prosecution for a number of offences followed the discovery by HMIP of 25 discharges breaching the release limit set for ammonia by an IPC authorisation held by the Cwm Coking Works of Coal Products Ltd. An enforcement notice was issued but

75 charges under Section 23(1)(a) of the EPA 1990 were also levied. Following a guilty plea the company was fined £22,500 with £10,000 costs. The fine amounts to about £300 per offence. Here the deterrent effect is questionable as the company had already been prosecuted twice for environmental offences.

Southern Refining Services Ltd, a solvent recovery firm with approximately £500,000 turnover and between £80,000 and £100,000 profit was fined £12,000 and ordered to pay costs of over £6,500. The single incident involved a release of noxious fumes, principally chlorine gas, for about 15 minutes. The company showed cooperation and responded quickly to the incident.

Vinamul Ltd, a Unilever subsidiary, was fined £19,000 for four breaches of its IPC authorisations. Part of the fine was imposed for failing to train staff sufficiently. Following two releases of substances into the atmosphere, an enforcement notice was served by HMIP requiring a study of potential hazards from operator intervention in computer-controlled processes. After further breaches, a further enforcement notice was served. Finally, prosecution followed under Section 23(1)(a) of the EPA 1990. Vinamul pleaded in mitigation that it had spent £1.5 million and was due to spend a further £5 million on environmental improvements. This illustrates the vast cost of complying with environmental legislation compared with the relatively minor fines for breach.

A failure to prevent the release of degraded organic peroxide and diluent from their Wilton Works led to a prosecution of ICI Chemicals and Polymers Ltd. The release was into the air from a bulk storage tank. The fine was £10,000 with costs awarded of about the same amount following a guilty plea.

Hickson Fine Chemicals, the Yorkshire chemical company, was fined £5,000 for breaching an IPC authorisation after it spilled timber treatment chemicals into a river. The spill was from a tanker and Hickson had been warned that a fully bunded loading area was required to operate the process. The loading area had been completed but the spill prompted full commissioning two days later. Again there was a guilty plea and costs were awarded. Once again deterrent appears to be slow in working here as Hickson already had three prosecutions with heavy fines prior to this incident.

The majority of the above cases proceeded with guilty pleas by the defendants. This is due to the ease of proving offences under Part I of the EPA 1990. The level of fines imposed by the Magistrates Courts are of a very similar level despite differences in the seriousness and number of breaches and the resources of the companies involved. The degree to which a fine hurts a company will clearly depend on the resources of the company and for much greater fines to be levied on large companies, cases will have to reach the Crown Court. At their present levels, fines can be insignificant in comparison with the cost of the measures required to ensure full compliance.

## REMEDIATION OF ENVIRONMENTAL DAMAGE

In addition to or instead of the penalties imposed for operating a prescribed process without authorisation, or failing to comply with or contravening any requirement or prohibition imposed by an enforcement or prohibition notice, the Court may order the person convicted of the offence to take specified action to remedy the matters that were the subject of the offence. Failure to comply with an Order of this type is also an offence (Section 23(1)(l)). The Court may fix a time within which such action must be taken, which may be extended by order of the Court on application by the person involved. However, the person will not commit any offence in respect of matters which continue during the time fixed by the Order.

HMIP may also arrange for any reasonable steps to be taken towards the remediation of any harm caused as the result of an offence and has the power to recover the costs of this action from the person convicted. This applies where a conviction is obtained for operating a prescribed process without authorisation or failing to comply with or contravening any requirement or prohibition imposed by an enforcement or prohibition notice. The Secretary of State must approve such action in writing and the permission of any occupier of land which will be affected by the action must be obtained.

## DIRECTORS' AND OFFICERS' LIABILITY

Company directors are, in law, persons distinct from the company but exercising control over it. A wide definition is given to "director" by Section 741 of the Companies Act 1985, including any person occupying the position of a director whatever the position is called, e.g. shadow directors and non-executive directors. Although so far, personal liability for members of the Board and senior management has arisen mainly in connection with health and safety matters there is potential for increased personal liability for people in such positions in the environmental field. Directors and officers may incur liability in a personal capacity by reason of their own actions, however, they may also be exposed to potential liability arising from their positions in a company.

### Individual Liability

Directors may clearly be liable for crimes which they commit as a principal in the course of running the company or where they deliberately commit the company to a criminal course of action. In addition, directors may also incur criminal liability as the result of giving directions for an act to be committed or through an omission to stop it. They may then be prosecuted as an aider, abetter, counsellor or procurer and therefore be tried as a principal offender.

Section 157(1) of the EPA 1990 imposes personal liability on directors and other officers where there has been some element of fault on their part enabling them to be prosecuted along with the company itself. The text of this provision is as follows:

"Where an offence under any provision of this Act which has been committed by a body corporate is proved to have been committed with the consent or connivance of, or to have been attributable to any neglect on the part of, any director, manager, secretary or other similar officer of the body corporate or a person who was purporting to act in any such capacity, he as well as the body corporate shall be guilty of that offence and shall be liable to be proceeded against and punished accordingly."

The meaning of the wording is fairly clear. However some clarification of the precise degree of fault needed for the provision to operate is required.

### Consent

Consent requires knowledge of the relevant matters along with affirmative action or approval. It has been held in a case under the

Customs and Excise Act 1952 that "where a director consents to the commission of an offence by his company he is well aware of what is going on and agrees to it". The Courts have indicated that turning a blind eye to the obvious or allowing action likely to cause contravention while ignoring the consequences may amount to consent. An indifferent director therefore cannot escape liability.

### Connivance

The meaning of "connivance" is less clear but is taken to imply knowledge of, and acquiescence in, the offence committed. One judge has stated that "where he (the director) connives at the offence committed by the company, he is equally well aware of what is going on but his agreement is tacit; not actively encouraging what happens but letting it continue and saying nothing about it". This provision may well catch non-executive directors.

### Neglect

There is a greater degree of understanding of the meaning of neglect, although judges have shown some reluctance to pronounce on its meaning without recourse to judicial authority. It has been said to imply "failure to perform a duty which the person knows or ought to know".

### Offences

Section 157 relates back to offences prescribed in both Part I (Integrated Pollution Control) and Part II (Waste on Land) of the EPA 1990. The offences concerning IPC to which Section 157 relates are contained in Section 23 (see earlier in this Chapter). Breach by a director of this provision may give rise to liability under Section 157.

To date, there have been no prosecutions of directors or senior management in relation to breaches of IPC legislation, probably because IPC is still in its infancy but also possibly because of the difficulty in proving beyond all reasonable doubt that a director or other officer had consented, connived or been negligent. Some commentators regard this as a lack of will on the part of HMIP to prosecute individuals.

Chapter 6

# ACCESS TO INFORMATION RELATING TO IPC

## INTRODUCTION

Public accountability and accessibility are central to the IPC system. In order to maintain public confidence in the regulation of the most potentially polluting industrial operations, it is important that the decision making process is transparent and that individuals or organisations wishing to take part in that process have the opportunity to do so. The advertising and public consultation procedures associated with applications for authorisations or variations of authorisations and appeals have been described in Chapter 4. Through this procedure, the public is notified of developments and given the opportunity to make representations to HMIP or the Secretary of State. In order that the system operates properly, it is important that members of the public have access to sufficient information to enable them to make informed decisions on the environmental effects of processes and to put forward meaningful and valuable representations. Such information is provided through the public register maintained by HMIP which contains a wide range of information on the operation and environmental effects of prescribed processes and the actions taken by HMIP. Data on releases from IPC processes is included in the Chemical Release Inventory and other relevant information is available through HMIP's "ECOfacts by Fax service".

These services have been developed specifically to provide access to information concerning HMIP's activities and IPC. Information on IPC processes can also be obtained from other sources, using powers intended to increase public access to all types of environmental information. The information available can be divided into that held by official bodies (concerning their policies or activities, or consisting of data supplied by companies) and that provided directly by companies about their own processes and activities. It may be made available through statutory provisions or under voluntary schemes.

Information held by official bodies will include that obtainable using the powers of access provided for by The Environmental Information Regulations 1992 and the Code of Practice on Access to Government Information. At EU level, institutions have codes of practice on access to information and the European Commission is developing proposals for an emissions inventory which may parallel the CRI in the UK. Information on IPC processes provided directly by companies includes that contained in environmental annual reports and the environmental statements published in connection with environmental audits.

## PUBLIC REGISTERS

HMIP is required to maintain a public register containing information on the operation of IPC, including details of the processes regulated and action taken by HMIP. Provisions to set up the public register were included in the EPA 1990 to ensure that the IPC system is as transparent as possible and that the general public has access to information on the environmental effects of industrial processes. The Applications, Appeals and Registers Regulations set out the information to be included in the public register.

The public register must contain information relating to the following.

· Applications for authorisations.

· Notices issued by HMIP to applicants requesting additional information on a prescribed process and the information provided in response to such notices.

· Representations made by statutory consultees in response to the notification of an application for authorisation or the variation of an authorisation.

· Granted authorisations.

· Variation notices.

· Enforcement notices.

· Prohibition notices.

· Notices issued to withdraw prohibition notices.

· Notifications to the holders of authorisations that a change to a process will represent a substantial change (following the serving of a variation notice).

· Applications for the variation of authorisations (where HMIP has notified the holder of the authorisation that a proposed change will constitute a substantial change).

· Revocations of authorisations.

· Notices of appeal against a decision of HMIP in connection with authorisations, or variation, enforcement or prohibition notices, together with details of the grounds for that appeal, any relevant correspondence and decisions or notices about which the appeal is brought, any written notification from the Secretary of State determining the appeal and any report accompanying that notification.

· Convictions for any offences committed in connection with IPC, including details of the offender's name, date of conviction, Court and penalty imposed.

· Monitoring information concerning the operation of a prescribed process, either through HMIP's monitoring activities or provided by an operator to satisfy a condition of an authorisation or in response to a request from HMIP. Where monitoring information is not included for reasons of commercial confidentiality, HMIP will include a statement indicating whether the operator is in compliance with any relevant conditions of that authorisation.

· Reports published by HMIP assessing the local environmental consequences of the operation of a prescribed process.

· Directions issued to HMIP by the Secretary of State concerned with any aspect of IPC (except in relation to the exclusion of information affecting national security from the public register).

The Department of the Environment has made a number of proposals which would increase the amount of information placed on the public register, including the name of the operator's ultimate holding company, a copy of the advertisement concerning an application for authorisation or the variation of an authorisation, the information required as a condition of a variation, enforcement or prohibition notice, notices of the transfer of authorisations and representations made by the public. Information is also to be removed, including that relating to withdrawn applications which have not yet been determined and processes no longer subject to IPC because of legislative amendments.

Provision is made for information which is commercially confidential or could affect national security to be excluded from the public register. The Secretary of State may direct that specific information be removed from the public register which is not prescribed for inclusion or which should have been excluded for reasons of national security or commercial confidentiality.

Monitoring information and superseded information may be removed if it has been present on the register for a period of four years. An exception to this rule has been proposed for aggregated monitoring data (i.e. that on the CRI) to allow yearly comparisons to be made.

It is interesting to note that the Applications, Appeals and Registers Regulations require "all particulars" of applications, notices etc. and "details" of convictions to be placed on the public register. There is therefore no specific requirement for the entire documents to be included. In practice, however, the public register consists of photocopies of the actual documents because transcribing particulars onto the register would be too time consuming. This approach has the additional advantage that the public can access the actual documents, not facts extracted from them.

There is no specified time limit for HMIP to place such information on the public register although its policy is to do this as soon as practically possible after the document concerned has been received or issued. It should however be in place in time for members of the public who are alerted by the advertisement of an application to gain access to it. A time limit of 14 days has been proposed where applications for authorisations or variations of authorisations are concerned. There will be delays where information may be excluded from the register for reasons of commercial confidentiality or national security.

HMIP's public register can be accessed at its regional offices in Leeds, Bedford, Bristol, Fleet, Cardiff, Warrington and Sutton Coldfield. Each office holds documents relevant to the processes operated in that region: these are the only HMIP offices where documents can be accessed. HMIP's London Headquarters maintains a national index to all IPC regulated sites but does not store the actual documents. Each regional office also holds an index to the sites in that region and a copy of the national index. The addresses of these offices can be found in Appendix IV.

The EPA 1990 provides that the public register may be kept in any form, for example on computer or in a filing cabinet etc. In practice, HMIP's public register is paper based, at least for the present. The information is kept in a uniform and structured way to facilitate enquiries (by operator name in alphabetical order). Information included in the CRI (see later in this Chapter) is in computerised form and can be searched in conjunction with the public register. HMIP must make the public register available to the public at all reasonable times. This is generally interpreted as being available during normal working hours (9.30 am to 4.30 pm) on weekdays. HMIP recommends that before visiting to make a search, prior arrangements are made by telephone. Access to the public register is free of charge and facilities to make photocopies of register entries are provided, for which a small charge is made.

It is not necessary to visit an HMIP office to find out whether information on a particular company is kept. Enquiries can be conducted in the CRI over the telephone and the national index to IPC regulated sites is also available through HMIP's ECOfacts by Fax service (see later in this Chapter).

HMIP sends copies of all the documents to be placed on the register to the local authority in whose area the IPC process is located. Members of the public can access these documents at district or borough council offices. This information will usually be held by the Environmental Health Department. Where a prescribed process involves discharges to controlled waters, HMIP provides a copy of the relevant documentation to the regional office of the NRA for inclusion on the public register maintained there. When the functions of HMIP and the NRA are merged on the formation of the Environment Agency, these registers may be held on the same premises and may even be merged.

### Information not Included on the Public Register

Not all information must be included on the public register. Exemptions from this requirement exist for information which may affect national security and commercially confidential information. Where information is excluded for reasons of commercial confidentiality, a statement that such information exists should be placed on the public register.

### Information Affecting National Security

Information will not be placed on the public register if the Secretary of State considers that its inclusion would be contrary to the interests of national security. It is also possible for any other person to apply for such information to be excluded.

The Secretary of State can direct HMIP that specific information or information of a specific description should be excluded. Alternatively, information of a specific description can be referred to him for determination and will not be placed on the register until its inclusion has been cleared by the Secretary of State. Where HMIP excludes information in response to such directions, the Secretary of State should be informed.

Any other person who believes that information should be excluded for reasons of national security can apply to the Secretary of State giving details of the information concerned. HMIP should also be notified and such information will not be placed on the public register until the Secretary of State has made his determination. The procedure associated with applications containing such information is given in Chapter 4.

### Commercially Confidential Information

Information may be withheld from the public register if it is commercially confidential in relation to any individual or person and its disclosure would prejudice the commercial interests of that individual or person to an unreasonable degree. HMIP has a strict interpretation of this in practice: "IPC - A Practical Guide" states that the applicant should be able to demonstrate that the:

"disclosure of the information would negate or diminish a commercial advantage, or produce or increase a commercial disadvantage which is unreasonable given the nature of the information and the financial effect of disclosure".

In view of this, operators should be careful to ensure that only information specifically required by HMIP is supplied with applications etc. (see details of the appeal by National Power below).

A person supplying information to HMIP in connection with:

· an application for authorisation or for the variation of an authorisation;

· compliance with any condition attached to an authorisation; or

· compliance with a notice from HMIP requiring information to enable it to discharge its functions;

can request that this information is excluded from the public register because it is commercially confidential to himself or some other person. The procedure for doing so is detailed in Chapter 4.

The decision as to whether information is indeed commercially confidential will be made by HMIP or, on appeal, by the Secretary of State. Where information is deemed to be commercially confidential it may not be placed on the public register without the consent of the individual concerned or the person conducting the business concerned. However, in certain circumstances, the Secretary of State may direct that certain information or information of a particular description, regardless of whether it is commercially confidential, should not be excluded because its inclusion on the register is in the public interest.

A determination on the confidential nature of the information must be made by HMIP within 14 days of the application for commercial confidentiality. If HMIP fails to make its determination within this period, the information will be deemed to be commercially confidential.

This process can also be initiated by HMIP if it considers that information it has obtained may be commercially confidential (other than information obtained in the circumstances listed above). In such circumstances, HMIP will inform the person or business concerned that, unless excluded for reasons of commercial confidentiality, the information will be placed on the register. They will then have the opportunity to object to its inclusion on the grounds of commercial confidentiality and make representations to HMIP to justify this. HMIP will make its determination, taking these representations into account. Information which is not judged to be commercially confidential will be placed on the register 21 days after HMIP's decision is notified to the operator. During this period it is possible to appeal to the Secretary of State against HMIP's determination, both when the operator applies for an exclusion and where the process is initiated by HMIP. It is important to recognise that once HMIP has made its determination that information is not commercially confidential, it cannot change this opinion. Therefore, information must be placed on the public register unless a successful appeal is made.

If an appeal is brought, the information will not be included on the public register until either the appeal is finally determined or withdrawn. An appeal to the Secretary of State follows the general procedure outlined in Chapter 4 but the interested parties participation procedures will not be followed. The Department of the Environment has proposed that no information relating to an application for authorisation or variation of an authorisation will be placed on the public register until a decision is reached. However, a note will be placed on the register to indicate that an application or appeal has been made.

Information which is judged to be commercially confidential will be excluded for a period of four years from the date on which it was determined as such. At the end of this period, it will no longer be deemed to be confidential. However, it is open to the operator to apply to HMIP for the information to continue to be excluded, on the grounds that it is still commercially confidential. HMIP will, once again, determine whether this is the case. The same requirements relating to the time period for placing information on the register and appeals will apply in relation to this re-determination.

In practice, industry has made considerable use of these commercial confidentiality provisions. As the first applications for authorisations were made during 1991-1992, numerous applications for commercial confidentiality were also made. Although some applications were granted, many others were rejected, including those made by the electricity generators National Power and Powergen. These companies were the first to appeal against HMIP's determinations in relation to commercial confidentiality. The Secretary of State's decisions on the appeals were announced in November 1992.

Powergen's appeal to prevent the disclosure of information on forecasts of sulphur dioxide and nitrogen oxide emissions for 1991 was heard in a private hearing. Although the inspector at the hearing recommended that the appeal be upheld, it was subsequently dismissed by the Secretary of State who did not consider that the inclusion of the information on the public register was prejudicial to an unreasonable degree to the commercial interests of Powergen.

In contrast, the Secretary of State allowed National Power's appeal against placing data on the specification and quantity of its future fuel inputs on the public register. The company had argued that this would allow fuel suppliers to increase prices and would be advantageous to competitors. National Power's appeal was heard by way of written representations. The Secretary of State concluded that the information supplied by National Power was not directly relevant to the determination of the application for the IPC authorisation or the conditions likely to be imposed and was not necessary to enable the public to comment effectively on the application. It was not the type of information intended by the legislation to be made available. In view of this, he decided that any prejudice to the company's commercial interests would be unreasonable.

This decision caused some controversy and the Secretary of State was accused by pressure groups of restricting public access to information. However, following the announcement of the appeal decision, it was disclosed that, after supplying the information subject to the appeal, National Power had sent a second set of information on the proposed fuel inputs to HMIP which could be placed on the public register. The appeal was in respect of the first set of information which was commercially confidential to National Power. However, it was not possible to withdraw this and therefore, to ensure its exclusion, it was necessary for National Power to appeal against HMIP's determination.

## CHEMICAL RELEASE INVENTORY

The information relating to prescribed processes available on the public register is complemented by details of releases from processes regulated by IPC which can be accessed through the CRI. The CRI is a computerised database containing details of annual emissions of over 370 substances released from authorised processes. This includes releases of prescribed substances, releases of substances for which limits are included in IPC authorisations and releases of substances which operators are required to monitor. Information is continually being added to the CRI as authorisations are granted and data is received on the operation of prescribed processes. Operators are required to provide emissions data to HMIP on a regular basis. The CRI also contains details of radioactive substances regulated by HMIP under the Radioactive Substances Act 1993.

An inventory of substances released from industrial processes is not a new concept, although this is the first time that such information has been made available in this way in the UK. A Toxics Release Inventory which requires some industrial companies of above a certain size to report releases of specific substances has operated in the United States since 1987. The European Commission is also considering the introduction of a Polluting Emissions Register (see later in this Chapter) and the proposal for a Directive on IPPC provides for the development of an inventory of releases from installations subject to this regulatory system.

Release inventories are seen as having several major benefits. Firstly, publishing details of releases promotes efforts to reduce, control and eliminate such pollution. Either independently, or in response to pressure from interest groups, many companies have set improvement targets which can then be measured against the data published in subsequent years. The collation of data also identifies pollution "black spots", thereby allowing both industry and the regulatory authorities to target resources to address particularly severe environmental problems.

The information contained in the CRI can be accessed in two ways: through the printed "Annual Report" of releases which is produced from the CRI database; and through a search in the database itself. In September 1994, the first CRI Annual Report was published containing data on emissions produced in the period 1992-1993. This covered processes in the fuel and power, waste disposal and mineral industry sectors, together with some chemical industry processes. Future reports will include information on the remainder of the processes regulated by IPC. The 1992-1993 Annual Report provided details of releases for each substance, organised by industry sector and local authority area. Copies can be obtained from the Department of the Environment Publications Department. It is intended that the publication of the CRI Annual Report will eventually be only three to four months after the end of each reporting year.

Obviously, in a publication of this type, the quantity of information provided and the organisation of that information is constrained by limitations on size. For more detailed information, searches in the CRI database can be carried out for members of the public by HMIP staff and the resulting information presented in a wide range of formats. The CRI is available at the seven HMIP offices holding the public register and search requests may be made in writing or over the telephone. It is also possible to visit HMIP offices although prior arrangements should be made by telephone. A charge is made for the information printed out but not for the actual search. This service is generally available between 9.30am to 4.30pm on weekdays.

The search criteria which can be used to interrogate the CRI are listed in Table 11; these give an indication of the type of information included in the database. A combination of criteria can be used to locate very specific information, e.g. those operators discharging substances to water in a particular region of HMIP. The information retrieved can be displayed and printed out in a variety of formats, e.g. in order of operator, substance, local authority or county. For each substance, the CRI contains details of the release limits imposed, actual releases of substances and any unauthorised releases.

## TABLE 11

### SEARCH CRITERIA USED IN THE CRI

| SEARCH CRITERIA |
| --- |
| Substance |
| Substance Group |
| Environmental Medium |
| Operator |
| Country |
| County |
| HMIP Division |
| HMIP Region |
| Local Authority |
| Industry |
| Process Type |
| Process |
| Process Code |

The actual release quantity included in the CRI will be that provided by the operator as part of his monitoring activities or, if it is not possible to measure releases directly, that calculated or estimated by HMIP using methods agreed with the operator. Operators are required to report releases exceeding authorised limits and releases of substances which are not included in the authorisation, at the time when such releases occur. This information is added to the CRI.

Reaction towards the CRI has been mixed. Some companies and trade associations already report on annual emissions on an independent basis, through environmental annual reports or industry schemes. For such companies, emissions reporting is seen as a beneficial exercise and the introduction of the CRI is merely formalising their actions. In contrast, other companies are opposed in principle to the CRI and argue that the provision of raw emissions data to the public without explanation or analysis may be misleading. It is also seen as being an unnecessary and additional burden on industry which is not in accordance with the Government's deregulatory policy.

There has been particular criticism of the fact that the CRI only covers emissions from processes regulated by IPC and details of premises holding radioactive substances. Some industry sectors, for example the chemical industry, claim that this will make their releases seem disproportionately high and support the expansion of the CRI to other industry sectors. HMIP has warned against interpreting the emissions totals contained in the CRI as being representative of the total emissions of such substances in England and Wales. Although IPC regulates the most potentially polluting industrial processes, some pollutants are produced in large quantities by other sectors which are not subject to IPC, e.g. transport and agriculture. For example, the total level of methane emissions reported in the CRI is only a very small proportion of the actual national total because major sources of methane are agriculture and landfill sites. For other pollutants, e.g. sulphur dioxide, the total in the CRI is more representative of the national total as the majority of emissions are produced from processes regulated by IPC.

The CRI does not cover discharges to water consented by the NRA or air emissions regulated by local authorities under the APC system. HMIP believes that extending the CRI to cover such releases would place an unreasonable burden on small and medium sized companies. There would also be considerable problems in integrating this data as a variety of collection methodologies is used by the different authorities. However, HMIP has stressed that the development of the CRI is in its pilot phase at present and has not ruled out its extension to other industry sectors and regulatory systems in the future. This integration may be facilitated by the creation of the Environment Agency.

The incomplete nature of the CRI has also been seen as a problem. As a result of the phased introduction of the IPC system, it will be some considerable time before the CRI contains data on all IPC processes. It is thus difficult to identify trends and draw meaningful conclusions. The comparability of the data has also been questioned because of its reliance on monitoring methodologies which may be unreliable in some cases.

Although the information contained in the CRI can be accessed through both the computerised database and the published Annual Report, it is this latter format which will be used most widely by the public. However, because the Annual Report effectively represents the results of a search in the CRI database, the range of data included is limited. In particular, there has been criticism that the Annual Report for 1992-1993 does not explicitly provide emissions data for individual companies, although such information can be accessed through the CRI database.

Finally, because the CRI is restricted to IPC, there are fears that it will not dovetail with the European Commission's proposed Polluting Emissions Register which could cover a wider range of substances and industry sectors. Similarly, the CRI may have to be adapted to implement the requirement for an emissions inventory under the IPPC proposal (see later in this Chapter).

## HMIP ECOFACTS BY FAX SERVICE

Information on HMIP's activities can be obtained through its ECOfacts by Fax service. This is a computerised information system which automatically faxes documents to telephone callers. The service is available 24 hours a day, all year. Callers dial the system and order documents using a push button phone; selected documents are then received by fax within a few minutes. The ECOfacts telephone number is: 0881 882288.

A variety of information concerning IPC is available.

· Index to the information held on the public register relating to applications for IPC authorisations.

· HMIP public register contacts.

· Background information on the HMIP public register and index.

· References to HMIP guidance documents, including CIGNs and Technical Guidance Notes.

· HMIP prosecution guidelines and details of latest prosecutions.

· HMIP Scheme of Fees and Charges.

· Map of HMIP regions and offices.

· HMIP latest Quarterly Report.

· "Pollution Prevention - Our Common Concern" - HMIP's code of conduct under the Citizen's Charter.

· Catalogue of currently available HMIP fact sheets, Quarterly Reports, Bulletin articles and press releases.

· Information on the ECOfacts by Fax service.

ECOfacts by Fax was launched in April 1994 and, following a successful trial period, the range of information included is to increase.

## INFORMATION ON THE INTERNET

HMIP has also placed background information on its operations and activities, and details of the ECOfacts by Fax service on the Internet. This can be accessed at http:\\www.open.gov.uk\hmip\ hmiphone.wtp.

## GENERAL ACCESS TO INFORMATION

The information services discussed above relate specifically to the operation of the IPC system. Information relating to HMIP and IPC can also be obtained using powers providing access to environmental information in general or any information held by official bodies.

### Environmental Information

The Freedom of Access to Information on the Environment Directive (90/313/EEC) was adopted to increase the amount of environmental information available to the public and to harmonise access procedures throughout the EU. This Directive is implemented in Great Britain by The Environmental Information Regulations 1992 which came into force on 31st December 1992. The Regulations place a duty on certain "relevant persons" to make environmental information which they have in their possession available to the public. The definition of "relevant persons" includes Ministers of the Crown, Government departments, local authorities and certain categories of bodies with public administration functions in relation to the environment, and bodies with public responsibilities in relation to the environment that do not come within these earlier categories but which are under the control of such authorities. Certainly, HMIP, the NRA and local authorities fall within this definition. However, the rules relating to other bodies, e.g. the privatised water companies, are less clear.

Any request for information received from a member of the public must be replied to as soon as possible and no later than two months after the request is made. Reasonable charges may be made for the information supplied. Requests for information must be made directly to the body concerned.

The powers provided by these Regulations do not reduce other rights of access, e.g. access to statutory public registers of environmental information. They provide an additional right of access to environmental information which is not held on such registers. Where other statutory provisions provide for more information to be made available than is provided for in these Regulations, the more liberal regime will have precedence.

The bodies ("relevant persons") concerned have discretion to refuse access to certain types of information, including information relating to international relations, national defence or public security, legal or other proceedings, internal communications, unfinished documents, or commercially confidential information. Access to information which has been supplied on a voluntary basis or which is personal information must not be disclosed unless agreement of the person who supplied it has been obtained. Similarly, information must not be disclosed if this would contravene a legal requirement or agreement, or lead to the likelihood of environmental damage. Requests may also be refused if they are unreasonable or too general. Any refusal must be made in writing and give reasons for that refusal. An appeal may then be made to the body concerned, a Member of Parliament or legal action may be taken.

## Information Held by Official Bodies

Information relating to IPC and HMIP's activities may also be obtained through the public's right to access certain information held by official bodies.

In the UK, a Code of Practice on Access to Government Information came into effect in April 1994. This supports the Government's policy under the Citizen's Charter of extending access to official information and responding to requests for such information. It requires Government departments and public bodies under the jurisdiction of the Parliamentary Commissioner for Administration (the Ombudsman) to publish facts and analysis considered relevant and important in relation to major policy proposals and decisions; to publish or otherwise make available explanatory material on departments' dealings with the public (including rules, procedures, internal guidance etc.); to give reasons for administrative decisions to those affected; to publish information on the operation of public services; and to release information relating to policies, actions, decisions and other matters in response to specific requests.

Under this scheme, the Department of the Environment has issued its own Code of Practice on Access to Government Information detailing the types of information which will be released. Where requests are made for information, this will be provided as soon as practicable. The target for responses to simple requests is twenty working days from the date of receipt. Where information cannot be provided, an explanation will be given. In general, no charge will be made for simple requests that will cost less than £50 to complete, although where more complex requests which require extensive searches or the collation of information are made, a fee reflecting reasonable costs will be charged. The Code of Practice is not intended to override existing statutory provisions on access to public records. Complaints about information provision should be made initially to the relevant body, or, through a Member of Parliament, to the Ombudsman.

There are exemptions for certain types of confidential information, including information which if released would harm national security or international relations or inhibit internal discussions and advice, information concerned with law enforcement and legal proceedings, information which would prejudice the effective management and operation of public service bodies, information which is to be published in the near future, personal information about a third party, commercially confidential information or information given in confidence. An index to explanatory material on how the Department of the Environment deals with the public has been published in conjunction with this Code of Practice. This includes documents published by HMIP.

## Developments in Access to Information at EU Level

In addition to the Freedom of Access to Information on the Environment Directive (90/313/EEC), there has been a general trend towards increasing public access to information in all subject areas, including documents held by EU institutions.

The European Commission's Fifth Action Programme on the Environment states that:

"it is essential that the citizen be enabled to participate in the process of setting conditions for operating licences and Integrated Pollution Control, and be facilitated in judging the actual performance of public and private enterprises through access to inventories of emissions, discharges and wastes and to environmental audits".

The proposal for an IPPC Directive requires the establishment and maintenance of inventories containing information on releases of substances from industrial installations, subject to a number of exemptions including commercial confidentiality and information affecting national security. The European Commission has been developing a proposal for a Polluting Emissions Register for some time. In 1993, a consultation document outlining a mandatory Polluting Emissions Register was produced and discussions were held between representatives from governments, industry and environmental pressure groups. It was proposed that the Polluting Emissions Register would contain information collected from EU and possibly other European countries, with companies providing details of releases of specific substances above threshold levels on a plant by plant basis. The arguments for and against this proposal are similar to those put forward in relation to HMIP's CRI. During discussions, a voluntary approach was also considered and a European Commission working group was appointed to examine the various options in this area. In 1994, a draft proposal was produced. However, it is possible that work on this project will be held in abeyance for some time, pending the development of the inventories required under the IPPC Directive (see Chapter 8).

## INFORMATION PROVIDED BY COMPANIES

### Environmental Annual Reports

Information on the environmental performance of industrial operations (including processes regulated under IPC) is available in the environmental annual reports produced by some companies and through schemes operated by some industry associations. The Confederation of British Industry's Environment Business Forum has a number of membership requirements, including the publication of an annual report on a company's environmental performance. Similarly, the Chemical Industries Association's Responsible Care Programme requires that member companies submit data to allow the preparation of indicators of environmental performance for the chemical industry. This is published in the form of national aggregate figures. The format of environmental annual reports varies considerably, although there have been moves towards standardisation. Recently, a number of guides to environmental reporting have been published, including those produced by the World Industry Council on the Environment and the Public Environmental Reporting Initiative.

### Environmental Auditing

Many of the industry sectors regulated under the IPC system are covered by the EU Eco Management and Audit Scheme ("EMAS"). Although a voluntary scheme, a company must comply with the requirements set out in the Regulation (1836/93) establishing EMAS if it is to register. EMAS was launched in the UK in April 1995 and provides for the continuous improvement of the environmental performance of companies and the provision of information to the public. Companies wishing to register under EMAS must adopt an environmental policy, conduct an initial review, introduce environmental programmes and management systems, set improvement targets and conduct audits on the effectiveness of these measures. After the initial review and each audit, an environmental statement must be produced for every site registered under the Scheme and information disseminated to the public. This will be verified by an independent third party before registration is permitted. The statement will therefore contain information on the operations conducted at a site which can be compared to other information, for example that found on the public register, to ascertain whether a company is meeting its objectives.

Chapter 7

# RELATIONSHIP BETWEEN IPC AND OTHER REGULATORY SYSTEMS

## INTRODUCTION

Although IPC aims to centralise pollution control and streamline regulatory requirements for operators, some overlap or duplication with other statutory controls is inevitable as certain aspects of the operation of a process or its environmental effects will potentially be the responsibility of other regulatory authorities. It can often be difficult to determine the boundaries between IPC and other regulatory systems, particularly where prescribed and non-prescribed processes are operated together.

There are two types of situation in which conflict can arise: those where controls over a particular process could potentially be duplicated by two or more regulatory systems and it is necessary to determine which system will take precedence; and those situations where two or more regulatory systems could function in parallel and the relationship between these systems must be defined.

Such problems are overcome using a variety of mechanisms. The legislation establishing each regulatory system will often include provisions setting out the boundaries of that system and its relationship with other regimes. Section 28 of Part I of the EPA 1990 sets out rules governing the relationship between IPC and other regulatory systems. Similar provisions are contained elsewhere in the EPA 1990 and in other statutes, including the Water Resources Act 1991 and the Water Industry Act 1991. Advice is given in official guidance and, in at least one case, guidance has also been provided by way of legal precedent. "Memoranda of Understanding" have been drawn up between different authorities where frequent overlap is anticipated and such arrangements can be reviewed by joint committees. There are also procedures to coordinate enforcement action. Finally, the "statutory consultee" system alerts relevant bodies, e.g. the NRA and the HSE of applications for authorisations, applications for variations of authorisations or appeals under the IPC system. This gives such authorities the opportunity to make representations to HMIP in connection with developments likely to impact on matters over which they have control.

Some administrative issues may be simplified when the NRA and the waste regulation authorities are combined with HMIP to form the Environment Agency in April 1996. However, as the regulatory systems will continue to operate separately, some overlap will always remain.

The regulatory systems with which IPC most frequently overlaps are listed in Table 12. The mechanisms used to define the relationships between these systems will now be discussed in greater detail.

## TABLE 12

## OVERLAP OF IPC WITH OTHER REGULATORY SYSTEMS

| REGULATORY SYSTEM | REGULATORY AUTHORITY | LEGISLATIVE PROVISIONS |
|---|---|---|
| Disposal of waste to land | Waste regulation authority* | Part II EPA 1990 |
| Discharges into controlled waters | National Rivers Authority* | Water Resources Act 1991 |
| Discharges into sewers | Sewerage undertaker | Water Industry Act 1991 |
| Air pollution control | Local authority | Part I EPA 1990 |
| Statutory nuisances | Local authority | Part III EPA 1990 |
| Clean air | Local authority | Clean Air Act 1993 |
| Radioactive materials and waste | HMIP | Radioactive Substances Act 1993 |
| Health and safety | Health and Safety Executive | Health and Safety at Work Etc. Act 1974 |
| Land use planning | Local planning authority | Town and Country Planning Act 1990 |

* to be combined with HMIP to form the Environment Agency

## DISPOSAL OF WASTE TO LAND

Under Section 28(1) of the EPA 1990, no condition may be attached to an IPC authorisation so as to regulate or apply to the final disposal of waste by deposit in or on land. In circumstances where a prescribed process will involve such activities, HMIP must inform the relevant waste regulation authority. The operator will then be licensed by that authority under the waste management licensing regime introduced by Part II of the EPA 1990. This regime, which controls the treatment, keeping and disposal of waste, was brought into effect on 1st May 1994 by The Waste Management Licensing Regulations 1994.

Conversely, the waste management licensing regime does not apply to the recovery or disposal of waste where that activity is or forms part of a prescribed process designated for IPC, e.g. certain incineration processes. This exemption does not apply however if the activity involves the final disposal of waste by deposit in or on land. However, a waste management licence may be required for activities carried out before the exempted operation, e.g. the preparation of waste for incineration and Section 33(1)(c) of the EPA 1990, which provides that a person shall not treat, keep or dispose of controlled waste in a manner likely to cause pollution of the environment or harm to human health, will apply. Department of the Environment Circular 11/94 on the Waste Management Licensing System and Waste Management Paper No. 4 "Licensing of Waste Management Facilities" provide guidance in this area.

Although a waste management licence is not required where a prescribed process involves the recovery or disposal of waste, HMIP has a duty to exercise its powers to achieve certain objectives set out in The Waste Management Licensing Regulations 1994. HMIP must ensure that waste is recovered or disposed of without endangering human health and without using processes or methods which could harm the environment and, in particular, without risk to water, air, soil, plants or animals; or causing nuisance through noise or odours; or adversely affecting the countryside or places of special interest. Any provisions of a waste management plan must be implemented. However, HMIP is not required to consider the prevention of detriment to the amenities of the locality where the process is or is to be situated, if planning permission is in force or will be in force before the process is operated.

The waste management licensing regime introduced by Part II of the EPA 1990 has generally replaced the previous waste disposal licensing system which operated under Part I of the COPA 1974. Waste disposal licences will automatically be treated as waste management licences under the new system. However, waste disposal licences may still be held for activities which are part of processes subject to IPC but for which an application for authorisation is not yet required under the IPC implementation timetable. Once such processes are authorised, a waste management licence will not be required, in accordance with the exemptions discussed above. The waste disposal licence will apply until IPC authorisation is granted and then be surrendered to the waste regulation authority, without the necessity for compliance with the new requirements relating to the surrender of licences which have been introduced under the waste management licensing system. If the authorisation is refused and the process remains licensable, the waste disposal licence will be treated as a waste management licence from the date on which the IPC authorisation is refused.

## DISCHARGES INTO CONTROLLED WATERS

Where a prescribed process releases substances into controlled waters (i.e. groundwater and surface, territorial and coastal waters) a separate NRA discharge consent will not be required and control will remain with HMIP. If the discharge is made in compliance with the IPC authorisation, it will not constitute an offence under Section 85 of the Water Resources Act 1991. Under the statutory consultee arrangements, the NRA will be notified where a process releases substances to controlled waters. HMIP must refuse to grant an authorisation if the NRA certifies that, in its opinion, the release of a substance into controlled waters from the IPC process will result in, or contribute to, a failure to achieve any water quality objective. The NRA is able to specify conditions relating to water pollution control to be included in the IPC authorisation although HMIP is able to impose more stringent conditions if it believes this is appropriate. The NRA can also require HMIP to serve a variation notice on the operator of a prescribed process in order to prevent water pollution. NRA offices will place information supplied by HMIP on IPC processes involving releases to water on their public register.

If a facility contains both prescribed and non-prescribed processes, HMIP will regulate releases from those subject to IPC and the remainder will be controlled by the NRA. HMIP and the NRA have entered into a Memorandum of Understanding on the regulation of releases to controlled waters to clarify their responsibilities and to provide a working arrangement between the two authorities for situations, e.g. where effluent from prescribed and non-prescribed processes is released to controlled waters through a common pipeline. In such cases, HMIP will impose and enforce any conditions relating to the maintenance and operation of the pipeline. The NRA will have responsibility for the effluent from the non-prescribed processes at the distal end of the pipeline and HMIP will control the effluent arising from the prescribed processes at any convenient juncture in the pipework. The NRA will normally monitor the receiving waters although HMIP also has powers to do so. The Memorandum of Understanding also covers information provision and exchange, enforcement action and the arrangements for the recovery of any costs incurred by the NRA in relation to IPC processes. A Joint Review Committee oversees these procedures.

## DISCHARGES INTO SEWERS

Trade effluent discharged into sewers from IPC processes will be controlled by HMIP through the conditions attached to the authorisation. Consent will also be required from the sewerage undertaker which may require the inclusion of a variety of conditions, e.g. relating to the volume, composition and temperature of the effluent. Sewerage undertakers are statutory consultees for all processes involving releases into sewers. However, there is no provision in the legislation (mainly the Water Industry Act 1991) which sets out the powers of the sewerage undertakers in this regard. It is simply left as a matter of negotiation and, hopefully agreement, between HMIP and the sewerage undertaker.

## AIR POLLUTION CONTROL

The APC system administered by local authorities has been described briefly in Chapter 2 as, in many respects, it parallels the IPC system. Much of the legislation establishing the APC system is shared with IPC. However, it is important to emphasise that APC regulates emissions to air only, whilst IPC is concerned with emissions to air, water and land. APC processes are those set out in Part B of Schedule 1 to the Prescribed Processes and Substances Regulations. Where a process involves two or more process descriptions coming within both Part A (relating to IPC processes) and Part B of the same section of Schedule 1 to these Regulations, all the processes will be regarded as part of the Part A process and subject to IPC. Conversely, where the Part A and Part B process descriptions fall into different sections of Schedule 1, each process will be subject to the appropriate regulatory system. The Secretary of State can direct that an individual Part B process or category of APC process be transferred from local authority to HMIP control.

A Memorandum of Understanding has been agreed by the HMIP/ Local Authority Enforcement Liaison Committee to facilitate cooperation between these organisations when regulating IPC and APC processes respectively. HMIP is required to liaise with the relevant local authority where it judges that an IPC process may have a significant impact on the local environment and to inform the local authority of any important regulatory developments, e.g. if an IPC authorisation condition is breached. The Memorandum of Understanding sets out procedures for dealing with public complaints about IPC and APC processes. Where HMIP receives a justifiable compliant in relation to an IPC process, the relevant local authority should be informed of this and also of the outcome of any subsequent investigation. If a complaint is received by HMIP in relation to an APC process, this should be passed to the local authority. Similarly, where a local authority receives a complaint about an IPC process, this should be directed to HMIP which must then keep the local authority informed of subsequent developments. There are also provisions to foster contacts between the two types of authority: a local authority should be provided with the name of the HMIP inspector with responsibility for each IPC process in its area. HMIP will provide the local authority with documents for inclusion on the authority's public register which relate to IPC processes carried out in its area.

## STATUTORY NUISANCES

Part III of the EPA 1990 provides local authorities with powers to control specific statutory nuisances which are prejudicial to health or a nuisance, e.g. noise, dust, smoke etc. However, a local authority cannot initiate summary proceedings in relation to certain types of statutory nuisances without consent from the Secretary of State if proceedings might be instituted under Part I of the EPA 1990, i.e. where the nuisance is connected with a prescribed process. The statutory nuisances to which this applies are: smoke emitted from premises; any dust, steam, smell or other effluvia arising on industrial, trade or business premises; and any accumulation or deposit. The HMIP/Local Authority Enforcement Liaison Committee Memorandum of Understanding (see earlier in this Chapter) also covers the overlap between IPC and the regulation of statutory nuisances and requires liaison and the exchange of information between these authorities.

## CLEAN AIR

The Clean Air Act 1993 ("CAA 1993") gives local authorities the power to control emissions of smoke, grit, dust and fumes. Section 41 of the CAA 1993 provides that clean air controls will not apply to any process regulated by IPC as appropriate controls will be incorporated into the IPC authorisation.

## RADIOACTIVE MATERIALS AND WASTE

A prescribed process comprising activities involving radioactive materials or radioactive waste may be regulated by both an IPC authorisation and a registration (for the use of radioactive materials) or authorisation (for the storage or disposal of radioactive waste) granted under the Radioactive Substances Act 1993. These regulatory systems are both administered by HMIP. If different requirements are imposed by conditions under the two regulatory systems with regard to the same matter, the conditions imposed by the IPC authorisation will be treated as not binding on the operator and the requirements of the radioactive substances regulatory system will take precedence.

## HEALTH AND SAFETY

The operation of most industrial processes will involve some risks to the health and safety of both workers at the facility and the general public. To prevent overlap between IPC and the provisions of the HSWA 1974, no condition may be attached to an IPC authorisation with the sole purpose of protecting the health of workers. The HSE is a statutory consultee for all IPC authorisations and will be consulted on the content of CIGNs. A Memorandum of Understanding has been drawn up between HMIP and the HSE to coordinate the regulation of facilities where both environmental protection and the protection of workers and the general public are important, from the initial design of the plant to its decommissioning. This covers a range of issues, including operational matters, enforcement, incidents of non-compliance, technical standards and the disclosure of information. If environmental protection requires more stringent standards than would normally be used for worker protection, such standards may be applied provided that they do not impact adversely on health and safety at work. Arrangements also exist to ensure consistency between the responses of these authorities during consultation by planning authorities in areas such as environmental impact assessment and the regulation of facilities holding and using large quantities of hazardous materials. A Joint Review Group oversees these procedures.

## LAND USE PLANNING

In order to construct and operate an industrial facility involving prescribed processes planning approval will generally be required. The planning application for an IPC process will usually need to be accompanied by an environmental statement prepared under The Town and Country Planning (Assessment of Environmental Effects) Regulations 1988, either because the project is one of those for which the preparation of a statement is mandatory or because it is likely to have significant environmental effects by virtue of factors such as its nature, size or location. The environmental statement must be provided to the local planning authority either with the planning application or shortly after it is submitted.

The operation of the IPC and planning systems is essentially independent. HMIP can have an input into some planning issues, e.g. the preparation of development plans. It must be consulted in relation to the environmental impact assessment of some types of project and must provide any relevant information to the developers of such projects on request. Planning authorities are not consulted during the determination of applications for IPC authorisations. Planning permission is not a prerequisite for an IPC authorisation to be granted and HMIP can refuse to grant authorisation for a facility if it considers that the conditions attached to that authorisation will not be met, even if the facility has been granted planning permission. However, there are several areas of potential conflict associated with the interface between IPC and planning controls.

Firstly, there can be duplication between the requirements of the two regulatory systems. There is considerable overlap between the lists of projects subject to IPC and to environmental impact assessment. Some developments will therefore require an environmental statement to be submitted with the planning application to assess its environmental impact and a separate assessment of the environmental effects of releases from the prescribed process and the BPEO for their control as part of the application for IPC authorisation. These assessment reports will generally have some areas in common which can lead to duplication, although in practice, as they are prepared for different authorities and for different purposes, their coverage and depth of detail is likely to vary.

Secondly, the conditions imposed by planning authorities and HMIP on planning permissions and IPC authorisations respectively may conflict as some matters can be determined by both regulatory authorities. Planning permission will cover a range of issues, including the siting, design, external appearance and means of access to a site. As discussed in Chapter 3, the conditions attached to an IPC authorisation require that BATNEEC is used to prevent, minimise or render harmless releases into the environment. The definition of BAT refers, in addition to the techniques to be used and the personnel involved, to the design, construction and layout of the premises in which the prescribed process is operated. However, the requirements for site design and layout set out by each regulatory system may differ: it is unlikely that the design with least visual impact will be exactly the same as that involving the least risk to the environment. For example, where a facility includes a chimney in its design, the planning authority will favour a short chimney for reasons of visual amenity, but this is likely to be at odds with the requirement of HMIP for a high stack which is most effective at dispersing pollutants. Where such conflict arises and full planning permission has been obtained, the applicant may have to re-apply to re-design the site.

Finally, there are problems relating to the timescale within which applications for planning permission and IPC authorisation are made. It is usual for a developer to apply for planning permission at a relatively early stage of the project, but the application for IPC authorisation is usually submitted at a later stage when the details of the facility design are complete. Even if the application for authorisation is made at an earlier stage of the project, HMIP will be unable to determine it because there will not be sufficient information available to allow this. The staged application procedure discussed in Chapter 4 provides some assistance, but it still cannot give a definite indication of whether the process would eventually be authorised and the final conditions to be attached. If HMIP is able to specify BATNEEC for a particular process when the planning permission is determined, this might not constitute BATNEEC when the application for IPC authorisation is determined because, by its very nature, BATNEEC is developing continuously and could change in the intervening period. Similarly, if a long period of time elapses between the granting of the IPC authorisation and the commencement of operations, the authorisation may need to be varied to take account of changes in BATNEEC and other standards. As a result, the planning authority is frequently forced to make its decision without knowing the precise details of the pollution control techniques to be used at the facility. It may respond to local concerns and attempt to address pollution control issues by seeking assurances on the environmental effects of the proposed development. Traditionally, the Secretary of State has taken the approach that planning controls are unnecessary where this would duplicate other, more specific controls. However, this has been a significant problem in recent years and was the subject of a Court of Appeal action in 1994 in which the opinion of the Secretary of State was questioned by a local authority.

The Department of the Environment has issued a Planning Policy Guidance Note "Planning and Pollution Control" ("PPG 23") which considers the relationship between the planning system and other regulatory systems, including IPC. However, this is only guidance and, in practice, it will be for the Courts to deal with issues of law. The overlap between IPC and planning controls was considered in some detail in *Gateshead Metropolitan Borough Council v. Secretary of State for the Environment and Northumbrian Water Group*. The publication of the final version of PPG 23 was delayed to incorporate the implications of this judgement.

The Gateshead case concerned a planning application with pollution control implications. Northumbrian Water Group applied to the planning authority for permission to build a clinical waste incinerator near Gateshead. Outline planning permission was refused following a planning inquiry. The inspector at the inquiry concluded that although the incinerator could be constructed to meet emission standards, the impact on air quality and agriculture in the semi-rural location was insufficiently defined and public concerns over potential pollution could not be allayed sufficiently to make the site acceptable. This recommendation was rejected by the Secretary of State for the Environment who noted that IPC authorisation from HMIP was also necessary for the operation of the incinerator and the pollution concerns would be addressed by that regulatory system. He found that it would be possible to design and operate the proposed incinerator to meet the standards required by HMIP. The Secretary of State's decision was challenged by the planning authority. His decision was upheld by the High Court and subsequently by the Court of Appeal.

In the Court of Appeal, Gateshead MBC argued that if planning permission was granted, HMIP would not refuse to grant an authorisation to operate the plant, that even the use of BATNEEC might still result in environmental damage and that IPC was not adequate to deal with the issues raised by the inspector. The judge accepted that the issues raised were material planning considerations and that if the inquiry had found evidence that emissions were bound to be unacceptable and HMIP would not have granted the application for authorisation, planning permission could have been refused. However, he found that because there was no clear evidence that air quality at the site would be adversely affected, pollution matters could be left to HMIP. Although public concern was a material planning consideration, if it was not justified, it could not be conclusive. It was emphasised that HMIP has a right to refuse an IPC authorisation if it considers that this is the proper course and that it should not consider that the grant of planning permission inhibits it from doing so.

In both Courts, it was emphasised that there is overlap and no clear dividing line between the IPC and planning control systems. The power of HMIP to refuse an authorisation was emphasised: this shifts responsibility to HMIP and makes it more difficult for a planning authority to refuse a planning application on pollution grounds in the absence of conclusive evidence to support its decision.

PPG 23 incorporates this decision and provides guidance on the relationship between planning laws and pollution control legislation. It follows the Court of Appeal's decision in the Gateshead case and emphasises that the regulatory systems established by such legislation are separate, but complementary, in that both are designed to protect the environment from potential harm. However, they have different objectives. The planning system controls the development and use of land and determines the location of development. It is concerned with whether a development is an acceptable use of land. In contrast, the pollution control system controls the processes carried out on the land or substances produced by the development.

PPG 23 advises that planning authorities should not seek to duplicate controls which are the statutory responsibility of other bodies and that planning controls are not appropriate for regulating the detailed characteristics of potentially polluting activities. It should be assumed that the relevant pollution controls will be properly applied and enforced. Therefore, planning authorities should not attempt to substitute their own judgement for that of the pollution control authorities on such issues. However, it is acknowledged that there is not always a clear dividing line between planning and pollution control and that some matters may be relevant to both regulatory systems. Much depends on the scope of the pollution control system in each particular case.

PPG 23 advises that to minimise these potential problems, consultation, cooperation and coordination between all the parties concerned is essential. Specifically, Annex 8 makes a number of recommendations concerning liaison between HMIP and planning authorities. Planning authorities should consult with HMIP over projects subject to IPC to take account of the scope of the pollution controls likely to be imposed. The applicant should show the proposed design to both authorities and incorporate their comments. This will minimise the potential for conflicting requirements and duplication of controls. HMIP will be able to supply a range of information to the planning authority, including its responsibilities in relation to that type of process, the applicable standards and the likelihood that it will receive IPC authorisation or if it has already done so.

Although the two regulatory systems are independent, applications should be submitted in parallel wherever possible to reduce delays and allow likely pollution controls, e.g. chimney heights, to be taken into account by the planning authority. In any event, the applicant should ensure that once agreement is reached on planning permission, the application for IPC authorisation is submitted as soon as possible. If HMIP is consulted by the planning authority but is not yet aware of an application for IPC authorisation, it will contact the developer for pre-application discussions.

HMIP has recently produced a guidance note "Planning Liaison with Local Authorities" setting out the arrangements for coordination between itself and local planning authorities. This stresses that applications for IPC authorisations should be prepared at the same time as planning applications and emphasises the importance of pre-application consultations with both authorities.

Chapter 8

# DEVELOPMENTS IN IPC AT INTERNATIONAL LEVEL

## INTRODUCTION

A lthough this book concentrates on the situation in England and Wales, it is important to recognise that the development of an integrated approach to pollution control has not been restricted to this jurisdiction. Regulatory regimes based on the IPC and BPEO concepts exist in many other countries although the nomenclature used and specific details vary. On a worldwide scale, there has been a general move towards more integrated environmental management and the problems identified and addressed by IPC have also been recognised by international bodies.

In 1987, the World Commission on Environment and Development published "Our Common Future"; generally termed the "Brundtland Report" after its Chairman Gro Harlem Brundtland. This criticised the existing pollution regulatory systems and institutions as being too independent, fragmented and narrow in their responsibilities, in contrast to the integrated and inter-dependent nature of environmental problems. The Brundtland Report concluded that if such problems were to be effectively tackled, then the policy and institutions involved in combating pollution must change. In 1991, the Organisation for Economic Cooperation and Development recommended that member countries should practice integrated pollution prevention and control and adopt or amend appropriate legislative provisions if necessary.

## IPC IN THE EUROPEAN UNION

Regulatory systems similar to IPC which control releases to the environment in an integrated manner are in existence in a number of other European countries. In addition to the implementation of such national measures, developments are taking place at EU level. EU environmental policy places particular emphasis on preventing, reducing and eliminating pollution at source and promoting the sensible management of raw material resources, in line with the "polluter pays" principle. One area of special importance is IPC which is seen as an important part of the move towards more sustainable development. IPC has been a priority of the European Commission for some time and is designated as a priority field of action in its Fifth Action Programme on the Environment which covers the period to the year 2000. This concludes that improved management and control of production processes including a system of licensing linked to integrated pollution prevention and control will give a new sense of direction and thrust to the environmental/industrial policy interface.

At present, EU legislation exists to control pollution from operations discharging to air and water, and to require authorisation for such operations (the Air Framework Directive (84/360/EEC) and the Dangerous Substances into Water Directive (76/464/EEC)). No such legislation exists in relation to the control of pollution to land, although the proposed Landfill Directive contains relevant provisions. A proposal for a Directive on IPPC is currently under discussion which will harmonise the IPC systems already in place in EU member states and require the introduction of integrated measures in other member states.

The proposed IPPC Directive was first drafted in September 1991 and has been in development for some time. Following a lengthy consultation phase in which the text of the draft proposal was revised many times, an "official" proposal was adopted in September 1993. The legal basis for this proposal is Article 130s of the Treaty of Rome, the Treaty which established the European Economic Community in 1957. Article 130s is concerned with the adoption of legislation which has environmental protection as its primary aim.

Proposals put forward under this Article will follow the "cooperation procedure" which gives the European Parliament an important role in determining the final form of legislation. Under the cooperation procedure, a proposal put forward by the European Commission will be discussed by the European Parliament at a first reading stage and any amendments resolved upon will be submitted to the European Commission for consideration. The Economic and Social Committee is also able to give its opinion at this stage. The proposal will then be sent to the Council of Ministers. This body consists of a representative from the government of each member state and its composition is dependent upon the subject under discussion. The "Environment Council" is comprised of the national ministers with responsibility for environmental matters and meets several times a year. It is through this body that member state governments have the opportunity to modify and adopt proposals for EU legislation. The Council of Ministers is represented in ongoing negotiations by a Committee of Permanent Representatives and therefore considerable discussion will have taken place before the Council meets.

The Council of Ministers will discuss the proposal and reach agreement on a Common Position. This will then be passed to the European Parliament for a second reading. The outcome of the legislative process will depend on whether the European Parliament is completely satisfied with the proposal or wishes to amend or reject it, and the Council of Ministers' reaction to this. The final stage is the adoption of the legislation by the Council of Ministers. This legislative procedure for environmental issues is intended to increase the input of directly elected MEPs in the decision making process. However, although the European Parliament can influence the final form of the legislation to a significant degree, the balance of power still lies with the Council of Ministers and it is this body that generally has the final decision on the adoption of environmental legislation.

The IPPC proposal is a Directive, one of a number of legislative instruments used by the EU. Directives are used frequently in the environmental area. They are binding as to the results to be achieved by national legislation, but provide a high degree of flexibility to accommodate existing national laws and variations in the nature of member states' legal systems.

There is an increased emphasis on shared competence between the EU and member states, in line with the "subsidiarity principle", whereby the EU will take action relating to the environment only where its objectives can be attained better at EU level than at the level of individual member states. Thus, policy is determined at EU level whilst allowing decisions on more specific matters to be taken at member state level. The provisions of the proposed IPPC Directive are in line with this principle; broad objectives are included in the proposal, but specific details, e.g. emission limits and the nature of the Best Available Techniques ("BAT") to be used, will be set at member state level. Member states will then report back to the European Commission to ensure that national measures are consistent throughout the EU.

The provisions of the proposed IPPC Directive have proved to be quite contentious and considerable negotiation has been required to allow agreement on a Common Position to be reached by the Council of Ministers. The scope of the proposal, the timetable for the upgrading of existing installations and the need for EU emission limit values have been subject to considerable discussion. Opinions have also differed on the definition of BAT to be used to control pollution from installations. The UK has been anxious that a consideration of the costs and benefits associated with measures be included, whilst other member states prefer a requirement to use the best, state of the art techniques. When selecting BAT, account will be taken of local conditions, although environmental quality standards must not be breached and a high level of environmental protection must be achieved. The southern member states, where environmental quality is higher, have argued that in some circumstances, pollution controls less stringent than BAT should be allowed. However, northern member states have been against this and believe that the requirement to use BAT should take priority to prevent wide variations in pollution control standards within the EU.

This proposal received its first reading in the European Parliament at the end of December 1994 and political agreement on a Common Position on the Directive was reached by the Council of Ministers in June 1995. It will now be considered at a second reading in the European Parliament. It is unlikely that any significant amendments put forward by the European Parliament will be accepted by the European Commission in view of the delicate nature of the compromise reached by the Council of Ministers on the Common Position. It is possible that a final decision on this proposed Directive may be reached by the end of 1995 or early in 1996. Once adopted, member states will have three years to implement its provisions into national law.

It would appear that the IPPC Directive may be used as the basis for future legislation. The European Commission has proposed that the Large Combustion Plants Directive (88/609/EEC) should be replaced by a daughter directive made under the IPPC Directive. This follows a review of the existing controls relating to such plants. It is possible that this legislation may be drafted by the end of 1995. Regardless of this development, it is likely that future legislation put forward by the European Commission will incorporate a more integrated approach to pollution control.

## PROVISIONS OF THE IPPC PROPOSAL

The proposed IPPC Directive aims to achieve integrated prevention and control of pollution from certain types of industrial installations by providing for measures to prevent or, where this is not practicable, to reduce emissions into air, water and land in order to achieve a high level of protection for the environment as a whole. The IPPC proposal will apply to those industrial installations with the greatest potential to cause pollution, covering mainly the manufacturing industries but also energy production, waste management and some forms of intensive animal farming. Annex I to the proposal lists the categories of industrial activities coming within the new system (see Table 13). IPPC will operate at the level of "installations", that is stationary technical units where one or more of the activities listed in Annex I are conducted. The installation will include any other directly associated activities with a technical connection with the activities conducted on the site which could have an impact on the emissions or pollution produced. In some cases, whether an installation is subject to IPPC will depend on whether a particular aspect of the activity carried out (usually production capacity or output) is above a threshold level. Where an operator carries out several activities under the same heading of Annex I or several activities are operated at the same site, the cumulative capacity of those activities should be measured against the threshold level.

### New and Existing Installations

A permit will be required to operate the industrial installations coming under the proposed Directive. For new installations, a permit will be required immediately that the provisions of the Directive are implemented into national law (subject to some exemptions for large combustion plants). Existing installations must have permits meeting the requirements of this legislation no later than eight years after the Directive is implemented. Existing installations are those already in operation or authorised by existing legislation or the subject of a full request for authorisation, provided that the installation is put into operation no later than one year after the date on which the Directive is brought into effect. However, certain provisions of the proposed Directive will apply to existing installations from the date of its implementation, e.g. existing installations undergoing "substantial change" during the eight year transitional period will require a permit when that change takes place.

### Basic Obligations

Operators of installations must meet a number of basic obligations to ensure that:

· all appropriate preventative measures are taken against pollution, in particular through the use of BAT;

· no significant pollution is caused;

· waste production is prevented in accordance with the Waste Framework Directive (75/442/EEC);

· waste which is produced is recovered;

· waste which is impossible to recover for technical and economic reasons is disposed of whilst avoiding or reducing any impact on the environment;

· energy is used efficiently;

· necessary measures are taken to prevent accidents and to limit their consequences; and

· necessary measures are taken to avoid any risk of pollution and to return the site to a satisfactory state following the final cessation of activities.

These basic obligations will be taken into account by the regulatory authority when the conditions of the permit for the installation are determined.

### Applying for a Permit

In addition to introducing IPPC, the proposed Directive aims to harmonise permitting procedures throughout the EU. The application for a permit must be submitted to a regulatory authority or authorities designated by the member state. Where a number of authorities are involved in the issuing of a permit, this procedure and the conditions attached to the permit must be coordinated to ensure an integrated approach. This allows separate permits to be issued by different authorities for different environmental media. Although those installations already subject to IPC in England and

Wales receive a single authorisation from HMIP, it is possible that processes not currently subject to IPC, but which come under the IPPC proposal, will receive permits from several authorities.

The application for a permit should contain details of:

· the installation and its activities;

· the raw and auxiliary materials, other substances and the energy used in or generated by the installation;

· the sources of emissions from the installation;

· the condition of the installation site;

· the nature and quantities of foreseeable emissions from the installation into air, water and land;

· the significant environmental effects of such emissions;

· the technology and other techniques to be used to prevent or reduce emissions;

· where necessary, the measures to be used for waste prevention and the recovery of any waste produced;

· any additional measures required to allow compliance with the basic obligations placed on the operator (see earlier in this Chapter); and

· the arrangements for monitoring emissions.

The application may include or have attached to it any relevant information supplied in accordance with the Environmental Impact Assessment Directive (85/337/EEC) or with a safety report submitted under the Major Accident Hazards Directive (the "Seveso" Directive, 82/501/EEC).

**Conditions of Permits**

The regulatory authority will grant the permit subject to conditions which will ensure that the installation complies with requirements of the proposed Directive. If the installation will not comply with these requirements, the permit will be refused. All granted permits must include details of the measures required to comply with the basic obligations placed on the operator and to meet applicable environmental quality standards. The permit will ensure that long range or transboundary pollution is minimised and that a high level of protection is achieved for the environment as a whole. For new installations or existing installations undergoing substantial change, any information or conclusions arising out of an environmental impact assessment conducted in accordance with the Environmental Impact Assessment Directive (85/337/EEC) will be taken into account during the consideration of the application for a permit.

The conditions of the permit must include emission limit values, at least for the pollutants listed in Annex III to the proposal (see Table 14) which are likely to be produced by the installation in significant quantities, and measures to prevent the transfer of pollution between the different environmental media. If appropriate, emission limit values can be supplemented or replaced by equivalent parameters or technical measures.

Emission limit values, and equivalent parameters and techniques will be based on the use of BAT. As is the case with IPC in England and Wales, the definition of BAT is crucial to the implementation of this regulatory system. The IPPC proposal defines "Best Available Techniques" as:

"the most effective and advanced stage in the development of activities and their methods of operation which indicate the practical suitability of particular techniques for providing in principle the basis for emission limit values designed to prevent and, where that is not practicable, generally to reduce emissions and the impact on the environment as a whole.

"Techniques" include both the technology used and the way in which the installation is designed, built, maintained, operated and decommissioned.

"Available" techniques means those developed on a scale which allows implementation in the relevant industry sector, under economically and technically viable conditions, taking into consideration the costs and advantages, whether or not the techniques are used or produced inside the member state in question, as long as they are reasonable accessible to the operator.

"Best" means the most effective in achieving a high general level of protection of the environment as a whole.

No specific technique or technology is to be prescribed by the permit, allowing the operator choice in this matter. When selecting BAT for a particular activity, special consideration must be given to the following factors:

· the use of low waste technology;

· the use of less hazardous substances;

· where appropriate, the furthering of recovery and recycling of substances produced and used in the process, and of waste;

· comparable processes, facilities or methods of operation which have been tried with success on an industrial scale;

· technological advances and changes in scientific knowledge and understanding;

· the nature, effects and volume of the emissions concerned;

· the commissioning dates for new or existing installations;

· the length of time needed to introduce BAT;

· the consumption and nature of raw materials (including water) used in the process and their energy efficiency;

· the need to prevent or reduce to a minimum the overall impact of the emissions on the environment and the risks to it;

· the need to prevent accidents and to minimise the consequences for the environment;

· the information published by the European Commission or by international organisations on BAT and monitoring.

The likely costs and benefits of such measures and the principles of prevention and precaution must be taken into account, as should the technical characteristics of the installation, its geographical location and local environmental conditions around the installation.

Details of national emission limit values and, if appropriate, the BAT from which these are derived, will be submitted to the European Commission to ensure harmonisation. Regulatory authorities are under a duty to monitor developments in BAT and the European Commission will organise the exchange of information on BAT and monitoring techniques.

If EU emission limit values are not adopted (see later in this Chapter), the emission limit values defined in the permit must take as a minimum those values specified in existing EU environmental legislation. Where any environmental quality standard requires stricter conditions than those achievable through the use of BAT, additional measures may be specified in the permit.

If necessary, the permit may include conditions relating to the protection of soil and groundwater and the management of waste produced at the installation. The permit will set out requirements for situations other than normal operating conditions where there is a risk of environmental damage, including the start up and shut down of operations, leaks, malfunctions, short stoppages and the permanent cessation of operations at the installation.

In some cases, conditions may be set for categories of installations in general binding rules, rather than including these in individual permits. However, each installation must still be issued with a permit. It is possible that such binding rules may be used in England and Wales for IPPC installations not currently subject to IPC.

Permits will specify the methodology, frequency and analytical techniques to be used in programmes for monitoring emissions from installations. To enable the regulatory authority to check operators' compliance with the conditions of the permit, operators must regularly inform the regulatory authority of the results of monitoring programmes and, without delay, of any incidents or accidents which would significantly affect the environment. They must also assist the regulatory authority during the inspection of installations, the taking of samples and the gathering of information.

### Changes to Installations

If the operator proposes to make any change to the operation of an installation, the regulatory authority must be informed and the permit or the conditions attached to it may be amended accordingly. A "change" in these circumstances will constitute a change in the nature or functioning, or an extension, of the installation which may have consequences for the environment. A "substantial change" is a change in the operation which, in the opinion of the regulatory authority, may have significant negative effects on human beings or the environment. Any substantial change to an installation will require a permit from the regulatory authority.

### Reviewing Permits

Permit conditions will also be reviewed periodically and, where necessary, updated. In any event, the conditions must be reviewed where new or revised emission limit values need to be included in the permit in view of the pollution produced from an installation, where substantial changes in BAT enable emissions to be reduced significantly without imposing excessive costs, where operational safety requires new techniques to be used or where EU or national legislation requires this.

### Access to Information

Applications for permits for new or substantially changed installations must be made available for public comment for an appropriate time before the regulatory authority reaches its decision. The public will also have access to that decision, a copy of the permit and any subsequent revisions, and the results of emissions monitoring carried out under permit conditions, subject to some exemptions, e.g. on the grounds of commercial confidentiality and national security. Every three years an inventory of principal emissions and the sources of such emissions will be published by the European Commission, based on information supplied by member states. The European Commission will ensure that the data provided by each member state is comparable and complementary. This provision for an inventory may mean that the European Commission's work on a Polluting Emissions Register may now be set aside (see Chapter 6).

### Transboundary Effects

The proposed Directive is able to make provision for the control of the transboundary effects of pollution. If one member state is aware that the operation of an installation is likely to have significant negative effects on the environment of another member state, the information supplied by the operator in the application for the permit must be sent to the affected member state at the same time as this information is made available to the public. The member state affected may also request this information to be forwarded. The public in the affected member state has the right to comment on the proposed installation before a decision is made on the granting of a permit.

### EU Emission Limit Values

Legislation may be adopted by the Council of Ministers in the future to set emission limit values for the installations listed in Annex I (see Table 13) and the polluting substances referred to in Annex III (see Table 14). It is important to recognise that this provision only gives the Council the power to adopt such measures; as yet no EU emission limit values have been set.

### Status of Existing Legislation

Until existing installations have been granted permits, the provisions of the Air Framework Directive (84/360/EEC), certain provisions of the Dangerous Substances into Water Directive (76/464/EEC) and the provisions of other environmental directives relating to authorisation systems will apply. For new installations, the provisions relating to authorisation systems in these directives will not apply. The Air Framework Directive will lapse at the end of the eight year transitional period for the permitting of existing installations.

## RELATIONSHIP WITH IPC IN ENGLAND AND WALES

To a large extent, the provisions of the IPPC proposal, as currently drafted, are similar to those of the IPC system in England and Wales. However, there are several important distinctions. In particular, there is variation between the processes and substances prescribed for control. The range of polluting substances set out for water in the IPPC proposal is wider than that of the prescribed substances for water under IPC. It is estimated that at least an additional 5,000 processes will be brought under IPC as a result of this legislation, including intensive livestock units, food and drink manufacturers and other manufacturing companies currently subject to APC in England and Wales.

There are also differences in the definitions used in the two sets of legislation and where definitions are common to both there are variations in terminology. For example, the IPPC proposal includes noise in its definition of "pollution" and this is not the case for the EPA 1990. Conversely, the definition of "substances" in the EPA 1990 is wider. There is variation between the definitions of BAT used in the IPPC proposal and the concept of BATNEEC.

An IPPC permit would include post-operation conditions to ensure that installations that have ceased to operate do not cause any environmental damage. There are no corresponding provisions under Part I of the EPA 1990. The implementation dates for the two systems also differ. These variations would require the amendment of the existing national legislation in this area. The Department of the Environment will produce a consultation paper containing proposals to implement the provisions of the IPPC Directive in England and Wales.

## TABLE 13

### ANNEX I TO THE IPPC PROPOSAL

### CATEGORIES OF ACTIVITIES AND PROCESSES

| CATEGORIES OF INDUSTRIAL ACTIVITIES | |
| --- | --- |
| 1. | **Energy Industries** |
| 1.1 | Combustion installations with a rated thermal input exceeding 50 MW (the material requirements of the Large Combustion Plants Directive (88/609/EEC) for existing installations still apply until 31st December 2003). |
| 1.2 | Mineral oil and gas refineries. |
| 1.3 | Coke ovens. |
| 1.4 | Coal gasification and liquefication plants. |
| 2. | **Production and Processing of Metals** |
| 2.1 | Metal ore (including sulphide ore) roasting or sintering installations. |

| | |
|---|---|
| 2.2 | Installations for the production of pig iron or steel (primary or secondary fusion) including continuous casting, with a capacity exceeding 2.5 tonnes per hour. |
| 2.3 | Installations for the processing of ferrous metals: |
| (a) | hot-rolling mills with a capacity exceeding 20 tonnes of crude steel per hour. |
| (b) | smitheries with hammers the energy of which exceeds 50 kilojoule per hammer, where the calorific power used exceeds 20 MW. |
| (c) | application of protective fused metal coats with an input exceeding 2 tonnes of crude steel per hour. |
| 2.4 | Ferrous metal foundries with a production capacity exceeding 20 tonnes per day. |
| 2.5 | Installations: |
| (a) | for the production of non-ferrous crude metals from ore, con centrates or secondary raw materials by metallurgical, chemical or electrolytic processes. |
| (b) | for the smelting, including the alloyage, of non-ferrous metals, including recovered products, (refining, foundry casting etc.) with a melting capacity exceeding 4 tonnes for lead and cadmium or 20 tonnes for all other metals per day. |
| 2.6 | Installations for surface treatment of metals and plastic materials using an electrolytic or chemical process where the volume of the treatment vats exceed 30 m$^3$. |
| 3. | **Mineral Industry** |
| 3.1 | Installations for the production of cement clinker in rotary kilns with a production capacity exceeding 500 tonnes per day or lime in rotary kilns with a production capacity exceeding 50 tonnes per day or in other furnaces with a production capacity exceeding 50 tonnes per day. |

| | |
|---|---|
| 3.2 | Installations for the production of asbestos and manufacture of asbestos-based products. |
| 3.3 | Installations for the manufacture of glass including glass fibre with a smelting capacity exceeding 20 tonnes per day. |
| 3.4 | Installations for smelting mineral substances including the production of mineral fibres with a smelting capacity exceeding 20 tonnes per day. |
| 3.5 | Installations for the manufacture of ceramic products by burn ing in particular roofing tiles, bricks, refractory bricks, tiles, stoneware or porcelain, with a production capacity exceeding 75 tonnes per day, and/or with a kiln capacity exceeding 4 m³ and exceeding a loading density of 300 kg/m³. |
| **4.** | **Chemical Industry** |
| | Production within the meaning of the categories of activities contained in Section 4 means the production on an industrial scale by chemical processing of substances or groups of substances listed in Sections 4.1 to 4.6. |
| 4.1 | Chemical installations for the production of basic organic chemicals, such as: |
| (a) | simple hydrocarbons (linear or cyclic, saturated or unsaturated aliphatic or aromatic); |
| (b) | oxygen-containing hydrocarbons such as alcohols, aldehydes, ketones, carboxylic acids, esters, acetates, ethers, peroxides, epoxy resins; |
| (c) | sulphurous hydrocarbons; |
| (d) | nitrogenous hydrocarbons such as amines, amides, nitrous compounds, nitro compounds or nitrate compounds, nitriles, cyanates, isocyanates; |
| (e) | phosphorus-containing hydrocarbons; |
| (f) | halogenic hydrocarbons; |

| | |
|---|---|
| (g) | organometallic compounds; |
| (h) | basic plastic materials, (polymers,) synthetic fibres and cellulose-based fibres; |
| (i) | synthetic rubbers; |
| (j) | dyes and pigments; |
| (k) | surface-active agents and surfactants. |
| 4.2 | Chemical installations for the production of basic inorganic chemicals, such as: |
| (a) | gases, such as ammonia, chlorine or hydrogen chloride, fluorine or hydrogen fluoride, carbon oxides, sulphur compounds, nitrogen oxides, hydrogen, sulphur dioxide, carbonyl chloride; |
| (b) | acids, such as chromic acid, hydrofluoric acid, phosphoric acid, nitric acid, hydrochloric acid, sulphuric acid, oleum, sulphurous acids; |
| (c) | bases, such as ammonium hydroxide, potassium hydroxide, sodium hydroxide; |
| (d) | salts, such as ammonium chloride, potassium chlorate, potassium carbonate, sodium carbonate, perborate, silver nitrate; |
| (e) | non-metals, metal oxides or other inorganic compounds such as calcium carbide, silicon, silicon carbide. |
| 4.3 | Chemical installations for the production of phosphorus, nitrogen or potassium-based fertilisers (simple or compound fertilisers). |
| 4.4 | Chemical installations for the production of basic plant health products and of biocides. |
| 4.5 | Installations using a chemical or biological process for the production of basic pharmaceutical products. |

| 4.6 | Chemical installations for the production of explosives. |
|-----|----------------------------------------------------------|
| 5. | **Waste Management** |
| | Without prejudice to Article 11 of the Waste Framework Directive (91/156/EEC, as amending 75/442/EEC) or Article 3 of the Hazardous Waste Directive (91/689/EEC): |
| 5.1 | Installations for the disposal or recovery of hazardous waste referred to in the Hazardous Waste List (Decision 94/904/EC) as defined in Annexes IIA and IIB (operations R1, R5, R6, R8 and R9) to the Waste Framework Directive (75/442/EEC) and to the Waste Oils Directive (75/439/EEC), with a capacity exceeding 10 tonnes per day. |
| 5.2 | {...} |
| 5.3 | Installations for the incineration of municipal waste as defined in the Municipal Incinerator Directives (89/369/EEC and 89/429/EEC) with a capacity exceeding 3 tonnes per hour. |
| 5.4 | Installations for the disposal or recovery of non-hazardous waste as defined in Annex IIA to the Waste Framework Directive (75/442/EEC) under headings D8, D9, with a capacity exceeding 50 tonnes per day. |
| 5.5 | Landfills receiving more than 10 tonnes per day or with a total capacity exceeding 25,000 tonnes, as defined in Article 2(b) of the proposed Landfill Directive excluding the sites listed in Article 3(3)(a) of that Directive and landfills of inert waste. |
| 6. | **Other Activities** |
| 6.1 | Industrial plants for the: |
| (a) | production of pulp from timber or similar fibrous materials; |
| (b) | production of paper and board with a production capacity exceeding 20 tonnes per day. |

| 6.2 | Plants for the pre-treatment (operations such as washing, bleaching, mercerisation) or dyeing of fibres or textiles where the treatment capacity exceeds 10 tonnes per day. |
|---|---|
| 6.3 | Plants for the tanning of hides and skins where the treament capacity exceeds 12 tonnes of finished products per day. |
| 6.4 | (a) slaughterhouses with a carcase production capacity greater than 50 tonnes per day; |
| | (b) treatment and processing intended for the production of food products from: |
| | · animal raw materials (other than milk) with a finished product production capacity greater than 75 tonnes per day; |
| | · vegetable raw materials with a finished product production capacity greater than 300 tonnes per day (average value on a quarterly basis); |
| | (c) treatment and processing of milk, the quantity of milk received being greater than 200 tonnes per day (average value on a quarterly basis). |
| 6.5 | Installations for the disposal or recycling of animal carcases and animal waste with a treatment capacity exceeding 10 tonnes per day. |
| 6.6 | Installations for the intensive rearing of poultry or pigs with more than: |
| (a) | 40,000 places for poultry; |
| (b) | 2,000 places for production pigs (over 30 kg); or |
| (c) | 750 places for sows. |
| 6.7 | Installations for the surface treatment of substances, objects or products using organic solvents, in particular for dressing, printing, coating, degreasing, waterproofing, sizing, paint ing, cleaning or impregnating, with a solvent input of more than 150 kg per hour or more than 200 tonnes per year. |

| 6.8 | Installations for the production of carbon (hard-burnt coal) or electrographite by means of incineration or graphitisation. |

**Note**

1. Installations or parts of installations used for research, development and testing of new products and processes are not covered by this Directive.

2. The threshold values given below generally refer to production capacities or outputs. Where one operator carries out several activities falling under the same heading in the same installation or on the same site, the capacities of such activities are added together.

## TABLE 14

## ANNEX III TO THE IPPC PROPOSAL

| **INDICATIVE LIST OF THE MAIN PARAMETERS AND POLLUTING SUBSTANCES TO BE TAKEN INTO ACCOUNT IF THEY ARE RELEVANT FOR FIXING EMISSION LIMIT VALUES** |
| --- |
| Air |
| Sulphur dioxide and other sulphur compounds. |
| Oxides of nitrogen and other nitrogen compounds. |
| Carbon monoxide. |
| Volatile organic compounds. |
| Metals and their compounds. |
| Dust. |
| Asbestos (suspended particulates, fibres). |
| Chlorine and its compounds. |

Fluorine and its compounds.

Arsenic and its compounds.

Cyanides.

Substances and preparations which have been proved to possess carcinogenic or mutagenic properties or properties which may affect reproduction via the air.

Polychlorinated dibenzodioxins and polychlorinated dibenzofurans.

## Water

Organohalogen compounds and substances which may form such compounds in the aquatic environment.

Organophosphorus compounds.

Organotin compounds.

Substances and preparations which have been proved to possess carcinogenic or mutagenic properties or properties which may affect reproduction in or via the aquatic environment.

Persistent hydrocarbons and persistent and bioaccumulable organic toxic substances.

Cyanides.

Metals and their compounds.

Arsenic and its compounds.

Biocides and plant health products.

Materials in suspension.

Substances which contribute to eutrophication (nitrates and phosphates).

Substances which have an unfavourable influence on the oxygen balance (and can be measured using parameters such as BOD, COD, etc.).

# APPENDIX I

# THE ENVIRONMENTAL PROTECTION ACT 1990 PART I

## INTEGRATED POLLUTION CONTROL AND AIR POLLUTION CONTROL BY LOCAL AUTHORITIES

**Preliminary**

1. (1) The following provisions have effect for the interpretation of this Part.

   (2) The "environment" consists of all, or any, of the following media, namely, the air, water and land; and the medium of air includes the air within buildings and the air within other natural or man-made structures above or below ground.

   (3) "Pollution of the environment" means pollution of the environment due to the release (into any environ mental medium) from any process of substances which are capable of causing harm to man or any other living organisms supported by the environment.

   (4) "Harm" means harm to the health of living organ isms or other interference with the ecological systems of which they form part and, in the case of man, includes offence caused to any of his senses or harm to his property; and "harmless" has a corresponding meaning.

   (5) "Process" means any activities carried on in Great Britain, whether on premises or by means of mobile plant, which are capable of causing pollution of the environment and "prescribed process" means a proc ess prescribed under section 2(1) below.

   (6) For the purposes of subsection (5) above -

   "activities" means industrial or commercial activities or activities of any other nature whatsoever (including, with or without other activities, the keeping of a substance);

"Great Britain" includes so much of the adjacent territorial sea as is, or is treated as, relevant territo rial waters for the purposes of Chapter 1 of Part III of the Water Resources Act 1991, or, as respects Scotland, Part II of the Control of Pollution Act 1974; and "mobile plant" means plant which is designed to move or to be moved whether on roads or otherwise.

(7) The "enforcing authority", in relation to England and Wales, is the chief inspector or the local authority by whom, under section 4 below, the functions conferred or imposed by this Part otherwise than on the Secre tary of State are for the time being exercisable in rela tion respectively to releases of substances into the en vironment or into the air; and "local enforcing authority" means any such local authority.

(8) The "enforcing authority", in relation to Scotland, is

(a) in relation to releases of substances into the environ ment, the chief inspector or the river purification au thority (which in this Part means a river purification authority within the meaning of the Rivers (Prevention of Pollution) (Scotland) Act 1951),

(b) in relation to releases of substances into the air, the local authority, by whom, under section 4 below, the functions conferred or imposed by this Part otherwise than on the Secretary of State are for the time being exercisable; and "local enforcing authority" means any such local authority.

(9) "Authorisation" means an authorisation for a process (whether on premises or by means of mobile plant) granted under section 6 below; and a reference to the conditions of an authorisation is a reference to the con ditions subject to which at any time the authorisation has effect.

(10)   A substance is "released" into any environmental medium whenever it is released directly into that medium whether it is released into it within or outside Great Britain and "release" includes -

(a)   in relation to air, any emission of the substance into the air;

(b)   in relation to water, any entry (including any discharge) of the substance into water;

(c)   in relation to land, any deposit, keeping or disposal of the substance in or on land;

and for this purpose "water" and "land" shall be con strued in accordance with subsections (11) and (12) below.

(11)   For the purpose of determining into what medium a substance is released -

(a)   any release into -

(i)   the sea or the surface of the seabed,

(ii)   any river, watercourse, lake, loch or pond (whether natural or artificial or above or below ground) or reservoir or the surface of the river bed or of other land supporting such waters, or

(iii)   ground waters,

is a release into water;

(b)   any release into -

(i)   land covered by water falling outside paragraph (a) above or the water covering such land; or

(ii)   the land beneath the surface of the seabed or of other land supporting waters falling within paragraph (a)(ii) above, is a release into land; and

(c)     any release into a sewer (within the meaning of the Water Industry Act 1991 or, in relation to Scotland, of the Sewerage (Scotland) Act 1968) shall be treated as a release into water;
but a sewer and its contents shall be disregarded in determining whether there is pollution of the environment at any time.

(12)    In subsection (11) above "ground waters" means any waters contained in underground strata, or in -

(a)     a well, borehole or similar work sunk into underground strata, including any adit or passage constructed in connection with the well, borehole or work for facilitating the collection of water in the well, borehole or work; or

(b)     any excavation into underground strata where the level of water in the excavation depends wholly or mainly on water entering it from the strata.

(13)    "Substance" shall be treated as including electricity or heat and "prescribed substance" has the meaning given by section 2(7) below.

## Prescribed Processes and Prescribed Substances

2.      (1)     The Secretary of State may, by regulations, prescribe any description of process as a process for the carrying on of which after a prescribed date an authorisation is required under section 6 below.

(2)     Regulations under subsection (1) above may frame the description of a process by reference to any characteristics of the process or the area or other circumstances in which the process is carried on or the description of person carrying it on.

(3)     Regulations under subsection (1) above may prescribe or provide for the determination under the regulations of different dates for different descriptions of persons and may include such transitional provisions as the Secretary of State considers necessary or expedient as

respects the making of applications for authorisations and suspending the application of section 6(1) below until the determination of applications made within the period allowed by the regulations.

(3)     Regulations under subsection (1) above shall, as re spects each description of process, designate it as one for central control or one for local control.

(4)     The Secretary of State may, by regulations prescribe any description of substance as a substance the release of which into the environment is subject to control under sections 6 and 7 below.

(6)     Regulations under subsection (5) above may -

(a)     prescribe separately, for each environmental medium, the substances the release of which into that medium is to be subject to control; and

(b)     provide that a description of substance is only pre scribed, for any environmental medium, so far as it is released into that medium in such amounts over such periods, in such concentrations or in such other circums- tances as may be specified in the regulations;

and in relation to a substance of a description which is prescribed for releases into the air, the regulations may designate the substance as one for central control or one for local control.

(7)     In this Part "prescribed substance" means any substance of a description prescribed in regulations under subsec tion (5) above or, in the case of a substance of a descr- iption prescribed only for releases in circumstances specified under subsection (6)(b) above, means any sub stance of that description which is released in those circumstances.

## Emission etc. Limits and Quality Objectives

3.      (1)     The Secretary of State may make regulations under subsection (2) or (4) below establishing standards, ob

jectives or requirements in relation to particular pre scribed processes or particular substances.

(2)     Regulations under this subsection may -

(a)     in relation to releases of any substance from prescribed processes into any environmental medium, prescribe standard limits for -

(i)     the concentration, the amount or the amount in any period of that substance which may be so released; and

(ii)     any other characteristic of that substance in any circumstances in which it may be so released;

(b)     prescribe standard requirements for the measurement or analysis of, or of releases of, substances for which limits have been set under paragraph (a) above; and

(c)     in relation to any prescribed process, prescribe stand ards or requirements as to any aspect of the process.

(3)     Regulations under subsection (2) above may make dif ferent provision in relation to different cases, including different provision in relation to different processes, descriptions of person, localities or other circumstances.

(4)     Regulations under this subsection may establish for any environmental medium (in all areas or in specified areas) quality objectives or quality standards in relati on to any substances which may be released into that or any other medium from any process.

(5)     The Secretary of State may make plans for -

(a)     establishing limits for the total amount, or the total amount in any period, of any substance which may be released into the environment in, or in any area within, the United Kingdom;

(b) allocating quotas as respects the release of substances to persons carrying on processes in respect of which any such limit is established;

(c) establishing limits of the descriptions specified in sub section (2)(a) above so as progressively to reduce pollu tion of the environment;

(d) the progressive improvement in the quality objectives and quality standards established by regulations un- der subsection (4) above;

and the Secretary of State may, from time to time, revise any plan so made.

(6) Regulations or plans under this section may be made for any purposes of this Part or for other purposes.

(7) The Secretary of State shall give notice in the London, Edinburgh and Belfast Gazettes of the making and the revision of any plan under subsection (5) above and shall make the documents containing the plan, or the plan as so revised, available for inspection by members of the public at the places specified in the notice.

(8) Subject to any Order made after the passing of this Act by virtue of subsection (1)(a) of section 3 of the North- ern Ireland Constitution Act 1973, the making and revision of plans under subsection (5) above shall not be a transferred matter for the purposes of that Act but shall for the purposes of subsection (2) of that section be treated as specified in Schedule 3 to that Act.

## Discharge and Scope of Functions

4. (1) This section determines the authority by whom the functions conferred or imposed by this Part otherwise than on the Secretary of State are exercisable for the purposes for which they are exercisable.

(2) Those functions, in their application to prescribed proc esses designated for central control, shall be functions of the chief inspector appointed for England and Wales

by the Secretary of State under section 16 below and, in relation to Scotland of the Chief Inspector so appointed from Scotland or of the river purification au thority, as determined under regulations made under section 5(1) below, and shall be exercisable for the purpose of preventing or minimising pollution of the environment due to the release of substances into any environmental medium.

(3)    Subject to subsection (4) below, those functions, in their application to prescribed processes designated for local control, shall be functions of -

(a)    in the case of a prescribed process carried on (or to be carried on) by means of mobile plant, the local author ity in whose area the person carrying on the process has his principal place of business; and

(b)    in any other cases, the local authority in whose area the prescribed processes are (or are to be) carried on;

and the functions applicable to such processes shall be exercisable for the purpose of preventing or minimising pollution of the environment due to the release of substances into the air (but not into any other environmental medium).

(4)    The Secretary of State may, as respects the functions under this Part being exercised by a local authority specified in the direction, direct that those functions shall be exercised instead by the chief inspector while the direction remains in force or during a period specified in the direction.

(5)    A transfer of functions under subsection (4) above to the chief inspector does not make them exercisable by him for the purpose of preventing or minimising pollu tion of the environment due to releases of substances into any other environmental medium than the air.

(6)    A direction under subsection (4) above may transfer those functions as exercisable in relation to all or any description of prescribed processes carried on by all or

any description of persons (a "general direction") or in relation to a prescribed process carried on by a specified person (a "specific direction").

(7)    A direction under subsection (4) above may include such saving and transitional provisions as the Secretary of State considers necessary or expedient.

(8)    The Secretary of State, on giving or withdrawing a direction under subsection (4) above, shall -

(a)    in the case of a general direction -

(i)    forthwith serve notice of it on the chief inspector and on the local enforcing authorities affected by the direction; and

(ii)    cause notice of it to be published as soon as practicable in the London Gazette or, as the case may be, in the Edinburgh Gazette and in at least one newspaper circulating in the area of each authority affected by the direction;

(b)    in the case of a specific direction -

(i)    forthwith serve notice of it on the chief inspector, the local enforcing authority and the person carrying on or appearing to the Secretary of State to be carrying on the process affected, and

(ii)    cause notice of it to be published as soon as practicable in the London Gazette or, as the case may be, in the Edinburgh Gazette and in at least one newspaper circulating in the authority's area;

and any such notice shall specify the date at which the direction is to take (or took) effect and (where appropriate) its duration.

(9)    It shall be the duty of the chief inspector or, in Scot land, of the chief inspector and river purification authorities to follow developments in technology and tech-

niques for preventing or reducing pollution of the environment due to releases of substances from prescribed processes; and the local enforcing authorities shall follow such of those developments as concern releases into the air of substances from prescribed processes designated for local control.

(10)  It shall be the duty of the chief inspector, river purification authorities and the local enforcing authorities to give effect to any directions given to them under any provision of this Part.

(11)  In this Part "local authority" means, subject to subsection (12) below -

(a)  in Greater London, a London borough council, the Common Council of the City of London, the Sub-Treasurer of the Inner Temple and the Under Treasurer of the Middle Temple;

(b)  in England, outside Greater London, a district council and the Council of the Isles of Scilly, in Wales, a county council or county borough council; and

(c)  in Scotland, a council constituted under Section 2 of the Local Government (Scotland) Act 1994.

(12)  Where, by an order under section 2 of the Public Health (Control of Disease) Act 1984, a port health authority has been constituted for any port health district, the port health authority shall have by virtue of this sub section, as respects its district, the functions conferred or imposed by this Part and no such order shall be made assigning those functions; and "local authority" and "area" shall be construed accordingly.

## Further Provisions as to Discharge and Scope of Functions: Scotland

5.  (1)  For the purposes of section 4(2) above in its application to Scotland, the Secretary of State shall make regulations prescribing -

(a)    the method and arrangements for determining whether the functions referred to in that subsection shall be functions of the chief inspector or of a river purification authority;

(b)    if the functions are determined under paragraph (a) above to be functions of a river purification authority, the river purification authority by whom they are to be exercised.

(2)    The Secretary of State may make regulations prescribing -

(a)    the circumstances and manner in which consultation shall be carried out between -

(i)    whichever of the chief inspector or river purifica tion authority is determined under regulations made under subsection (1) above to be the enforcing authority, and

(ii)    the other (the "consulted authority"),

before granting, varying, transferring or revoking an authorisation or serving an enforcement or prohibition notice;

(b)    the circumstances in which the consulted authority may require the enforcing authority to include, in an au thorisation, conditions which the consulted authority reasonably believe will achieve the objectives specified in section 7(2) below.

(3)    Regulations under this section may contain such incidental, supplemental and consequential provision as the Secretary of State considers appropriate.

(4)    This section applies to Scotland only.

## AUTHORISATIONS

### Authorisations: General Provisions

**6.**  (1)    No person shall carry on a prescribed process after the date prescribed or determined for that description of process by or under regulations under section 2(1) above (but subject to any transitional provision made by the regulations) except under an authorisation granted by the enforcing authority and in accordance with the conditions to which it is subject.

     (2)    An application for an authorisation shall be made to the enforcing authority in accordance with Part I of Schedule 1 to this Act and shall be accompanied by the fee prescribed under section 8(2)(a) below.

     (3)    Where an application is duly made to the enforcing authority, the authority shall either grant the authorisation subject to the conditions required or authorised to be imposed by section 7 below or refuse the application.

     (4)    An application shall not be granted unless the enforcing authority considers that the applicant will be able to carry on the process so as to comply with the conditions which would be included in the authorisation.

     (5)    The Secretary of State may, if he thinks fit in relation to any application for an authorisation, give to the enforcing authority directions as to whether or not the authority should grant the authorisation.

     (6)    The enforcing authority shall, as respects each authorisation in respect of which it has functions under this Part, from time to time but no less frequently than once in every period of four years, carry out a review of conditions of the authorisation.

     (7)    The Secretary of State may, by regulations, substitute for the period for the time being specified in subsection

(6) above such other period as he thinks fit.

(8)    Schedule 1 to this Act (supplementary provisions) shall have effect in relation to authorisations.

## Conditions of Authorisations

7.    (1)    There shall be included in an authorisation -

(a)    subject to paragraph (b) below, such specific conditions as the enforcing authority considers appropriate, when taken with the general condition implied by subsection (4) below, for achieving the objectives specified in sub section (2) below;

(b)    such conditions as are specified in directions given by the Secretary of State under subsection (3) below; and

(c)    such other conditions (if any) as appear to the enforcing authority to be appropriate;

but no conditions shall be imposed for the purpose only of securing the health of persons at work (within the meaning of Part I of the Health and Safety at Work etc. Act 1974).

(2)    Those objectives are -

(a)    ensuring that, in carrying on a prescribed process, the best available techniques not entailing excessive cost will be used -

(i)    for preventing the release of substances prescribed for any environmental medium into that medium or, where that is not practicable by such means, for reducing the release of such substances to a minimum and for rendering harmless any such substances which are so released; and

(ii)    for rendering harmless any other substances which might cause harm if released into any environmental medium;

(b)     compliance with any directions by the Secretary of State given for the implementation of any obligations of the United Kingdom under the Community Treaties or international law relating to environmental protection;

(c)     compliance with any limits or requirements and achievement of any quality standards or quality objectives prescribed by the Secretary of State under any of the relevant enactments;

(d)     compliance with any requirements applicable to the grant of authorisations specified by or under a plan made by the Secretary of State under section 3(5) above.

(3)     Except as respects the general condition implied by subsection (4) below, the Secretary of State may give directions to the enforcing authorities as to the conditions which are, or are not, to be included in all authorisations, in authorisations of any specified description or in any particular authorisation.

(4)     Subject to subsections (5) and (6) below, there is implied in every authorisation a general condition that, in carrying on the process to which the authorisation applies, the person carrying it on must use the best available techniques not entailing excessive cost -

(a)     for preventing the release of substances prescribed for any environmental medium into that medium or, where that is not practicable by such means, for reducing the release of such substances to a minimum and for rendering harmless any such substances which are so released; and

(b)     for rendering harmless any other substances which might cause harm if released into any environmental medium.

(5)     In the application of subsections (1) to (4) above to authorisations granted by a local enforcing authority references to the release of substances into any environmental medium are to be read as references to the release of substances into the air.

(6) The obligation implied by virtue of subsection (4) above shall not apply in relation to any aspect of the process in question which is regulated by a condition imposed under subsection (1) above.

(7) The objectives referred to in subsection (2) above shall, where the process -

(a) is one designated for central control; and

(b) is likely to involve the release of substances into more than one environmental medium;

include the objective of ensuring that the best available techniques not entailing excessive cost will be used for minimising the pollution which may be caused to the environment taken as a whole by the releases having regard to the best practicable environmental option available as respects the substances which may be released.

(8) An authorisation for carrying on a prescribed process may, without prejudice to the generality of subsection (1) above, include conditions -

(a) imposing limits on the amount or composition of any substance produced by or utilised in the process in any period; and

(b) requiring advance notification of any proposed change in the manner of carrying on the process.

(9) This section has effect subject to section 28 below and, in relation to Scotland, to any regulations made under section 5(2) above.

(10) References to the best available techniques not entailing excessive cost, in relation to a process, include (in addition to references to any technical means and technology) references to the number, qualifications, training and supervision of persons employed in the process and the design, construction, lay-out and maintenance of the buildings in which it is carried on.

(11)    It shall be the duty of enforcing authorities to have regard to any guidance issued to them by the Secretary of State for the purposes of the application of subsections (2) and (7) above as to the techniques and environmental options that are appropriate for any description of prescribed process.

(12)    In subsection (2) above "the relevant enactments" are any enactments or instruments contained in or made for the time being under -

(a)    section 2 of the Clean Air Act 1968;

(b)    section 2 of the European Communities Act 1972;

(c)    Part I of the Health and Safety at Work etc. Act 1974;

(d)    Parts II, III or IV of the Control of Pollution Act 1974;

(e)    Part III of the Water Resources Act 1991; and

(f)    section 3 of this Act.

## Fees and Charges for Authorisations

8.    (1)    There shall be charged by and paid to the enforcing authority such fees and charges as may be prescribed from time to time by a scheme under subsection (2) below (whether by being specified in or made calculable under the scheme).

(2)    The Secretary of State may, with the approval of the Treasury, make, and from time to time revise, a scheme prescribing -

(a)    fees payable in respect of applications for authorisations;

(b)    fees payable by persons holding authorisations in respect of, or of applications for, the variations of authorisations; and

(c)     charges payable by such persons in respect of the sub sistence of their authorisations.

(3)     The Secretary of State shall, on making or revising a scheme under subsection (2) above, lay a copy of the scheme or of the alterations made in the scheme or, if he considers it more appropriate, the scheme as revised before each House of Parliament.

(4)     The Secretary of State may make separate schemes for fees and charges payable to the chief inspector or, as the case may be, river purification authority and fees and charges payable to local enforcing authorities under this Part.

(5)     A scheme under subsection (2) above may, in particular -

(a)     make different provision for different cases, including different provision in relation to different persons, cir cumstances or localities;

(b)     allow for reduced fees or charges to be payable in respect of authorisations for a number of prescribed processes carried on by the same person;

(c)     provide for the times at which and the manner in which the payments required by the scheme are to be made; and

(d)     make such incidental, supplementary and transitional provision as appears to the Secretary of State to be appropriate.

(6)     The Secretary of State, in framing a scheme under subsection (2) above, shall, so far as practicable, secure that the fees and charges payable under the scheme are sufficient, taking one financial year with another, to cover the relevant expenditure attributable to authorisations.

(7)     The "relevant expenditure attributable to authorisations" is the expenditure incurred by the enforcing auth-

orities in exercising their functions under this Part in relation to authorisations together with the expenditure incurred by the National Rivers Authority in exercising the Authority's functions in relation to authorisations for processes which may involve the release of any substance into water.

(8) If it appears to the enforcing authority that the holder of an authorisation has failed to pay a charge due in consideration of the subsistence of the authorisation, it may, by notice in writing served on the holder, revoke the authorisation.

(9) The Secretary of State may make to the National Rivers Authority payments of such amounts as appear to him to be required to meet the estimated relevant expenditure of the Authority attributable to authorisations.

(10) Subsections (7) and (9) above shall not apply to Scotland, but in relation to Scotland the "relevant expenditure attributable to authorisations" is the expenditure incurred by the enforcing authorities in exercising their functions under this Part or in relation to consultation carried out under regulations made under section 5(2) above.

(11) In Scotland, the chief inspector may make to a river purification authority and a river purification authority may make to the chief inspector payments of such amounts as are appropriate to meet their estimated relevant expenditure attributable to authorisations, such amounts to be determined by the Secretary of State if the chief inspector and the authority fail to agree on an appropriate amount of payment.

## Transfer of Authorisations

9. (1) An authorisation for the carrying on of any prescribed process may be transferred by the holder to a person who proposes to carry on the process in the holder's place.

(2)     Where an authorisation is transferred under this section, the person to whom it is transferred shall notify
the enforcing authority in writing of that fact not later
than the end of the period of twenty-one days beginning with the date of the transfer.

(3)     An authorisation which is transferred under this section shall have effect on and after the date of the transfer as if it had been granted to that person under section 6 above, subject to the same conditions as were
attached to it immediately before that date.

## Variation of Authorisations by Enforcing Authority

10.   (1)     The enforcing authority may at any time, subject to
the requirements of section 7 above, and, in cases to
which they apply, the requirements of Part II of Schedule 1 to this Act, vary an authorisation and shall do so
if it appears to the authority at that time that that
section requires conditions to be included which are
different from the subsisting conditions.

(2)     Where the enforcing authority has decided to vary an
authorisation under subsection (1) above the authority
shall notify the holder of the authorisation and serve a
variation notice on him.

(3)     In this Part a "variation notice" is a notice served by
the enforcing authority on the holder of an authorisa
tion -

(a)     specifying variations of the authorisation which the
enforcing authority has decided to make; and

(b)     specifying the date or dates on which the variations
are to take effect;

and, unless the notice is withdrawn, the variations specified in a variation notice shall take effect on the date
or dates so specified.

(4)     A variation notice served under subsection (2) above
shall also -

(a)    require the holder of the authorisation, within such period as may be specified in the notice, to notify the authority what action (if any) he proposes to take to ensure that the process is carried on in accordance with the authorisation as varied by the notice; and

(b)    require the holder to pay the fee (if any) prescribed by a scheme under section 8 above within such period as may be specified in the notice.

(5)    Where in the opinion of the enforcing authority any action to be taken by the holder of an authorisation in consequence of a variation notice served under subsection (2) above will involve a substantial change in the manner in which the process is being carried on, the enforcing authority shall notify the holder of its opinion.

(6)    The Secretary of State may, if he thinks fit in relation to authorisations of any description or particular authorisations, direct the enforcing authorities -

(a)    to exercise their powers under this section, or to do so in such circumstances as may be specified in the directions, in such manner as may be so specified; or

(b)    not to exercise those powers, or not to do so in such circumstances or such manner as may be so specified;

and the Secretary of State shall have the corresponding power of direction in respect of the powers of the enforcing authorities to vary authorisations under section 11 below.

(7)    In this section and section 11 below a "substantial change", in relation to a prescribed process being carried on under an authorisation, means a substantial change in the substances released from the process or in the amount or any other characteristic of any substance so released; and the Secretary of State may give directions to the enforcing authorities as to what does or does not constitute a substantial change in relation

to processes generally, any description of process or any particular process.

(8)   In this section and section 11 below -

"prescribed" means prescribed in regulations made by the Secretary of State;
"vary", in relation to the subsisting conditions or other provisions of an authorisation, means adding to them or varying or rescinding any of them;

and "variation" shall be construed accordingly.

## Variation of Conditions etc.: Applications by Holders of Authorisations

11.   (1)   A person carrying on a prescribed process under an authorisation who wishes to make a relevant change in the process may at any time -

(a)   notify the enforcing authority in the prescribed form of that fact, and

(b)   request the enforcing authority to make a determination, in relation to the proposed change, of the matters mentioned in subsection (2) below;

and a person making a request under paragraph (b) above shall furnish the enforcing authority with such information as may be prescribed or as the authority may by notice require.

(2)   On receiving a request under subsection (1) above the enforcing authority shall determine-

(a)   whether the proposed change would involve a breach of any condition of the authorisation;

(b)   if it would not involve such a breach, whether the authority would be likely to vary the conditions of the authorisation as a result of the change;

(c)    if it would involve such a breach, whether the authority would consider varying the conditions of the authorisation so that the change may be made; and

(d)    whether the change would involve a substantial change in the manner in which the process is being carried on;

and the enforcing authority shall notify the holder of the authorisation of its determination of those matters.

(3)    Where the enforcing authority has determined that the proposed change would not involve a substantial change, but has also determined under paragraph (b) or (c) of subsection (2) above that the change would lead to or require the variation of the conditions of the authorisation, then -

(a)    the enforcing authority shall (either on notifying its determination under that subsection or on a subsequent occasion) notify the holder of the authorisation of the variations which the authority is likely to consider making; and

(b)    the holder may apply in the prescribed form to the enforcing authority for the variation of the conditions of the authorisation so that he may make the proposed change.

(4)    Where the enforcing authority has determined that a proposed change would involve a substantial change that would lead to or require the variation of the conditions of the authorisation, then -

(a)    the authority shall (either on notifying its determination under subsection (2) above or on a subsequent occasion) notify the holder of the authorisation of the variations which the authority is likely to consider making; and

(b)    the holder of the authorisation shall, if he wishes to proceed with the change, apply in the prescribed form to the enforcing authority for the variation of the conditions of the authorisation.

(5)     The holder of an authorisation may at any time, unless he is carrying on a prescribed process under the authorisation and wishes to make a relevant change in the process, apply to the enforcing authority in the prescribed form for the variation of the conditions of the authorisation.

(6)     A person carrying on a process under an authorisation who wishes to make a relevant change in the process may, where it appears to him that the change will require the variation of the conditions of the authorisation, apply to the enforcing authority in the prescribed form for the variation of the conditions of the authorisation specified in the application.

(7)     A person who makes an application for the variation of the conditions of an authorisation shall furnish the authority with such information as may be prescribed or as the authority may by notice require.

(8)     On an application for variation of the conditions of an authorisation under any provision of this section -

(a)     the enforcing authority may, having fulfilled the requirements of Part II of Schedule 1 to this Act in cases to which they apply, as it thinks fit either refuse the application or, subject to the requirements of section 7 above, vary the conditions or, in the case of an application under subsection (6) above, treat the application as a request for a determination under subsection (2) above; and

(b)     if the enforcing authority decides to vary the conditions, it shall serve a variation notice on the holder of the authorisation.

(9)     Any application to the enforcing authority under this section shall be accompanied by the applicable fee (if any) prescribed by a scheme made under section 8 above.

(10)    This section applies to any provision other than a condition which is contained in an authorisation as it applies to a condition with the modification that any

reference to the breach of a condition shall be read as a reference to acting outside the scope of the authorisation.

(11) For the purposes of this section a relevant change in a prescribed process is a change in the manner of carrying on the process which is capable of altering the substances released from the process or of affecting the amount or any other characteristic of any substance so released.

## Revocation of Authorisation

12. (1) The enforcing authority may at any time revoke an authorisation by notice in writing to the person holding the authorisation.

(2) Without prejudice to the generality of subsection (1) above, the enforcing authority may revoke an authorisation where it has reason to believe that a prescribed process for which the authorisation is in force has not been carried on or not for a period of twelve months.

(3) The revocation of an authorisation under this section shall have effect from the date specified in the notice; and the period between the date on which the notice is served and the date so specified shall not be less than twenty-eight days.

(4) The enforcing authority may, before the date on which the revocation of an authorisation takes effect, withdraw the notice or vary the date specified in it.

(5) The Secretary of State may, if he thinks fit in relation to an authorisation, give to the enforcing authority directions as to whether the authority should revoke the authorisation under this section.

## ENFORCEMENT
## Enforcement Notices

13. (1) If the enforcing authority is of the opinion that the person carrying on a prescribed process under an

authorisation is contravening any condition of the authorisation, or is likely to contravene any such condition, the authority may serve on him a notice ("an enforcement notice").

(2)    An enforcement notice shall-

(a)    state that the authority is of the said opinion;

(b)    specify the matters constituting the contravention or the matters making it likely that the contravention will arise, as the case may be;

(c)    specify the steps that must be taken to remedy the contravention or to remedy the matters making it likely that the contravention will arise, as the case may be; and

(d)    specify the period within which those steps must be taken.

(3)    The Secretary of State may, if he thinks fit in relation to the carrying on by any person of a prescribed process, give to the enforcing authority directions as to whether the authority should exercise its powers under this section and as to the steps which are to be required to be taken under this section.

## Prohibition Notices

14.    (1)    If the enforcing authority is of the opinion, as respects the carrying on of a prescribed process under an authorisation, that the continuing to carry it on, or the continuing to carry it on in a particular manner, involves an imminent risk of serious pollution of the environment the authority shall serve a notice (a "prohibition notice") on the person carrying on the process.

(2)    A prohibition notice may be served whether or not the manner of carrying on the process in question

contravenes a condition of the authorisation and may relate to any aspects of the process, whether regulated by the conditions of the authorisation or not.

(3)   A prohibition notice shall -

(a)   state the authority's opinion;

(b)   specify the risk involved in the process;

(c)   specify the steps that must be taken to remove it and the period within which they must be taken; and

(d)   direct that the authorisation shall, until the notice is withdrawn, wholly or to the extent specified in the notice cease to have effect to authorise the carrying on of the process;

and where the direction applies to part only of the process it may impose conditions to be observed in carrying on the part which is authorised to be carried on.

(4)   The Secretary of State may, if he thinks fit in relation to the carrying on by any person of a prescribed process, give to the enforcing authority directions as to -

(a)   whether the authority should perform its duties under this section; and

(b)   the matters to be specified in any prohibition notice in pursuance of subsection (3) above which the authority is directed to issue.

(5)   The enforcing authority shall, as respects any prohibition notice it has issued to any person, by notice in writing served on that person, withdraw the notice when it is satisfied that the steps required by the notice have been taken.

## Appeals as Respects Authorisations and Against Variation, Enforcement and Prohibition Notices

**15.** (1) The following persons, namely -

(a) a person who has been refused the grant of an authorisation under section 6 above;

(b) a person who is aggrieved by the conditions attached, under any provision of this Part, to his authorisation;

(c) a person who has been refused a variation of an authorisation on an application under section 11 above;

(d) a person whose authorisation has been revoked under section 12 above;

may appeal against the decision of the enforcing authority to the Secretary of State (except where the decision implements a direction of his).

(2) A person on whom a variation notice, an enforcement notice or a prohibition notice is served may appeal against the notice to the Secretary of State.

(3) Where an appeal under this section is made to the Secretary of State -

(a) the Secretary of State may refer any matter involved in the appeal to a person appointed by him for the purpose; or

(b) the Secretary of State may, instead of determining the appeal himself, direct that the appeal or any matter involved in it shall be determined by a person appointed by him for the purpose;

and a person appointed under paragraph (b) above for the purpose of an appeal shall have the same powers under subsection (5), (6) or (7) below as the Secretary of State.

(4)     An appeal under this section shall, if and to the extent required by regulations under subsection (10) below, be advertised in such manner as may be prescribed by regulations under that subsection.

(5)     If either party to the appeal so requests or the Secretary of State so decides, an appeal shall be or continue in the form of a hearing (which may, if the person hearing the appeal so decides, be held, or held to any extent, in private).

(6)     On determining an appeal against a decision of an enforcing authority under subsection (1) above, the Secretary of State -

(a)     may affirm the decision;

(b)     where the decision was a refusal to grant an authorisation or a variation of an authorisation, may direct the enforcing authority to grant the authorisation or to vary the authorisation, as the case may be;

(c)     where the decision was as to the conditions attached to an authorisation, may quash all or any of the conditions of the authorisation;

(d)     where the decision was to revoke an authorisation, may quash the decision;
and where he exercises any of the powers in para graphs (b), (c) or (d) above, he may give directions as to the conditions to be attached to the authorisation.

(7)     On the determination of an appeal under subsection (2) above the Secretary of State may either quash or af firm the notice and, if he affirms it, may do so either in its original form or with such modifications as he may in the circumstances think fit.

(8)     Where an appeal is brought under subsection (1) above against the revocation of an authorisation, the revocation shall not take effect pending the final determination or the withdrawal of the appeal.

(9)     Where an appeal is brought under subsection (2) above against a notice, the bringing of the appeal shall not

have the effect of suspending the operation of the notice.

(10)    Provision may be made by the Secretary of State by regulations with respect to appeals under this section and in particular -

(a)    as to the period within which and the manner in which appeals are to be brought; and

(b)    as to the manner in which appeals are to be considered.

## Appointment of Chief Inspector and Other Inspectors

**16.**    (1)    The Secretary of State may appoint as inspectors (under whatever title he may determine) such persons having suitable qualifications as he thinks necessary for carrying this Part into effect in relation to prescribed processes designated for central control or for the time being transferred under section 4(4) above to central control, and may terminate any appointment made under this subsection.

(2)    The Secretary of State may make to or in respect of any person so appointed such payments by way of remuneration, allowances or otherwise as he may with the approval of the Treasury determine.

(3)    In relation to England and Wales the Secretary of State shall constitute one of the inspectors appointed under subsection (1) above to be the Chief Inspector for England and Wales and in relation to Scotland the Secretary of State shall constitute one of the said inspectors to be the Chief Inspector for Scotland.

(4)    The functions conferred or imposed by or under this Part on the Chief Inspector as the enforcing authority may, to any extent, be delegated by him to any other inspector appointed under subsection (1) above.

(5)    A river purification authority may appoint as inspectors (under whatever title the authority may determine) such persons having suitable qualifications as the authority thinks necessary for carrying this Part into

effect in relation to prescribed processes designated for central control and may terminate any appointment made under this subsection.

(6)     Any local authority may appoint as inspectors (under whatever title the authority may determine) such persons having suitable qualifications as the authority think necessary for carrying this Part into effect in the authority's area in relation to prescribed processes designated for local control (and not so transferred), and may terminate any appointment made under this subsection.

(7)     An inspector shall not be liable in any civil or criminal proceedings for anything done in the purported performance of his functions under section 17 or 18 below if the court is satisfied that the act was done in good faith and that there were reasonable grounds for doing it.

(8)     In the following provisions of this Part "inspector" means a person appointed as an inspector under subsection (1), (5) or (6) above.

## Powers of Inspectors and Others

17.    (1)     An inspector may, on production (if so required) of his authority, exercise any of the powers in subsection (3) below for the purposes of the discharge of the functions of the enforcing authority.

(2)     Those powers, so far as exercisable in relation to premises, are exercisable in relation -

(a)     to premises on which a prescribed process is, or is believed (on reasonable grounds) to be, carried on; and

(b)     to premises on which a prescribed process has been carried on (whether or not the process was a prescribed process when it was carried on) the condition of which is believed (on reasonable grounds) to be such as to give rise to a risk of serious pollution of the environment.

(3)     The powers of an inspector referred to above are -

(a)     at any reasonable time (or, in a situation in which in his opinion there is an immediate risk of serious pollution of the environment, at any time) to enter premises which he has reason to believe it is necessary for him to enter;

(b)     on entering any premises by virtue of paragraph (a) above to take with him -

(i)     any person duly authorised by the Chief Inspector, the river purification authority or, as the case may be, the local enforcing authority and, if the inspector has reasonable cause to apprehend any serious obstruction in the execution of his duty, a constable; and

(ii)     any equipment or materials required for any purpose for which the power of entry is being exercised;

(c)     to make such examination and investigation as may in any circumstances be necessary;

(d)     as regards any premises which he has power to enter, to direct that those premises or any part of them, or anything in them, shall be left undisturbed (whether generally or in particular respects) for so long as is reasonably necessary for the purpose of any examination or investigation under paragraph (c) above;

(e)     to take such measurements and photographs and make such recordings as he considers necessary for the purpose of any examination or investigation under paragraph (c) above;

(f)     to take samples of any articles or substances found in or on any premises which he has power to enter, and of the air, water or land in, on, or in the vicinity of, the premises;

(g)     in the case of any article or substance found in or on any premises which he has power to enter, being an article or substance which appears to him to have caused or to be likely to cause pollution of the environment, to cause it to be dismantled or subjected to any process or test (but not so as to damage or destroy it unless this is necessary);

(h)    in the case of any such article or substance as is mentioned in paragraph (g) above, to take possession of it and detain it for so long as is necessary for all or any of the following purposes, namely -

(i)    to examine it and do to it anything which he has power to do under that paragraph;

(ii)    to ensure that it is not tampered with before his examination of it is completed;

(iii)    to ensure that it is available for use as evidence in any proceedings for an offence under section 23 below or any other proceedings relating to a variation notice, an enforcement notice or a prohibition notice;

(i)    to require any person whom he has reasonable cause to believe to be able to give any information relevant to any examination or investigation under paragraph (c) above to answer (in the absence of persons other than a person nominated to be present and any persons whom the inspector may allow to be present) such questions as the inspector thinks fit to ask and to sign a declaration of the truth of his answers;

(j)    to require the production of, or where the information is recorded in computerised form, the furnishing of extracts from, any records which are required to be kept under this Part or it is necessary for him to see for the purposes of an examination or investigation under paragraph (c) above and to inspect and take copies of, or of any entry in, the records;

(k)    to require any person to afford him such facilities and assistance with respect to any matters or things within that person's control or in relation to which that person has responsibilities as are necessary to enable the inspector to exercise any of the powers conferred on him by this section;

(l) any other power for the purpose mentioned in subsection (1) above which is conferred by regulations made by the Secretary of State;
and in so far as any of the powers specified above are applicable in relation to mobile plant an inspector shall have, in circumstances corresponding to those specified in subsection (2) above, powers corresponding to those powers.

(4) The Secretary of State may by regulations make provision as to the procedure to be followed in connection with the taking of, and the dealing with, samples under subsection (3)(f) above.

(5) Where an inspector proposes to exercise the power conferred by subsection (3)(g) above in the case of an article or substance found on any premises, he shall, if so requested by a person who at the time is present on and has responsibilities in relation to those premises, cause anything which is to be done by virtue of that power to be done in the presence of that person.

(6) Before exercising the power conferred by subsection (3)(g) above in the case of any article or substance, an inspector shall consult such persons as appear to him appropriate for the purpose of ascertaining what dangers, if any, there may be in doing anything which he proposes to do under the power.

(7) Where under the power conferred by subsection (3)(h) above an inspector takes possession of any article or substance found on any premises, he shall leave there, either with a responsible person or, if that is impracticable, fixed in a conspicuous position, a notice giving particulars of that article or substance sufficient to identify it and stating that he has taken possession of

it under that power; and before taking possession of any such substance under that power an inspector shall, if it is practical for him to do so, take a sample of it and give to a responsible person at the premises a portion of the sample marked in a manner sufficient to identify it.

(8)    No answer given by a person in pursuance of a requirement imposed under subsection (3)(i) above shall be admissible in evidence in England and Wales against that person in any proceedings, or in Scotland against that person in any criminal proceedings.

(9)    The powers conferred by subsection (3)(a), (b)(ii), (c), (e) and (f) above shall also exercisable (subject to sub section (4) above) by any person authorised for the purpose in writing by the Secretary of State.

(10)    Nothing in this section shall be taken to compel the production by any person of a document of which he would on grounds of legal professional privilege be entitled to withhold production on an order for discovery in an action in the High Court or, in relation to Scotland, or an order for the production of documents in an action in the Court of Session.

## Power to Deal with Cause of Imminent Danger of Serious Harm

18.    (1)    Where, in the case of any article or substance found by him on any premises which he has power to enter, an inspector has reasonable cause to believe that, in the circumstances in which he finds it, the article or substance is a cause of imminent danger of serious harm he may seize it and cause it to be rendered harmless (whether by destruction or otherwise).

(2)    Before there is rendered harmless under this section:-

(a)    any article that forms part of a batch of similar articles; or

(b)    any substance,

the inspector shall, if it is practicable for him to do so, take a sample of it and give to a responsible person at the premises where the article or substance was found by him a portion of the sample marked in a manner sufficient to identify it.

(3) As soon as may be after any article or substance has been seized and rendered harmless under this section, the inspector shall prepare and sign a written report giving particulars of the circumstances in which the article or substance was seized and so dealt with by him, and shall -

(a) give a signed copy of the report to a responsible person at the premises where the article or substance was found by him; and

(b) unless that person is the owner of the article or substance, also serve a signed copy of the report on the owner;

and if, where paragraph (b) above applies, the inspector cannot after reasonable inquiry ascertain the name or address of the owner, the copy may be served on him by giving it to the person to whom a copy was given under paragraph (a) above.

## Obtaining of Information from Persons and Authorities

**19.** (1) For the purposes of the discharge of his functions under this Part, the Secretary of State may, by notice in writing served on an enforcing authority, require the authority to furnish such information about the discharge of its functions as an enforcing authority under this Part as he may acquire.

(2) For the purposes of the discharge of their respective functions under this Part, the following authorities, that is to say -

(a) the Secretary of State,

(b)   a local enforcing authority,

(c)   the Chief Inspector, and

(d)   in relation to Scotland, a river purification authority,

may, by notice in writing served on any person, require that person to furnish to the authority such information which the authority reasonably considers that it needs as is specified in the notice, in such form and within such period following service of the notice as is so specified.

(3)   For the purposes of this section the discharge by the Secretary of State of an obligation of the United Kingdom under the Community Treaties or any inter national agreement relating to environmental protec tion shall be treated as a function of his under this Part.

## PUBLICITY

### Public Registers of Information

**20.**   (1)   It shall be the duty of each enforcing authority, as respects prescribed processes for which it is the enforc- ing authority, to maintain, in accordance with regula- tions made by the Secretary of State, a register conta- ining prescribed particulars of or relating to -

(a)   applications for authorisations made to that authority;

(b)   the authorisations which have been granted by that authority or in respect of which the authority has func- tions under this Part;

(c)   variation notices, enforcement notices and prohibition notices issued by that authority;

(d)   revocations of authorisations effected by that authority;

(e)   appeals under section 15 above;

(f)     convictions for such offences under section 23(1) below as may be prescribed;

(g)     information obtained or furnished in pursuance of the conditions of authorisations or under any provision of this Part;

(h)     directions given to the authority under any provision of this Part by the Secretary of State; and

(i)     such other matters relating to the carrying on of prescribed processes or any pollution of the environment caused thereby as may be prescribed;
        but that duty is subject to sections 21 and 22 below.

(2)     Subject to subsection (4) below, the register maintained by a local enforcing authority shall also contain prescribed particulars of such information contained in any register maintained by the Chief Inspector or river purification authority as relates to the carrying on in the area of the authority of prescribed processes in relation to which the Chief Inspector or river purification authority has functions under this Part; and the Chief Inspector or river purification authority shall furnish each authority with the particulars which are necessary to enable it to discharge its duty under this subsection.

(3)     In Scotland, the register maintained by -

(a)     the Chief Inspector shall also contain prescribed particulars of such information contained in any register maintained by a river purification authority as relates to the carrying on in the area of the authority of prescribed processes in relation to which the authority has functions under this Part, and each authority shall furnish the Chief Inspector with the particulars which are necessary to enable him to discharge his duty under this section;

(b)     each river purification authority shall also contain prescribed particulars of such information contained in any register maintained by the Chief Inspector as relates to the carrying on in the area of the authority of prescribed processes in relation to which the Chief Inspector has functions under this Part, and the Chief Inspector shall furnish each authority with the particulars which are necessary to enable them to discharge their duty under this section.

(4)     Subsection (2) above does not apply to port health authorities but each local enforcing authority whose

area adjoins that of a port health authority shall include corresponding information in the register maintained by it; and the Chief Inspector shall furnish each such local enforcing authority with the particulars which are necessary to enable it to discharge its duty under this subsection.

(5)     Where information of any description is excluded from any register by virtue of section 22 below, a statement shall be entered in the register indicating the existence of information of that description.

(6)     The Secretary of State may give to enforcing authorities directions requiring the removal from any register of theirs of any specified information not prescribed for inclusion under subsection (1) or (2) above or which, by virtue of section 21 or 22 below, ought to have been excluded from the register.

(7)     It shall be the duty of each enforcing authority -

(a)     to secure that the registers maintained by them under this section are available, at all reasonable times, for inspection by the public free of charge; and

(b)     to afford to members of the public facilities for obtaining copies of entries, on payment of reasonable charges.

(8)     Registers under this section may be kept in any form.

(9)     For the purpose of enabling the National Rivers Authority to discharge its duty under section 190(1)(f) of the Water Resources Act 1991 to keep corresponding

particulars in registers under that section, the Chief Inspector shall furnish the Authority with the particulars contained in any register maintained by him under this section.

(10)　In this section "prescribed" means prescribed in regulations under this section.

## Exclusion from Registers of Information Affecting National Security

**21.**　(1)　No information shall be included in a register maintained under section 20 above if and so long as, in the opinion of the Secretary of State, the inclusion in the register of that information, or information of that description, would be contrary to the interests of national security.

(2)　The Secretary of State may, for the purpose of securing the exclusion from registers of information to which subsection (1) above applies, give to enforcing authorities directions -

(a)　specifying information, or descriptions of information, to be excluded from their registers; or

(b)　specifying descriptions of information to be referred to the Secretary of State for his determination;

and no information referred to the Secretary of State in pursuance of paragraph (b) above shall be included in any such register until the Secretary of State determines that it should be so included.

(3)　The enforcing authority shall notify the Secretary of State of any information it excludes from the register in pursuance of directions under subsection (2) above.

(4)　A person may, as respects any information which appears to him to be information to which subsection (1) above may apply, give a notice to the Secretary of State specifying the information and indicating its apparent nature; and, if he does so -

(a)    he shall notify the enforcing authority that he has done so; and

(b)    no information so notified to the Secretary of State shall be included in any such register until the Secretary of State has determined that it should be so included.

## Exclusion from Registers of Certain Confidential Information

**22.**    (1)    No information relating to the affairs of any individual or business shall be included in a register maintained under section 20 above, without the consent of that individual or the person for the time being carrying on that business, if and so long as the information -

(a)    is, in relation to him, commercially confidential; and

(b)    is not required to be included in the register in pursu ance of directions under subsection (7) below;

but information is not commercially confidential for the purposes of this section unless it is determined under this section to be so by the enforcing authority or, on appeal, by the Secretary of State.

(2)    Where information is furnished to an enforcing author- ity for the purpose of -

(a)    an application for an authorisation or for the variation of an authorisation;

(b)    complying with any condition of an authorisation; or

(c)    complying with a notice under section 19(2) above;

then, if the person furnishing it applies to the author- ity to have the information excluded from the register on the ground that it is commercially confidential (as regards himself or another person), the authority shall determine whether the information is or is not commercially confidential.

(3)     A determination under subsection (2) above must be made within the period of fourteen days beginning with the date of the application and if the enforcing authority fails to make a determination within that period it shall be treated as having determined that the information is commercially confidential.

(4)     Where it appears to an enforcing authority that any information (other than information furnished in circumstances within subsection (2) above) which has been obtained by the authority under or by virtue of any provision of this Part might be commercially confidential, the authority shall -

(a)     give to the person to whom or whose business it relates notice that that information is required to be included in the register unless excluded under this section; and

(b)     give him a reasonable opportunity -

(i)     of objecting to the inclusion of the information on the ground that it is commercially confidential; and
(ii)     of making representations to the authority for the purpose of justifying any such objection;

and, if any representations are made, the enforcing authority shall, having taken the representations into account, determine whether the information is or is not commercially confidential.

(5)     Where, under subsection (2) or (4) above, an authority determines that information is not commercially confidential -

(a)     the information shall not be entered on the register until the end of the period of twenty-one days beginning with the date on which the determination is notified to the person concerned;

(b)     that person may appeal to the Secretary of State against the decision;

and, where an appeal is brought in respect of any information, the information shall not be entered on the register pending the final determination or withdrawal of the appeal.

(6)    Subsections (3), (5) and (10) of section 15 above shall apply in relation to appeals under subsection (5) above.

(7)    The Secretary of State may give to the enforcing authorities directions as to specified information, or descriptions of information, which the public interest requires to be included in registers maintained under section 20 above notwithstanding that the information may be commercially confidential.

(8)    Information excluded from a register shall be treated as ceasing to be commercially confidential for the purposes of this section at the expiry of the period of four years beginning with the date of the determination by virtue of which it was excluded; but the person who furnished it may apply to the authority for the information to remain excluded from the register on the ground that it is still commercially confidential and the authority shall determine whether or not that is the case.

(9)    Subsections (5) and (6) above shall apply in relation to a determination under subsection (8) above as they apply in relation to a determination under subsection (2) or (4) above.

(10)    The Secretary of State may, by order, substitute for the period for the time being specified in subsection (3) above such other period as he considers appropriate.

(11)    Information is, for the purposes of any determination under this section, commercially confidential, in relation to any individual or person, if its being contained in the register would prejudice to an unreasonable degree the commercial interest of that individual or person.

## PROVISIONS AS TO OFFENCES

**Offences**

**23.** (1)   It is an offence for a person -

(a)   to contravene section 6(1) above;

(b)   to fail to give the notice required by section 9(2) above;

(c)   to fail to comply with or contravene any requirement or prohibition imposed by an enforcement notice or a prohibition notice;

(d)   without reasonable excuse, to fail to comply with any requirement imposed under section 17 above;

(e)   to prevent any other person from appearing before or from answering any question to which an inspector may by virtue of section 17(3) require an answer;

(f)   intentionally to obstruct an inspector in the exercise or performance of his powers or duties;

(g)   to fail, without reasonable excuse, to comply with any requirement imposed by a notice under section 19(2) above;

(h)   to make a statement which he knows to be false or misleading in a material particular, or recklessly to make a statement which is false or misleading in a material particular, where the statement is made -

(i)   in purported compliance with a requirement to furnish any information imposed by or under any provision of this Part; or

(ii)   for the purpose of obtaining the grant of an authorisation to himself or any other person or the variation of an authorisation;

(i)   intentionally to make a false entry in any record required to be kept under section 7 above;

(j)    with intent to deceive, to forge or use a document issued or authorised to be issued under section 7 above or required for any purpose thereunder or to make or have in his possession a document so closely resembling any such document as to be likely to deceive;

(k)    falsely to pretend to be an inspector;

(l)    to fail to comply with an order made by a court under section 26 below.

(2)    A person guilty of an offence under paragraph (a), (c) or (l) of subsection (1) above shall be liable-

(a)    on summary conviction, to a fine not exceeding £20,000;

(b)    on conviction on indictment, to a fine or to imprisonment for a term not exceeding two years, or to both.

(3)    A person guilty of an offence under paragraph (b), (g), (h), (i) or (j) of subsection (1) above shall be liable -

on summary conviction, to a fine not exceeding the statutory maximum;

(b)    on conviction on indictment, to a fine or to imprisonment for a term not exceeding two years, or to both.

(4)    A person guilty of an offence under paragraph (d), (e), (f) or (k) of subsection (1) above shall be liable, on summary conviction, to a fine not exceeding the statutory maximum.

(5)    In England and Wales an inspector, if authorised to do so by the Secretary of State, may, although not of counsel or a solicitor, prosecute before a magistrates' court proceedings for an offence under subsection (1) above.

## Enforcement by High Court

24.    If the enforcing authority is of the opinion that proceedings for an offence under section 23(1)(c) above would

afford an ineffectual remedy against a person who has failed to comply with the requirements of an enforcement notice or a prohibition notice, the authority may take proceedings in the High Court or, in Scotland, in any court of competent jurisdiction for the purpose of securing compliance with the notice.

## Onus of Proof as Regards Techniques and Evidence

25. (1) In any proceedings for an offence under section 23(1)(a) above consisting in a failure to comply with the general condition implied in every authorisation by section 7(4) above, it shall be for the accused to prove that there was no better available technique not entailing excessive cost than was in fact used to satisfy the condition.

 (2) Where-

 (a) an entry is required under section 7 above to be made in any record as to the observance of any condition of an authorisation; and

 (b) the entry has not been made;

 that fact shall be admissible as evidence that that condition has not been observed.

## Power of Court to Order Cause of Offence to be Remedied

26. (1) Where a person is convicted of an offence under section 23(1)(a) or (c) above in respect of any matters which appear to the court to be matters which it is in his power to remedy, the court may, in addition to or instead of imposing any punishment, order him, within such time as may be fixed by the order, to take such steps as may be specified in the order for remedying those matters.

 (2) The time fixed by an order under subsection (1) above may be extended or further extended by order of the court on an application made before the end of the time

as originally fixed or as extended under this subsection, as the case may be.

(3)     Where a person is ordered under subsection (1) above to remedy any matters, that person shall not be liable under section 23 above in respect of those matters in so far as they continue during the time fixed by the order or any further time allowed under subsection (2) above.

## Power of Chief Inspector to Remedy Harm

27.     (1)     Where the commission of an offence under section 23(1)(a) or (c) above causes any harm which it is possible to remedy, the Chief Inspector or, in Scotland, a river purification authority may, subject to subsection (2) below -

(a)     arrange for any reasonable steps to be taken towards remedying the harm; and

(b)     recover the cost of taking those steps from any person convicted of that offence.

(2)     The Chief Inspector or, as the case may be, the river purification authority shall not exercise their powers under this section except with the approval in writing of the Secretary of State and, where any of the steps are to be taken on or will affect land in the occupation of any person other than the person on whose land the prescribed process is being carried on, with the permission of that person.

# AUTHORISATIONS AND OTHER STATUTORY CONTROLS

## Authorisations and Other Statutory Controls

28.     (1)     No condition shall at any time be attached to an authorisation so as to regulate the final disposal by deposit in or on land of controlled waste (within the meaning of Part II), nor shall any condition apply to such a disposal; but the enforcing authority shall notify the authority which is the waste regulation

authority under that Part for the area in which the process is to be carried on of the fact that the process involves the final disposal of controlled waste by deposit in or on land.

(2) Where any of the activities comprising a prescribed process are regulated both by an authorisation granted by the enforcing authority under this Part and by a registration or authorisation under the Radioactive Substances Act 1993, then, if different obligations are imposed as respects the same matter by a condition attached to the authorisation under this Part and a condition attached to the registration or authorisation under that Act, the condition imposed by the authorisation under this Part shall be treated as not binding the person carrying on the process.

(3) Where the activities comprising a prescribed process designated for central control include the release of any substances into water included in waters which are controlled waters for the purposes of Chapter I of Part III of the Water Resources Act 1991, then -

(a) the enforcing authority shall not grant an authorisation under this Part if the National Rivers Authority certifies to the enforcing authority its opinion that the release will result in or contribute to a failure to achieve any water quality objective in force under Part III of that Act; and

(b) any authorisation that is granted shall, as respects such releases, include (with or without others appearing to the enforcing authority to be appropriate) such conditions as appear to the National Rivers Authority to be appropriate for the purposes of this Part as that Authority requires by notice in writing given to the enforcing authority;

but the enforcing authority may, if it appears to be appropriate to do so, make the authorisation subject to conditions more onerous than those (if any) notified to it under paragraph (b) above.

(4)     Where the activities comprising a prescribed process carried on under an authorisation include the release of any substances into water as mentioned in subsection (3) above then, if at any time it appears to the National Rivers Authority appropriate for the purposes of this Part that the conditions of the authorisation should be varied, the enforcing authority shall exercise its powers under section 10 above so as to vary the conditions of the authorisation as required by the National Rivers Authority by notice in writing given to the enforcing authority.

# APPENDIX II

## THE ENVIRONMENTAL PROTECTION (PRE-SCRIBED PROCESSES AND SUBSTANCES) REGULATIONS 1991

### Citation, Application and Commencement

1.　(1)　These Regulations may be cited as the Environmental Protection (Prescribed Processes and Substances) Regulations 1991.

　　(2)　These Regulations shall come into force in England and Wales on 1st April 1991 and in Scotland on 1st April 1992.

### Interpretation

2.　　　In these Regulations:

"the Act" means the Environmental Protection Act 1990;

"background concentration" has the meaning given to that term in regulation 4(7);

"Part A process" means a process falling within a description set out in Schedule 1 hereto under the head ing "Part A" and "Part B process" means a process falling within a description so set out under the heading "Part B"; and

"particulate matter" means grit, dust or fumes.

### Prescribed Provisions

3.　(1)　Subject to the following provisions of these Regulations, the descriptions of processes set out in Schedule 1 hereto are hereby prescribed pursuant to Section 2(1) of the Act as processes for the carrying on of which after the prescribed date an authorisation is required under Section 6.

(2)     Schedule 2 has effect for the interpretation of Schedule 1.

(3)     In paragraph (1), the prescribed date means the appropriate date set out or determined in accordance with Schedule 3.

## Exceptions

4.     (1)     Subject to paragraph (6), a process shall not be taken to be a Part A process if it has the following characteristics, namely:

(i)     that it cannot result in the release into the air of any substance prescribed by regulation 6(1) or there is no likelihood that it will result in the release into the air of any such substance except in a quantity which is so trivial that it is incapable of causing harm or its capacity to cause harm is insignificant; and

(ii)     that it cannot result in the release into water of any substance prescribe by regulation 6(2) except:

(a)     in a concentration which is no greater than the background concentration; or

(b)     in a quantity which does not, in any 12 month period, exceed the background quantity by more than the amount specified in relation to the description of substance in column 2 of Schedule 5; and

(iii)     that it cannot result in the release into land of any substance prescribed by regulation 6(3) or there is no likelihood that it will result in the release into land of any such substance except in a quantity which is so trivial that it is incapable of causing harm or its capacity to cause harm is insignificant.

(2)     Subject to paragraph (6), a process shall not be taken to be a Part B process unless it will, or there is a likelihood that it will, result in the release into the air of one or more substances prescribed by regulation 6(1) in a quantity greater than that mentioned in paragraph (1)(i) above.

(3)     A process shall not be taken to fall within a descrip
        tion in Schedule 1 if it is carried on in a working
        museum to demonstrate an industrial process of histo-
        ric interest or if it is carried on for educational purpo-
        ses in a school as defined in Section 144 of the Educa-
        tion Act 1944 or, in Scotland, Section 135(1) of the
        Education (Scotland) Act 1980.

(4)     The running on or within an aircraft, hovercraft,
        mechanically propelled road vehicle, railway locomo-
        tive or ship or other vessel of an engine which propels
        or provides electricity for it shall not be taken to fall
        within a description in Schedule 1.

(4A)    The running of an engine in order to test it before
        installation or in the course of its development shall
        not be taken to fall within a description in Schedule 1.

(4B)    The use of a fume cupboard shall not be taken to fall
        within a description in Schedule 1 if it is used as a
        fume cupboard in a laboratory for research or testing,
        and it is not:

(a)     a fume cupboard which is an industrial and continuous
        production process enclosure; or

(b)     a fume cupboard in which substances or materials are
        manufactured.

        In this paragraph, "fume cupboard" has the meaning
        given by the British Standard "Laboratory fume cup
        boards" published by the British Standards Institution
        numbered BS7258: Part 1: 1990.

(5)     A process shall not be taken to fall within a descrip-
        tion in Schedule 1 if it is carried on as a domestic
        activity in connection with a private dwelling.

(6)     Paragraphs (1) and (2) do not exempt any process
        described in Schedule 1 from the requirement for
        authorisation if the process may give rise to an offen
        sive smell noticeable outside the premises where the
        process is carried on.

(7)   In these Regulations:

"background concentration" means any concentration of the relevant substance which would be present in the release irrespective of any effect the process may have had on the composition of the release and, with out prejudice to the generality of the foregoing, includes such concentration of the substance as is referred to in paragraph (8) below; and

"background quantity" means such quantity of the relevant substance as is referred to in paragraph (8) below.

(8)   The concentration or, as the case may be, quantity mentioned in paragraph (7) above is such concentration or quantity as is present in:

(a)   water supplied to the premises where the process is carried on;

(b)   water abstracted for use in the process; and

(c)   precipitation onto the premises on which the process is carried on.

## Enforcement

5.   (1)   The descriptions of processes set out in Schedule 1 un der the heading 'Part A' are designated pursuant to Section 2(4) of the Act for central control.

(2)   The descriptions of processes set out in Schedule 1 under the heading 'Part B' are so designated for local control.

## Prescribed Substances: Release into the Air, Water or Land

6.   (1)   The description of substances set out in Schedule 4 are prescribed pursuant to Section 2(5) of the Act as substances the release of which into the air is subject to control under Sections 6 and 7 of the Act

(2)     The descriptions of substances set out in column 1 of Schedule 5 are so prescribed as substances the release of which into water is subject to control under those Sections.

(3)     The descriptions of substances set out in Schedule 6 are so prescribed as substances the release of which into land is subject to control under those Sections.

## SCHEDULE 1

## DESCRIPTIONS OF PROCESSES

**CHAPTER 1:     FUEL PRODUCTION PROCESSES, COMBUSTION PROCESSES (INCLUDING POWER GENERATION) AND ASSOCIATED PROCESSES.**

**Section 1.1 Gasification and Associated Processes**

## PART A

(a)     Reforming natural gas.

(aa)    Refining natural gas if that process is related to another Part A process or is likely to involve the use in any 12 month period of 1000 tonnes or more of natural gas.

(b)     Odourising natural gas or liquified petroleum gas if that process is related to another Part A process.

(c)     Producing gas from coal, lignite, oil or other carbonaceous material or from mixtures thereof other than from sewage or the biological degradation of waste unless carried on as part of a process which is a combustion process (whether or not that process falls within Section 1.3 of this Schedule)

(d)     Purifying or refining any product of any of the processes described in paragraphs (a), (b) or (c) or converting it into a different product.

In this Section, "carbonaceous material" includes such materials as charcoal, coke, peat and rubber.

## PART B

(a)     Odourising natural gas or liquified petroleum gas, except where that process is related to a Part A process.

(b)     Blending odorant for use with natural gas or liquified petroleum gas.

(c)     Any process for refining natural gas not falling within paragraph (aa) of Part A of this Section.

In this Section "refining natural gas" does not include refining mains gas.

### Section 1.2 Carbonisation and Associated Processes

## PART A

(a)     The pyrolysis, carbonisation, distillation, liquefaction, partial oxidation or other heat treatment of coal (other than the drying of coal), lignite, oil, other carbonaceous material (as defined in Section 1.1) or mixtures thereof otherwise than with a view to gasification or making of charcoal.

(b)     The purification or refining of any of the products of a process mentioned in paragraph (a) or its conversion into a different product.

Nothing in paragraph (a) or (b) refers to the use of any substance as a fuel or its incineration as a waste or to any process for the treatment of sewage.

In paragraph (a), the heat treatment of oil does not include heat treatment of waste oil or waste emulsions containing oil in order to recover the oil.

## PART B

## Nil

## Section 1.3 Combustion Processes

## PART A

(a)     Burning any fuel in a boiler or furnace with a net rated thermal input of 50 megawatts or more or, when the process is carried on by the same person at the same location, burning any fuel in any of two or more boilers or furnaces with an aggregate net rated thermal input of 50 megawatts or more (disregarding any boiler or furnace with a net rated thermal input of less than 3 megawatts);

(b)     burning any fuel in a gas turbine or compression ignition engine with a net rated thermal input of 50 mega watts or more or, when the process is carried on by the same person at the same location, burning any fuel in any of two or more such turbines or engines with an aggregate net rated thermal input of 50 megawatts or more (disregarding any such turbine or engine with a net rated thermal input of less than 3 megawatts);

(c)     burning any of the following in an appliance with a net rated thermal input of 3 megawatts or more otherwise than as a process which is related to a Part B process:

(i)     waste oil;

(ii)    recovered oil;

(iii)   any fuel manufactured from, or comprising any other waste.

Nothing in this Part of this Section applies to the burning of any fuel in a boiler, furnace or other appliance with a net rated thermal input of less than 3 megawatts.

# PART B

The following processes unless carried on in relation to and as part of any Part A process:

(a)   burning any fuel in a boiler or furnace with a net rated thermal input of not less than 20 megawatts (but less than 50 megawatts);

(b)   burning any fuel in a gas turbine or compression igni- tion engine with a net rated thermal input of not less than 20 megawatts (but less than 50 megawatts);

(c)   burning as fuel, in an appliance with a net rated ther- mal input of less than 3 megawatts, waste oil or recovered oil;

(d)   burning in an appliance with a net rated thermal input of less than 3 megawatts solid fuel which has been manufactured from waste by a process involving the application of heat;

(e)   burning, in any appliance, fuel manufactured from, or including, waste (other than waste oil or recovered oil or such fuel as is mentioned in paragraph (d)) if the appliance has a net rated thermal input of less than 3 megawatts but at least 0.4 megawatts or is used to gether with (whether or not it is operated simultane ously with) other appliances which have a net rated thermal input of less than 3 megawatts and the aggre- gate net rated thermal input of all the appliances is at least 0.4 megawatts.

In paragraph (c) of Part A and paragraph (e) of Part B, "fuel" does not include gas produced by biological degradation of waste; and for the purposes of this Section:

"net rated thermal input" is the rate at which fuel can be burned at the maximum continuous rating of the appliance multiplied by the net calorific value of the fuel and expressed as megawatts thermal; and "waste oil" means any mineral based lubricating or industrial oil which has become unfit for the use for which it was intended and, in particular, used combustion engine oil, gearbox oil, mineral lubricating oil, oil for turbines and hydraulic oil; and

"recovered oil" means waste oil which has been processed before being used.

### Section 1.4 Petroleum Processes

## PART A

(a)   The loading, unloading or other handling of, the storage of, or the physical, chemical or thermal treatment of:

(i)   crude oil;

(ii)   stabilised crude petroleum;

(iii)   crude shale oil;

(iv)   if related to another process described in this paragraph, any associated gas or condensate.

(b)   Any process not falling within any other description in this Schedule by which the product of any process described in paragraph (a) above is subject to further refining or conversion or is used (otherwise than as a fuel or solvent) in the manufacture of a chemical.

## PART B

## Nil

### CHAPTER 2:   METAL PRODUCTION AND PROCESSING

### Section 2.1 Iron and Steel

## PART A

(a)   Loading, unloading or otherwise handling or storing iron ore except in the course of mining operations

(b)    Loading, unloading or otherwise handling or storing burnt pyrites.

(c)    Crushing, grading, grinding, screening, washing or drying iron ore or any mixture of iron ore and other materials.

(d)    Blending or mechanically mixing grades of iron ore or iron ore with other materials.

(e)    Pelletising, calcining, roasting or sintering iron ore or any mixture of iron ore and other materials.

(f)    Making, melting or refining iron, steel or any ferrous alloy in any furnace other than a furnace described in Part B of this Section.

(g)    Any process for the refining or making of iron, steel or any ferrous alloy in which air or oxygen or both are used unless related to a process described in Part B of this Section.

(h)    The desulphurisation of iron, steel or any ferrous alloy made by a process described in this Part of this Section.

(i)    Heating iron, steel or any ferrous alloy (whether in a furnace or other appliance) to remove grease, oil or any other non-metallic contaminant (including such operations as the removal by heat of plastic or rubber covering from scrap cable), if related to another process described in this Part of this Section.

(j)    Any foundry process (including ancillary foundry operations such as the manufacture and recovery of moulds, the reclamation of sand, fettling, grinding and shot-blasting) if related to another process described in this Part of this Section.

(l)    Handling slag in conjunction with a process described in paragraph (f) or (g).

(m)     Any process for rolling iron, steel or any ferrous alloy carried on in relation to any process described in para graph (f) or (g), and any process carried on in conjunction with such rolling involving the scarfing or cutting with oxygen of iron, steel or any ferrous alloy.

Nothing in paragraph (a) or (b) of this Part of this Section applies to the handling or storing of other minerals in association with the handling or storing of iron ore or burnt pyrites.

A process does not fall within paragraph (a), (b) (c) or (d) of this Part of this Section unless:

(i)     it is carried on as part of or is related to a process falling within a paragraph of this Part of this Section other than paragraph (a), (b), (c) or (d); or

(ii)     it consists of, forms part of or is related to a process which is likely to involve the unloading in any 12 month period of more than 500,000 tonnes of iron ore or burnt pyrites or, in aggregate, both.

## PART B

(a)     Making, melting or refining iron, steel or any ferrous alloy in:

(i)     an electric arc furnace with a designed holding capacity of less than 7 tonnes; or

(ii)     a cupola, crucible furnace, reverberatory furnace, rotary furnace, induction furnace or resistance furnace

(b)     Any process for the refining or making of iron, steel or any ferrous alloy in which air or oxygen or both are used, if related to a process described in this Part of this Section.

(c)     The desulphurisation of iron, steel or any ferrous alloy, if the process does not fall within paragraph (h) of Part A of this Section.

(d)     Any such process as is described in paragraph (i) of Part A above, if not falling within that paragraph; but a process does not fall within this paragraph if:

    (i)     it is a process for heating iron, steel or any ferrous alloy in one or more furnaces or other appliances the primary combustion chambers of which have in aggregate a net rated thermal input of less than 0.2 megawatts;

    (ii)     it does not involve the removal by heat of plastic or rubber covering from scrap cable or of any asbestos contaminant; and

    (iii)     it is not related to any other process described in this Part of this Section.

(e)     Any foundry process (including ancillary foundry operations such as the manufacture and recovery of moulds, the reclamation of sand, fettling, grinding and shot-blasting) if related to another process described in this Part of this Section.

(f)     Any other process involving the casting of iron, steel or any ferrous alloy from deliveries of 50 tonnes or more at one time of molten metal.

Any description of a process in this Section includes, where the process produces slag, the crushing, screening or grading or other treatment of the slag if that process is related to the process in question.

In this Section "net rated thermal input" has the same meaning as in Section 1.3

In this Section and Section 2.2, "ferrous alloy" means an alloy of which iron is the largest constituent, or equal to the largest constituent, by weight, whether or not that alloy also has a non-ferrous metal content greater than any percentage specified in Section 2.2 below, and "non-ferrous metal alloy" shall be construed accordingly.

## Section 2.2 Non-ferrous Metals

## PART A

(a)  The extraction or recovery from any material:
(i)    by chemical means or the use of heat of any non-ferrous metal or alloy of non-ferrous metal or any com pound of a non-ferrous metal; or

(ii)   by electrolytic means, of aluminium,

if the process may result in the release into the air of particulate matter or any metal, metalloid or any metal or metalloid compound or in the release into water of a substance described in Schedule 5 or does not fall within paragraph (b) of Part B of this Section.

In this paragraph "material" includes ores, scrap and other waste.

(b)  The mining of zinc or tin where the process may result in the release into water of cadmium or any compound of cadmium.

(c)  The refining of any non-ferrous metal (other than the electrolytic refining of copper) or non-ferrous metal alloy except where the process is related to a process falling within a description in paragraphs (a), (c), or (d) or (g) of Part B of this Section.

(d)  Any process other than a process described in para graphs (b), (c), (d) or, except in the case of a process which produces any nickel alloy, (g) of Part B of this Section for making or melting any non-ferrous metal or non-ferrous metal alloy in a furnace, bath or other holding vessel if the furnace, bath or vessel employed has a designed holding capacity of 5 tonnes or more.

(e)  Any process for producing, melting or recovering by chemical means or by the use of heat lead or any lead alloy, if:

(i)    the process may result in the release into the air of particulate matter or smoke which contains lead; and

(ii)    in the case of lead alloy, the percentage by weight of lead in the alloy in molten form exceeds 23% if the alloy contains copper and 2% in other cases.

(ee)    Any process for recovering any of the elements listed below if the process may result in the release into the air of particulate matter or smoke which contains any of those elements:

gallium
indium
palladium
tellurium
thallium.

(f)    Any process for producing, melting or recovering (whether by chemical means or by electrolysis or by the use of heat) cadmium or mercury or any alloy con taining more than 0.05 per cent by weight of either of those metals or of both of those metals in aggregate.

(g)    Any manufacturing or repairing process involving the manufacture or use of beryllium or selenium or an alloy of one or both of those metals if the process may occasion the release into the air of any substance de scribed in Schedule 4, but a process does not fall within this paragraph by reason solely of its involving the melting of an alloy of beryllium if that alloy contains less than 0.1 per cent by weight of beryllium in molten form and the process falls within a description in para graph (a), (d) or (g) of Part B of this Section.

(h)    The heating in a furnace or other appliance of any non-ferrous metal or non-ferrous metal alloy for the purpose of removing grease, oil or any other non-me tallic contaminant (including such operations as the removal by heat of plastic or rubber covering from scrap cable), if related to another process described in this Part of this Section.

(i)   Any foundry process (including ancillary foundry operations such as the manufacture and recovery of moulds, the reclamation of sand, fettling, grinding and shot-blasting) if related to another process described in this Part of this Section.

(k)   Pelletising, calcining, roasting or sintering any non-ferrous metal ore or any mixture of such ore and other materials.

## PART B

(a)   The making or melting of any non-ferrous metal or non-ferrous metal alloy (other than tin or any alloy which, in molten form, contains 50% or more by weight of tin) in any furnace, bath or other holding vessel with a designed holding capacity of less than 5 tonnes (together with any incidental refining).

(b)   The extraction or recovery of copper, aluminium or zinc from mixed scrap by the use of heat.

(bb)  The fusion of calcined bauxite for the production of artificial corundum.

(c)   Melting zinc or a zinc alloy in conjunction with a galvanising process.

(d)   Melting zinc or aluminium or an alloy of one or both of these metals in conjunction with a die-casting process.

(e)   Any such process as is described in paragraph (h) of Part A above, if not related to another process described in that Part; but a process does not fall within this paragraph if:

(i)   it involves the use of one or more furnaces or other appliances the primary combustion chambers of which have in aggregate a net rated thermal input of less than 0.2 megawatts; and

(ii)    it does not involve the removal by heat of plastic
or rubber covering from scrap cable or of any asbestos
contaminant.

(f)    Any foundry process (including ancillary foundry
operations such as the manufacture and recovery of
moulds, the reclamation of sand, fettling, grinding and
shot-blasting) if related to another process described in
this Part of this Section.

(g)    Any process for producing or melting by chemical means
or by the use of heat any of the elements listed below
or any alloy containing any of those elements if the
process may result in the release into the air of
particulate matter or smoke which contains any of those
elements:

antimony
arsenic
chromium
magnesium
manganese
phosphorus
platinum

The processes describe in paragraphs (a), (c), (d) and (g) above
include any related process for the refining of any non-ferrous metal
or non-ferrous metal alloy.

In this Section "net rated thermal input" has the same meaning as
in Section 1.3.

Nothing in this Section shall be taken to prescribe the processes of
hand soldering or flow soldering.

## CHAPTER 3: MINERAL INDUSTRIES

### Section 3.1 Cement and Lime Manufacture and Associated Processes

### PART A

(a)    Making cement clinker.

(b)    Grinding cement clinker.

(c)    Any of the following processes, where the process is related to a process described in paragraph (a) or (b), namely, blending cement; putting cement into silos for bulk storage; removing cement from silos in which it has been stored in bulk; and any process involving the use of cement in bulk, including the bagging of cement and cement mixtures, the batching of ready-mixed concrete and the manufacture of concrete blocks and other cement products.

(d)    The heating of calcium carbonate or calcium magnesium carbonate for the purpose of making lime where the process is likely to involve the heating in any 12 month period of 5,000 tonnes or more of either substance or, in aggregate, of both.

(e)    The slaking of lime for the purpose of making calcium hydroxide or calcium magnesium hydroxide where the process is related to a process described in paragraph (d) above.

### PART B

(a)    Any of the following processes, if not related to a process falling within a description in Part A of this Section:

(i)    storing, loading or unloading cement or cement clinker bulk prior to further transportation in bulk;

(ii)    blending cement in bulk or using cement in bulk other than at a construction site, including the bagging of cement and cement mixtures, the batching of ready-mixed concrete and the manufacture of concrete blocks and other cement products.

(b)     The slaking of lime for the purpose of making calcium hydroxide of calcium magnesium hydroxide unless re lated to and carried on as part of a process falling within another description in this Schedule.

(c)     The heating of calcium carbonate or calcium magne- sium carbonate for the purpose of making lime where the process is not likely to involve the heating in any 12 month period of 5,000 tonnes or more of either substance or, in aggregate, of both.

## Section 3.2 Processes involving Asbestos

### PART A

(a)     Producing raw asbestos by extraction from the ore except where the process is directly associated with the mining of the ore.

(b)     The manufacture and, where related to the manufac- ture, the industrial finishing of the following products where the use of asbestos is involved:

asbestos cement
asbestos cement products
asbestos fillers
asbestos filters
asbestos floor coverings
asbestos friction products
asbestos insulating board
asbestos jointing, packaging and reinforcement matrial
asbestos packing
asbestos paper or card
asbestos textiles

(c)     The stripping of asbestos from railway vehicles except:

(i)     in the course of the repair or maintenance of the vehicle;

(ii)    in the course of recovery operations following an accident; or

(iii)   where the asbestos is permanently bonded in cement or in any other material (including plastic, rubber or a resin)

(d)    The destruction by burning of a railway vehicle if as bestos has been incorporated in, or sprayed on to, its structure.

## PART B

The industrial finishing of any product mentioned in paragraph (b) of Part A of this Section if the process does not fall within that paragraph.

In this Section, "asbestos" means any of the following fibrous silicates - actinolite, amosite, anthophyllite, chrysotile, crocidolite and tremolite.

### Section 3.3 Other Mineral Fibres

## PART A

Manufacturing:

(i)    glass fibre;

(ii)    any fibre from any mineral other than asbestos

## PART B

### Nil

### Section 3.4 Other Mineral Processes

## PART A

### Nil

## PART B

(a)     The crushing, grinding or other size reduction (other than the cutting of stone) or the grinding, screening or heating of any designated mineral or mineral product expect where:

    (i)     the process falls within a description in another Section of this Schedule;

    (ii)     the process is related to and carried on as part of another process falling within such a description; or

    (iii)     the operation of the process is unlikely to result in the release into the air of particulate matter.

(b)     Any of the following processes unless carried on at an exempt location or as part of a process falling within another description in this Schedule:

    (i)     crushing, grinding or otherwise breaking up coal or coke or any other coal product;

    (ii)     screening, grading or mixing coal, or coke or any other coal product;

    (iii)     loading or unloading petroleum coke, coal, or any other coal product except unloading on retail sale.

(c)     The crushing, grinding or other size reduction, with machinery designed for that purpose, of bricks, tiles or concrete.

(d)     Screening the product of any such process as is described in paragraph (c).

(e)     Coating roadstone with tar or bitumen.

(f)     Loading, unloading, or storing pulverised fuel ash in bulk prior to further transportation in bulk, unless carried on as part of or in relation to a process falling within another description in this Schedule

In this Section:

"coal" includes lignite; "designated mineral or mineral product" means:

(i)     clay, sand and any other naturally occurring mineral other than coal or lignite;

(ii)    metallurgical slag;

(iii)   boiler or furnace ash produced from the burning of coal, coke or any other coal product;

(iv)    gypsum which is a by-product of any process; and

"exempt location" means:

(i)     any premises used for the sale of petroleum coke, coal, coke, or any coal product where the throughput of such substances at those premises in any 12 month period is in aggregate likely to be less than 10,000 tonnes; or

(ii)    any premises to which petroleum coke, coal, coke, or any coal product is supplied only for use there;

"retail sale" means sale to the final consumer.

Nothing in this Section applies to any process carried on underground.

### Section 3.5 Glass Manufacture and Production

## PART A

The manufacture of glass frit or enamel frit and its use in any process where that process is related to its manufacture and the aggregate quantity of such substances manufactured in any 12 month period is likely to be 100 tonnes or more.

## PART B

(a)     The manufacture of glass at any location where the person concerned has the capacity to make 5,000 tonnes or more of glass in any 12 month period, and any process involving the use of glass which is carried on at any such location in conjunction with its manufacture.

(b)     The manufacture of glass where the use of lead or any lead compound is involved.

(c)     The making of any glass product where lead or any lead compound has been used in the manufacture of the glass except:

(i)     the making of products from lead glass blanks;

(ii)    the melting, or mixing with another substance, of glass manufactured elsewhere to produce articles such as ornaments or road paint;

(d)     Polishing or etching glass or glass products in the course of any manufacturing process if:

(i)     hydrofluoric acid is used; or

(ii)    hydrogen fluoride may be released into the air.

(e)     The manufacture of glass frit or enamel frit and its use in any process where that process is related to its manufacture if not falling within Part A of this Section.

## Section 3.6 Ceramic Production

### PART A

Firing heavy clay goods or refractory material in a kiln where a reducing atmosphere is used for a purpose other than coloration.

### PART B

(a)     Firing heavy clay goods or refractory material (other than heavy clay goods) in a kiln where the process does not fall within a description in Part A of this Section.

(b)     Vapour glazing earthenware or clay with salts.

In this Section:

"clay" includes a blend of clay with ash, sand or other materials;
"refractory material" means material (such as fireclay, silica,
magnesite, chrome-magnesite, sillimanite, sintered alumina,
beryllia and boron nitride) which is able to withstand high tem-
peratures and to function as a furnace lining or in other similar
high temperature applications.

## CHAPTER 4:    THE CHEMICAL INDUSTRY

(See paragraph 4 of Schedule 2 as to cases where processes described in this chapter of the Schedule fall within two or more
descriptions).

Except where paragraph 2 or 8 of Schedule 2 applies, nothing in
this chapter of this Schedule applies to the operation of waste
treatment plant.

### Section 4.1 Petrochemical Processes

## PART A

(a)    Any process for the manufacture of unsaturated hydro
carbons.

(b)    Any process for the manufacture of any chemical which
involves the use of a product of a process described in
paragraph (a).

(c)    Any process for the manufacture of any chemical which
involves the use of a product of a process described in
paragraph (b) otherwise than as a fuel or solvent.

(d)    Any process for the polymerisation or co-polymerisation of any unsaturated hydrocarbons or of a product of
a process mentioned in paragraph (b) or (c) which is
likely to involve, in any 12 month period, the polymerisation or co-polymerisation of 50 tonnes or more of
any of those materials or, in aggregate, of any combination of those materials.

## PART B

## Nil

## Section 4.2 The Manufacture and Use of Organic Chemicals

## PART A

Any of the following processes unless falling within a description set out in Section 6.8:

(a)    the manufacture of styrene or vinyl chloride;

(aa)    the polymerisation or co-polymerisation of styrene or vinyl chloride where the process is likely to involve, in any 12 month period, the polymerisation or co-polymerisation of 50 tonnes or more of either of those materials or, in aggregate, of both;

(b)    any process of manufacture involving the use of vinyl chloride;

(c)    the manufacture of acetylene, any aldehyde, amine, isocyanate, nitrile, any carboxylic acid or any anhydride of carboxylic acid any organic sulphur compound or any phenol, if the process may result in the release of any of those substances into the air.

(d)    any process for the manufacture of a chemical involv ing the use of any substance mentioned in paragraph

(c)    if the process may result in the release of any such substance into the air;

(e)    the manufacture or recovery of carbon disulphide;

(f)    any manufacturing process which may result in the release of carbon disulphide into the air;

(g)    the manufacture or recovery of pyridine, or of any substituted pyridines;

(h)    the manufacture of any organo-metallic compound;

(i)    the manufacture, purification or recovery of any designated acrylate;

(j)    any process for the manufacture of a chemical which is likely to involve the use in any 12 month period of 1 tonne or more of any designated acrylate or, in aggregate, of more than one such designated acrylate.

In this Part of this Section, "designated acrylate" means any of the following, namely, acrylic acid, substituted acrylic acids, the esters of acrylic acid and the esters of substituted acrylic acids

## PART B

## Nil

### Section 4.3 Acid Processes

## PART A

(a)    Any process for the manufacture, recovery, concentration or distillation of sulphuric acid or oleum.

(b)    Any process for the manufacture of any oxide of sulphur but excluding any combustion or incineration process other than the burning of sulphur.

(c)    Any process for the manufacture of a chemical which uses, or may result in the release into the air of, any oxide of sulphur but excluding any combustion or incineration process other than the burning of sulphur and excluding also any process where such a release could only occur as a result of the storage and use of $SO_2$ in cylinders.

(d)    Any process for the manufacture or recovery of nitric acid.

(e)    Any process for the manufacture of any acid-forming oxide of nitrogen.

(f)    Any other process (except the combustion or incineration of carbonaceous material as defined in Section 1.1. of this Schedule) which is not described in Part B of this Section, does not fall within a description in Section 2.1 or 2.2 of this Schedule and is not treated as so falling by virtue of the rules in Schedule 2, and which is likely to result in the release into the air of any acid-forming oxide of nitrogen.

(g)    Any process for the manufacture or purification of phosphoric acid.

## PART B

Any process for the surface treatment of metal which is likely to result in the release into the air of any acid-forming oxide of nitrogen and which does not fall within a description in Section 2.1 or 2.2 of this Schedule and is not treated as so falling by virtue of the rules in Schedule 2.

### Section 4.4 Processes involving Halogens

## PART A

The following processes if not falling within a description in any other Section of this Schedule:

(a)    any process for the manufacture of fluorine, chlorine, bromine or iodine or of any compound comprising only:

(i)    two or more of those halogens; or

(ii)    any one or more of those halogens and oxygen;

(b)    any process of manufacture which involves the use of, or which is likely to result in the release into the air or into water of, any of those four halogens or any of the compounds mentioned in paragraph (a) other than the use of any of them as a pesticide (as defined in Schedule 6) in water;

(c)  any process for the manufacture of hydrogen fluoride, hydrogen chloride, hydrogen bromide or hydrogen iodide or any of their acids;

(d)  any process for the manufacture of chemicals which may result in the release into the air of any of the four compounds mentioned in paragraph (c);

(e)  any process of manufacture (other than the manufacture of chemicals) involving the use of any of the four compounds mentioned in paragraph (c) or any of their acids which may result in the release of any of those compounds into the air, other than the coating, plating or surface treatment of metal.

## PART B

### Nil

## Section 4.5 Inorganic Chemical Processes

### PART A

(a)  The manufacture of hydrogen cyanide or hydrogen sulphide other than in the course of fumigation.

(b)  Any manufacturing process involving the use of hydrogen cyanide or hydrogen sulphide.

(c)  Any process for the manufacture of a chemical which may result in the release into the air of hydrogen cyanide or hydrogen sulphide.

(d)  The production of any compound containing any of the following:

antimony
arsenic
beryllium
gallium
indium
lead
palladium

platinum
selenium
tellurium
thallium

where the process may result in the release into the air of any of those elements or compounds or the release into water of any substance described in Schedule 5.

(e)    The recovery of any compound referred to in paragraph (d) where the process may result in any such release as is mentioned in that paragraph.

(f)    The use in any process of manufacture, other than the application of a glaze or vitreous enamel, of any element or compound referred to in paragraph (d) where the process may result in such a release as is mentioned in that paragraph.

(g)    The production or recovery of any compound of cadmium or mercury.

(h)    Any process of manufacture which involves the use of cadmium or mercury or of any compound of either of those elements or which may result in the release into the air of either of those elements or any of their compounds.

(i)    The production of any compound of:

chromium
manganese
nickel
zinc

(j)    The manufacture of any metal carbonyl

(k)    Any process for the manufacture of a chemical involving the use of a metal carbonyl.

(l)    The manufacture or recovery of ammonia.

(m)     Any process for the manufacture of a chemical which involves the use of ammonia or may result in the re lease or ammonia into the air other than a process in which ammonia is used only as a refrigerant.

(n)     The production of phosphorus or of any oxide, hydride or halide of phosphorus.

(o)     Any process for the manufacture of a chemical which involves the use of phosphorus or any oxide, hydride or halide of phosphorous or which may result in the re lease into the air of phosphorus or of any such oxide, hydride or halide.

(p)     The extraction of any magnesium compound from sea water.

## PART B

## Nil

## Section 4.6 Chemical Fertiliser Production

## PART A

(a)     The manufacture of chemical fertilisers.

(b)     The conversion of chemical fertilisers into granules.

In this Section, "chemical fertilisers" means any inorganic chemical to be applied to the soil to promote     plant growth; and "inorganic chemical" includes urea; and "manufacture of chemical fertilisers" shall be taken to include any process for blending chemical fertilisers which is related to a process for their manufacture.

## PART B

## Nil

## Section 4.7 Pesticide Production

### PART A

The manufacture or the formulation of chemical pesticides if the process may result in the release into water of any substance described in Schedule 5.

### PART B

### Nil

In this Section "pesticide" has the same meaning as in Schedule 6.

## Section 4.8 Pharmaceutical Production

### PART A

The manufacture or the formulation of a medicinal product if the process may result in the release into water of any substance described in Schedule 5.

### PART B

### Nil

In this Section, "medicinal product" means any substance or article (not being an instrument, apparatus or appliance) manufactured for use in one of the ways specified in Section 130(1) of the Medicines Act 1968.

## Section 4.9 The Storage of Chemicals in Bulk

### PART A

### Nil

### PART B

The storage in a tank or tanks, other than as part of a Part A process, and other than in a tank for the time being forming part of a powered vehicle, of any of the substances listed below except where the total capacity of the tanks installed at the location in question in which the relevant substance may be stored is less than the figure specified below in relation to that substance;

any one or more designated acrylates     20 tonnes
acrylonitrile     20 tonnes
anhydrous ammonia     100 tonnes
anhydrous hydrogen fluoride     1 tonnes
toluene di-isocyanate     20 tonnes
vinyl chloride monomer     20 tonnes
ethylene     8,000 tonnes

In this Section, "designated acrylate" has the same meaning as in Part A of Section 4.2.

## CHAPTER 5:    WASTE DISPOSAL AND RECYCLING

### Section 5.1 Incineration

### PART A

(a)    The destruction by burning in an incinerator of any waste chemicals or waste plastic arising from the manu facture of a chemical or the manufacture of a plastic.

(b)    The destruction by burning in an incinerator, other than incidentally in the course of burning other waste, of any waste chemicals being, or comprising in elemental or compound form, any of the following:

bromine
cadmium
chlorine
fluorine
iodine
lead
mercury
nitrogen
phosphorus
sulphur
zinc.

(c)    The destruction by burning of any other waste, including animal remains, otherwise than by a process related to and carried on as part of a Part B process, on premises where there is plant designed to incinerate such waste at a rate of 1 tonne or more per hour.

(d)    The cleaning for re-use of metal containers used for the transport or storage of a chemical by burning out their residual content.

## PART B

(a)    The destruction by burning in an incinerator other than an exempt incinerator of any waste, including animal remains, except where related to a Part A process.

(b)    The cremation of human remains.

In this Section:

"exempt incinerator" means any incinerator on premises where there is plant designed to incinerate waste including animal remains at a rate of not more than 50 kgs per hour, not being an incinerator employed to incinerate clinical waste, sewage sludge, sewage screenings or municipal waste (as defined in Article 1 of EC Directive 89/369/EEC); and for the purposes of this Section, the weight of waste shall be determined by reference to its weight as fed into the incinerator;

"waste" means solid or liquid wastes or gaseous wastes (other than gas produced by biological degradation of waste);

"clinical waste" means waste (other than waste consisting wholly of animal remains) which falls within sub-paragraph (a) or (b) of the definition of such waste in paragraph (2) of regulation 1 of the Controlled Waste Regulations 1992 (or would fall within one of those sub-paragraphs but for paragraph (4) of that regulation).

## Section 5.2 Recovery Processes

## PART A

(a)    The recovery by distillation of any oil or organic solvent.

(b)    The cleaning or regeneration of carbon, charcoal or ion exchange resins by removing matter which is, or includes, any substance described in Schedule 4,5 or 6.

Nothing in this Part of this Section applies to:

(i)    the distillation of oil for the production or cleaning of vacuum pump oil; or

(ii)    a process which is ancillary and related to another process which involves the production or use of the substance which is recovered, cleaned or regenerated.

## PART B

### Nil

## Section 5.3 The Production of Fuel from Waste

### PART A

Making solid fuel from waste by any process involving the use of heat other than making charcoal.

### PART B

### Nil

## CHAPTER 6:  OTHER INDUSTRIES

## Section 6.1 Paper and Pulp Manufacturing Processes

### PART A

(a)    The making of paper pulp by a chemical method if the person concerned has the capacity at the location in question to produce more than 25,000 tonnes of paper pulp in any 12 month period.

(b)    Any process associated with making paper pulp or pa per (including processes connected with the recycling or paper such as de-inking) if the process may result in the release into water of any substance described in Schedule 5.

In this paragraph "paper pulp" includes pulp made from wood, grass, straw and similar materials and references to the making of paper are to the making of any product using paper pulp.

## PART B

### Nil

### Section 6.2 Di-isocyanate Processes

## PART A

(a)    Any process for the manufacture of any di-isocyanate or a partly polymerised di-isocyanate.

(b)    Any manufacturing process involving the use of toluene di-isocyanate or partly polymerised toluene di-isocyanate if:

(i)    1 tonne or more of toluene di-isocyanate monomer is likely to be used in any 12 month period; and

(ii)    the process may result in a release into the air which contains toluene di-isocyanate.

(d)    The flame bonding of polyurethane foams or polyurethane elastomers, and the hot wire cutting of such substances where such cutting is related to any other Part A process.

## PART B

(a)    Any process not falling within any other description in this Schedule where the carrying on of the process by the person concerned at the location in question is likely to involve the use in any 12 month period of 5 tonnes or more of any di-isocyanate or of any partly polymerised di-isocyanate or, in aggregate, of both.

(b)  Any process not falling within any other description in this Schedule involving the use of toluene di-isocyanate or partly polymerised di-isocyanate if:

(i)  less than 1 tonne of toluene di-isocyanate monomer is likely to be used in any 12 month period; and

(ii)  the process may result in a release into the air which contains toluene di-isocyanate.

(c)  The hot wire cutting of polyurethane foams or polyurethane elastomers, except where this process is related to any other part A process.

### Section 6.3 Tar and Bitumen Processes

## PART A

Any process not falling within any other description in this Schedule involving:

(a)  the distillation of tar or bitumen in connection with any process of manufacture; or

(b)  the heating of tar or bitumen for the manufacture of electrodes or carbon-based refractory materials;

where the carrying on of the process by the person concerned at the location in question is likely to involve the use in any 12 month period of 5 tonnes or more of tar or of bitumen or, in aggregate, of both.

## PART B

Any process not falling within Part A of this Section or within any other description in this Schedule involving:

(a)  the heating, but not the distillation, of tar or bitumen in connection with any process of manufacture; or

(b)  (unless the process is related to and carried on as part of a process falling within Part A of Section 1.4 of this Schedule) the oxidation of bitumen by blowing air through it, where the carrying on of the process by the person concerned at the location in question is likely to in volve the use in any 12 month period of 5 tonnes or more of tar or bitumen or, in aggregate, of both.

In this Section the expressions "tar" and "bitumen" include pitch.

### Section 6.5 Coating Processes and Printing

## PART A

(a)  The application or removal of a coating material con taining one or more tributylin compounds or triphenyltin compounds, if carried out at a shipyard or boatyard where vessels of a length of 25 metres or more can be built or maintained or repaired.

(b)  The treatment of textiles if the process may result in the release into water of any substance described in Schedule 5.

## PART B

(a)  Any process (other than for the repainting or respraying of or of parts of aircraft or road or railway vehicles) for the application to a substrate of, or the drying or curing after such application of, printing ink or paint or any other coating material as, or in the course of, a manufacturing process where:

(i) the process may result in the release into the air of particulate matter or of any volatile organic compound; and

(ii) the carrying on of the process by the person concerned at the location in question is likely to in volve the use in any 12 month period of:

(aa) 20 tonnes or more applied in solid form of any printing ink, paint or other coating material; or

(bb) 20 tonnes or more of any metal coatings which are sprayed on in molten form; or (cc) 25 tonnes or more of organic solvents in respect of any cold set web offset printing process or any sheet fed offset litho printing process or, in respect of any other process, 5 tonnes or more of organic solvents.

(b)     Any process for the repainting or respraying of or of parts of roads vehicles if the process may result in the release into the air of particulate matter or of any volatile organic compound and the carrying on of the process by the person concerned at the location in question is likely to involve the use of 1 tonne or more of organic solvents in any 12 month period.

(c)     Any process for the repainting or respraying of or of parts of aircraft or railway vehicles if the process may result in the release into the air of particulate matter or of any volatile organic compound and the carrying on of the process by the person concerned at the loca tion in question is likely to involve the use in any 12 month period of:

(i) 20 tonnes or more applied in solid form of any paint or other coating material; or

(ii) 20 tonnes or more of any metal coatings which are sprayed on in molten form; or

(iii) 5 tonnes or more of organic solvents.

In this Section:

"aircraft" includes gliders and missiles;
"coating material" means paint, printing ink, varnish, lacquer, dye, any metal oxide coating, any adhesive coating, any elastomer coating, any metal or plastic coating and any other coating material; and the amount of organic solvents used in a process shall be calculated as:

(a)     the total input of organic solvents into the process, including both solvents contained in coating materials and solvents used for cleaning or other purposes; less

(b)    any organic solvents that are removed from the process for re-use or for recovery for re-use.

## Section 6.6 The Manufacture of Dyestuffs, Printing Ink and Coating Materials

### PART A

Any process for the manufacture of dyestuffs if the process involves the use of hexachlorobenzene.

### PART B

Any process:

(a)    for the manufacture or formulation of printing ink or any other coating material containing, or involving the use of, an organic solvent, where the carrying on of the process by the person concerned at the location in question is likely to involve the use of 100 tonnes or more of organic solvents in any 12 month period;

(b)    for the manufacture of any powder for use as a coating material where there is the capacity to produce 200 tonnes or more of such powder in any 12 month period.

In this Section, "coating material" has the same meaning as in Section 6.5, and the amount of organic solvents used in a process shall be calculated as:

(a)    the total input of organic solvents into the process, including both solvents contained in coating materials and solvents used for cleaning or other purposes; less

(b)    any organic solvents (not contained in coating materials) that are removed from the process for re-use or for recovery for re-use.

## Section 6.7 Timber Processes

### PART A

(a)    The curing or chemical treatment as part of a manu facturing process of timber or of products wholly or mainly made of wood if any substance described in Schedule 5 is used.

## PART B

The manufacture of products wholly or mainly of wood at any works if the process involves the sawing, drilling, sanding, shaping, turning, planing, curing or chemical treatment of wood ("relevant processes") and the throughput of the works in any 12 month period is likely to exceed:

(i)    10,000 cubic metres, in the case of works at which wood is sawed but at which wood is not subjected to any other relevant processes or is subjected only to relevant processes which are exempt processes; or

(ii)    1,000 cubic metres in any other case

For the purposes of this paragraph:

Relevant processes other than sawing are "exempt processes" where, if no sawing were carried on at the works, the activities carried on there would be treated as not falling within this Part of this Section by virtue of regulation 4(2);

"throughput" shall be calculated by reference to the amount of wood which is subjected to any of the relevant processes: but where, at the same works, wood is subject to two or more relevant processes, no account shall be taken of the second or any subsequent process;

"wood" includes any product consisting wholly or mainly of wood; and

"works" includes a sawmill or any other premises on which relevant processes are carried out on wood.

### Section 6.8 Processes involving Rubber

## PART A

## Nil

## PART B

(a)   The mixing, milling or blending of:
    (i)   natural rubber; or

    (ii)   synthetic organic elastomers,

if carbon black is used.

(b)   Any process which converts the product of a process falling within paragraph (a) into a finished product if related to a process falling within that paragraph.

## Section 6.9 The Treatment and Processing of Animal or Vegetable Matter

### PART A

Any of the following processes, unless falling within a description in another Section of the Schedule or an exempt process, namely, the processing in any way whatsoever, storing or drying by the application of heat of any dead animal (or part thereof) or any vegetable matter where the process may result in the release into water of a substance described in Schedule 5: but excluding any process for the treatment of effluent so as to permit its discharge into controlled waters or into a sewer unless the treatment process involves the drying of any material with a view to its use as an animal feedstuff.

### PART B

(a)   Any process mentioned in Part A, of this Section unless an exempt process:

    (i)   where the process has the characteristics described in regulation 4(1)(ii) above; but

    (ii)   may release into the air a substance described in Schedule 4 or any offensive smell noticeable outside the premises on which the process is carried on.

(b)   Breeding maggots in any case where 5 kg or more of animal or of vegetable matter or, in aggregate, of both are introduced into the process in any week.

In this Section:

"animal" includes a bird or a fish; and

"exempt process" means:

>   (i)   any process carried on on a farm or agricultural hold
>   ing other than the manufacture of goods for sale;
>
>   (ii)   the manufacture or preparation of food or drink for
>   human consumption but excluding:
>
>>   (a)   the extraction, distillation or purification of ani-
>>   mal or vegetable oil or fat otherwise than as a process
>>   incidental to the cooking of food for human consumption
>>   (b)   any process involving the use of green offal or
>>   the boiling of blood except the cooking of food (other
>>   than tripe) for human consumption;
>>
>>   (c)   the cooking of tripe for human consumption else
>>   where than on premises on which it is to be consumed;
>
>   (iii)   the fleshing, cleaning and drying of pelts of fur-bear
>   ing mammals;
>
>   (iv)   any process carried on in connection with the operation
>   of a knacker's yard, as defined in article 3(1) of the Animal
>   By-Products Order 1992(b);
>
>   (v)   any process for the manufacture of soap not falling
>   within a description in Part A of Section 4.2 of this Sched-
>   ule;
>
>   (vi)   the storage of vegetable matter otherwise than as part
>   of any prescribed process;
>
>   (vii)   the cleaning of shellfish shells;
>
>   (viii)   the manufacture of starch;
>
>   (ix)   the processing of animal or vegetable matter at premises
>   for feeding a recognised pack of hounds registered under ar
>   ticle 10 of the Animal By-products Order 1992;

(x)    the salting of hides or skins, unless related to any other prescribed process;

(xi)    any process for composting animal or vegetable matter or a combination of both, except where that process is carried on for the purposes of cultivating mushrooms;

(xii)    any process for cleaning, and any related process for drying or dressing, seeds, bulbs, corms or tubers;
(xiii)    the drying of grain or pulses;

(xiv)    any process for the production of cotton yarn from raw cotton or for the conversion of cotton yarn into cloth;

"food" includes drink, articles and substances of no nutritional value which are used for human consumption, and articles and substances used as ingredients in the preparation of food; and

"green offal" means the stomach and intestines of any animal, other than poultry or fish, and their contents.

## SCHEDULE 2

## RULES FOR THE INTERPRETATION OF SCHEDULE 1

1.    These rules apply for the interpretation of Schedule 1 subject to any specific provision to the contrary in that Schedule.

2.    (1)    Any description of a process includes any other process carried on at the same location by the same person as part of that process; but this rule does not apply in relation to any two or more processes described in different Sections of Schedule 1 which, accordingly, require distinct authorisation.

(2)    For the purposes of this paragraph, two or more processes which are described in Part A of different Sections of Chapter 4 of Schedule 1 shall be treated as if they were described in the same Section.

2.A    Notwithstanding the rule set out in paragraph 2, where a combustion process described in Part A of Section 1.3

of Schedule 1 is operated, or where one or more boilers, furnaces or other combustion appliances which are operated as part of a process so described are operated, as an inherent part of and primarily for the purpose of a process described in Part A of Section 1.1, Part A of Section 1.4, Part A of Section 6.3 or Part A of any Section of Chapter 4 of that Schedule ("the other process"), that combustion process or, as the case may be, the operation of those boilers, furnaces or appliances shall be treated as part of the other process and not as, or as part of, a separate combustion process.

**2.B**    Notwithstanding the rule set out in paragraph 2, where a process of reforming natural gas described in paragraph (a) of Part A of Section 1.1 of Schedule 1 is carried on as an inherent part of and primarily for the purpose of producing a feedstock for a process described in Part A of any Section of Chapter 4 of that Schedule ("the other process"), that reforming process shall be treated as part of the other process and not as a separate process.

**2.C**    Notwithstanding the rule set out in paragraph 2, where the same person carries on at the same location two or more Part B processes described in the provisions of Schedule 1 mentioned in any one of the following sub-paragraphs, those processes shall be treated as requiring authorisation as a single process falling within Part B of the Section first mentioned in the relevant sub-paragraph:

(a)    Section 2.1 and Section 2.2;

(b)    Section 3.1 and Section 3.4;

(c)    Section 3.6 and Section 3.4;

(d)    Section 6.5 and Section 6.6;

(e)    Section 6.7 and paragraph (e) of Part B of Section 1.3 insofar as it relates to any process for the burning of waste wood.

**3.**    Where a person carries on a process which includes two or more processes described in the same Section of Schedule 1 those processes shall be treated as requiring authorisation as a single process; and if the processes involved are described in both Part A and Part B of the same Section, they shall all be regarded as part of a Part A process and so subject to central control

**3A.**    Where a person carries on a process which includes two or more processes described in Part A of different Sections of Chapter 4 of Schedule 1, those processes shall be treated as a single process falling within a description determined in accordance with the rule set out in paragraph 4.

**3B.**  (1)  Where paragraph 3A does not apply, but:

(a)  two or more processes falling within descriptions in Part A of any Sections of Chapter 4 of Schedule 1 are carried on at the same location by the same person; and

(b)  the carrying on of both or all of those processes at that location by that person is not likely to produce more than 250 tonnes of relevant products in any 12 month period,

those processes shall be treated as a single process falling within the description in whichever relevant Section is first mentioned in the sequence set out in paragraph 4.

(2)  In sub-paragraph (1), "relevant products" means any products of the processes in question, other than:

(a)  solid, liquid or gaseous waste;

(b)  by-products, if the total value of all such by-products is insignificant in comparison to the total value of the output of the processes; or

(c)     any substance or material retained in or added to the final product formulation, not as an active ingredient, but as a diluent, stabiliser or preservative or for a similar purpose.

4.      Where a process falls within two or more descriptions in Schedule 1, that process shall be regarded as falling only within that description which fits it most aptly: but where two or more descriptions are equally apt and a process falls within descriptions in different Sections of Chapter 4, it shall be taken to fall within the description in whichever relevant Section is first mentioned in the sequence, 4.5; 4.2; 4.1; 4.4; 4.3; 4.6; 4.7; 4.8; 4.9.

5.      Notwithstanding the rules set out in paragraphs 2 and 3:

(a)     the processes described in Part B of Section 1.3 do not include the incidental storage, handling or shredding of tyres which are to be burned;

(b)     the process described in paragraph (b) of Part B of Section 2.2 does not include the incidental storage or handling of scrap which is to be heated other than its loading into a furnace;

(c)     the process described in paragraph (a) of Part B of Section 5.1 does not involve the incidental storage or handling of wastes and residues other than animal remains intended for burning in an incinerator used wholly or mainly for the incineration of such remains or residues from the burning of such remains in such an incinerator;

(d)     the process described in Part B of Section 6.5 does not include the cleaning of used storage drums prior to painting and their incidental handling in connection with such cleaning.

(e)     any description of a Part B process includes any related process which would fall within paragraph (c) of Part A of Section 1.3 if it were not so related.

6.          The unloading of coal, lignite, coke or any other coal product or iron ore or burnt pyrites for use in a prescribed process by a person other than the person carrying on the process at the place where the process is carried on shall be treated as part of the process.

7.    (1)    Where by reason of the use at different times of different fuels or different materials or the disposal at different times of different wastes, processes of different descriptions are carried out with the same plant or machinery and those processes include one or more Part A processes and one or more other processes, the other processes shall be regarded as within the descriptions of the Part A processes.

       (2)    Where by reason of such use or disposal as is mentioned in paragraph (1), processes of different descriptions are carried out with the same plant or machinery and those processes include one or more Part B processes and one or more other processes (but no Part A processes), all those processes shall be re garded as within the descriptions of the Part B processes.

       (3)    Where by reason of such use or disposal as is mentioned in sub-paragraph (1), processes of different descriptions are carried out with the same plant and machinery and those processes include Part B processes falling within different Sections of Schedule 1 (but no Part A processes), those processes shall, not withstanding the rule set out in paragraph 2, be treated as a single Part B process falling within the description in whichever of those Sections first appears in that Schedule.

7A.       The reference to "any other process" in paragraph 2 and the references to "other processes" in paragraph 7 do not include references to a process (other than one described in Schedule 1) of loading or unloading any ship or other vessel.

8.        Where in the course of, or as a process ancillary to, any prescribed process the person carrying on that process uses, treats or disposes of waste at the same location (whether as fuel or otherwise), the use, treatment or disposal of that waste shall, notwithstanding the rule set out in paragraph 2, be regarded as falling within the description of that process, whether the waste was produced by the person carrying on the process or acquired by him for such use, treatment or disposal.

9.        References in Schedule 1 and this Schedule to related processes are references to separate processes carried on by the same person at the same location.

10.        [Rule 10 omitted by SI 1994/1271].

11.        References to a process involving the release of a substance falling within a description in Schedule 4 or 5 hereto do not effect the application of paragraphs (1) and (2) of regulation 4.

## SCHEDULE 3

### (Date from which authorisation is required under Section 6 of the Act)

OMITTED

## SCHEDULE 4

### RELEASE INTO THE AIR: PRESCRIBED SUBSTANCES

Oxides of sulphur and other sulphur compounds
Oxides of nitrogen and other nitrogen compounds
Oxides of carbon
Organic compounds and partial oxidation products
Metals, metalloids and their compounds
Asbestos (suspended particulate matter and fibres), glass fibres and mineral fibres
Halogens and their compounds
Phosphorus and its compounds
Particulate matter

# SCHEDULE 5

## RELEASE INTO WATER: PRESCRIBED SUBSTANCES

| (1) | (2) |
| --- | --- |
| **Substance** | **Amount in excess of background quantity released in any 12 month period (Grammes)** |
| Mercury and its compounds | 200 (expressed as metal) |
| Cadmium and its compounds | 1000 (expressed as metal) |
| All isomers of hexachlorocyclohexane | 20 |
| All isomers of DDT | 5 |
| Pentachlorophenol and its compounds | 350 |
| Hexachlorobenzene | 5 |
| Hexachlorobutadiene | 20 |
| Aldrin | 2 |
| Dieldrin | 2 |
| Endrin | 1 |
| Polychlorinated Biphenyls | 1 |
| Dichlorvos | 0.2 |
| 1,2-Dichloroethane | 2000 |
| All isomers of trichlorobenzene | 75 |
| Atrazine | 350* |
| Simazine | 350* |
| Tributyltin compounds | 4 |
| Tiphenyltin compounds | 4 |
| Trifluralin | 20 |
| Fenitrothion | 2 |
| Azinphos-methyl | 2 |
| Malathion | 2 |
| Endosulfan | 0.5 |

* Where both Atrazine and Simazine are released, the figure in aggregate is 350 grammes.

# SCHEDULE 6

## RELEASE INTO LAND: PRESCRIBED SUBSTANCES

Organic solvents
Azides
Halogens and their covalent compounds
Metal carbonyls
Organo-metallic compounds
Oxidising agents
Polychlorinated dibenzofuran and any congener thereof
Polychlorinated dibenzo-p-dioxin and any congener thereof
Polyhalogenated biphenyls, terphenyls and naphthalenes
Phosphorus
Pesticides, that is to say, any chemical substance or preparation prepared or used for destroying any pest, including those used for protecting plants or wood or other plant products from harmful organisms; regulating the growth of plants; giving protection against harmful creatures; rendering such creatures harmless; controlling organisms with harmful or unwanted effects on water systems, buildings or other structures, or on manufactured products; or protecting animals against ectoparasites.

Alkali metals and their oxides and alkaline earth metals and their oxides.

# APPENDIX III

# CHIEF INSPECTOR'S GUIDANCE NOTES ARRANGED UNDER RELEVANT SECTION OF SCHEDULE 1 TO THE PRESCRIBED PROCESSES AND SUBSTANCES REGULATIONS

## FUEL PRODUCTION PROCESSES, COMBUSTION PROCESSES (INCLUDING POWER GENERATION) AND ASSOCIATED PROCESSES

| Section 1.1 | Gasification and Associated Processes |
|---|---|
| IPR 1/11 | Gasification of Solid and Liquid Feedstocks |
| IPR 1/12 | Refining of Natural Gas |
| IPR 1/13 | The Refining of Natural Gas at Liquefied Natural Gas Sites |
| IPR 1/14 | The Odourising of Natural Gas or Liquefied Petroleum Gas |

| Section 1.2 | Carbonisation and Associated Processes |
|---|---|
| IPR 1/9 | Coke Manufacture |
| IPR 1/10 | Smokeless Fuel, Activated Carbon and Carbon Black Manufacture |

| Section 1.3 | Combustion Processes |
|---|---|
| IPR 1/1 | Large Boilers and Furnaces 50MW(th) and Over |
| IPR 1/2 | Gas Turbines |
| IPR 1/3 | Compression Ignition Engines 50MW(th) and Over |
| IPR 1/4 | Waste and Recovered Oil Burners 3MW(th) and Over |

| | |
|---|---|
| IPR 1/5 | Combustion of Solid Fuel Manufactured from Municipal Waste in Appliances with a Net Rated Thermal Input of 3MW or More |
| IPR 1/6 | Combustion of Fuel Manufactured from or Comprised of Tyres, Tyre Rubber or Similar Rubber Waste in Appliances with a Net Rated Thermal Input of 3MW or More |
| IPR 1/7 | Combustion of Solid Fuel Manufactured from or Comprised of Poultry Litter in Appliances with a Net Rated Thermal Input of 3MW or More |
| IPR 1/8 | Combustion of Solid Fuel which is Manufactured from or is Comprised of Wood Waste or Straw in Appliances with a Net Rated Thermal Input of 3MW or More |
| IPR 1/15 | Crude Oil Refineries |
| IPR 1/17 | Reheat and Heat Treatment Furnaces 50MW(th) and Over |
| **Section 1.4** | **Petroleum Processes** |
| IPR 1/15 | Crude Oil Refineries |
| IPR 1/16 | On-shore Oil Production |
| **METAL PRODUCTION AND PROCESSING** | |
| **Section 2.1** | **Iron and Steel** |
| IPR 2/1 | Integrated Iron and Steel Works |
| IPR 2/2 | Ferrous Foundry Processes |
| IPR 2/3 | Processes for Electric Arc Steelmaking, Secondary Steelmaking and Special Alloy Production |

| Section 2.2 | Non-ferrous Metals |
|---|---|
| IPR 2/4 | Processes for the Production of Zinc and Zinc Alloys |
| IPR 2/5 | Processes for the Production of Lead and Lead Alloys |
| IPR 2/6 | Processes for the Production of Refractory Metals |
| IPR 2/7 | Processes for the Production, Melting and Re covery of Cadmium, Mercury and their Alloys |
| IPR 2/8 | Processes for the Production of Aluminium |
| IPR 2/9 | Processes for the Production of Copper and Copper Alloys |
| IPR 2/10 | Processes for the Production of Precious Metals and Platinum Group Metals |
| IPR 2/11 | The Extraction of Nickel by the Carbonyl Process and the Production of Cobalt and Nickel Alloys |
| IPR 2/12 | Tin and Bismuth Processes |
| **MINERAL INDUSTRIES** | |
| Section 3.1 | Cement and Lime Manufacture and Associated Processes |
| IPR 3/1 | Cement Manufacture and Associated Processes |
| IPR 3/2 | Lime Manufacture and Associated Processes |
| Section 3.2 | Processes Involving Asbestos |
| IPR 3/3 | Processes Involving Asbestos |

| | |
|---|---|
| **Section 3.3** | **Other Mineral Fibres** |
| IPR 3/4 | Glass Fibres and Non-Asbestos Mineral Fibres |
| **Section 3.4** | **Other Mineral Processes** |
| (Only APC Processes) | |
| **Section 3.5** | **Glass Manufacture and Production** |
| IPR 3/5 | Glass Frit and Enamel Frit |
| **Section 3.6** | **Ceramic Production** |
| IPR 3/6 | Ceramic Processes |
| **THE CHEMICAL INDUSTRY** | |
| **Section 4.1** | **Petrochemical Processes** |
| IPR 4/1 | Petrochemical Processes |
| IPR 4/6 | Production and Polymerisation of Organic Monomers |
| **Section 4.2** | **The Manufacture and Use of Organic Chemicals** |
| IPR 4/2 | Processes for the Production and Use of Amines, Nitriles, Isocyanates and Pyridines |
| IPR 4/3 | Processes for the Production or Use of Acetylene, Aldehydes etc. |
| IPR 4/4 | Processes for the Production or Use of Organic Sulphur Compounds, and Production, Use or Recovery of Carbon Disulphide |
| IPR 4/5 | Batch Manufacture of Organic Chemicals in Multipurpose Plant |
| IPR 4/6 | Production and Polymerisation of Organic Monomers |

| | |
|---|---|
| IPR 4/7 | Processes for the Manufacture of Organo-metallic Compounds |

**Section 4.3      Acid Processes**

| | |
|---|---|
| IPR 4/10 | Processes for the Manufacture, Use or Release of Oxides of Sulphur and the Manufacture, Recovery, Condensation or Distillation of Sulphuric Acid or Oleum |
| IPR 4/11 | Processes for the Manufacture or Recovery of Nitric Acid and Processes Involving the Manufacture or Release of Acid Forming Oxides of Nitrogen |
| IPR 4/12 | Processes for the Sulphonation or Nitration of Organic Chemicals |

**Section 4.4      Processes Involving Halogens**

| | |
|---|---|
| IPR 4/13 | Processes for the Manufacture of, or which Use or Release Halogens, Mixed Halogen Compounds or Oxohalocompounds |
| IPR 4/14 | Processes for the Manufacture of, or which Use or Release Hydrogen Halides or any of their Acids |
| IPR 4/15 | Processes for the Halogenation of Organic Chemicals |

**Section 4.5      Inorganic Chemical Processes**

| | |
|---|---|
| IPR 4/18 | Processes for the Manufacture of Ammonia |
| IPR 4/19 | Processes for the Use, Release or Recovery of Ammonia |
| IPR 4/20 | The Production of and the Use of, in any Process for the      Manufacture of a Chemical, Phosphorus and any Oxide, Hydride, or Halide of Phosphorus |
| IPR 4/21 | Processes Involving the Manufacture, Use or Release of Hydrogen Cyanide or Hydrogen Sulphide |

| | |
|---|---|
| IPR 4/22 | Processes Involving the Use or Release of Antimony, Arsenic, Beryllium, Gallium, Indium, Lead, Palladium, Selenium, Tellurium, Thallium, or their Compounds |
| IPR 4/23 | Processes Involving the Use or Release of Cadmium or any Compounds of Cadmium |
| IPR 4/24 | Processes Involving the Use or Release of Mercury or any Compounds of Mercury |
| IPR 4/25 | Processes for the Production of Compounds of Chromium, Magnesium, Manganese, Nickel and Zinc |

**Section 4.6    Chemical Fertiliser Production**

| | |
|---|---|
| IPR 4/16 | Processes for the Manufacture of Chemical Fertilisers or their Conversion into Granules |

**Section 4.7    Pesticide Production**

| | |
|---|---|
| IPR 4/8 | Pesticide Processes |

**Section 4.8    Pharmaceutical Production**

| | |
|---|---|
| IPR 4/9 | Pharmaceutical Processes |

**Section 4.9    The Storage of Chemicals in Bulk**

(Only APC Processes)

**WASTE DISPOSAL AND RECYCLING**

**Section 5.1    Incineration**

| | |
|---|---|
| IPR 5/1 | Merchant and In-house Chemical Waste Incineration |
| IPR 5/2 | Clinical Waste Incineration |
| IPR 5/3 | Municipal Waste Incineration |

| | |
|---|---|
| IPR 5/4 | Animal Carcase Incineration |
| IPR 5/5 | The Burning Out of Metal Containers |
| IPR 5/11 | Sewage Sludge Incineration |
| **Section 5.2** | **Recovery Processes** |
| IPR 5/7 | Cleaning and Regeneration of Carbon |
| IPR 5/8 | Recovery of Organic Solvents by Distillation |
| IPR 5/9 | Regeneration of Ion Exchange Resins |
| IPR 5/10 | Recovery of Oil by Distillation |
| **Section 5.3** | **The Production of Fuel from Waste** |
| IPR 5/6 | Making Solid Fuel from Waste |
| **OTHER INDUSTRIES** | |
| **Section 6.1** | **Paper and Pulp Manufacturing Processes** |
| IPR 6/8 | The Making of Paper Pulp by Chemical Methods |
| IPR 6/9 | Papermaking and Related Processes, including Mechanical Pulping, Recycled Fibre and De-Inking |
| **Section 6.2** | **Di-isocyanate Manufacture** |
| IPR 6/4 | Di-isocyanate Manufacture |
| IPR 6/5 | Toluene Di-isocyanate Use and Flame Bonding of Polyurethanes |
| **Section 6.3** | **Tar and Bitumen Processes** |
| IPR 6/2 | Tar and Bitumen Processes |

| | |
|---|---|
| **Section 6.5** | **Coating Processes and Printing** |
| IPR 6/1 | The Application or Removal of Tributyltin or Triphenyltin Coatings at Shipyards or Boatyards |
| IPR 6/6 | Textile Treatment Processes |
| **Section 6.6** | **The Manufacture of Dyestuffs, Printing Ink and Coating Materials** |
| IPR 6/6 | Textile Treatment Process |
| **Section 6.7** | **Timber Processes** |
| IPR 6/3 | Timber Preservation Processes |
| **Section 6.9** | **The Treatment and Processing of Animal or Vegetable Matter** |
| IPR 6/7 | Processing of Animal Hides and Skins |

# APPENDIX IV

# LOCATION OF HMIP OFFICES

## HEADQUARTERS

Romney House
43 Marsham Street
London    SW1P 3PY

Tel:  0171 276 8061
Fax:  0171 276 8605

## NORTH EAST

Stockdale House
1st Floor
8 Victoria Road
Headingley
Leeds    LS6 1PF

Tel:   0113 280 2514
Fax:  0113 274 0464

Don House
Pennine Centre
20-22 Hawley Street
Sheffield    S1 1HD

Tel:   0114 270 0459
Fax:  0114 276 2398

Swan House
Merchants Wharf
Westpoint Road
Thornaby, Stockton
Cleveland    TS17 6BP

Tel:   01642 633753
Fax:  01642 608659

## NORTH WEST

Mitre House
Church Street
Lancaster    LA1 1BG

Tel:   01524 382100
Fax:  01524 382642

PO Box 142
Warrington    WA4 1HJ

Tel:   01925 655211
Fax:  01925 655876

## SOUTH WEST

Highwood Pavilions *
Jupiter Road
Patchway
Bristol    BS12 5SN

Tel:   0117 931 9600
Fax:  0117 931 9650

## ANGLIAN

Howard House *
40-64 St John's Street
Bedford    MK42 0DL

Tel:   01234 272112
Fax:  01234 277046

Mill House
4th Floor
Brayford Side North
Lincoln    LN1 1YW

Tel:   01522 512666
Fax:  01522 546544

## SOUTHERN

Millennium House
Unit 2
Fleetwood Park
Barley Way
Fleet    GU13 8UT

Tel:   01252 776600
Fax:  01252 776611

3 East Grinstead House
London Road
East Grinstead    RH10 1RR

Tel:   01342 312016
Fax:  01342 311565

## MIDLANDS

Unit 15-17
Wrens Court
Lower Queen Street
Sutton Coldfield
West Midlands    B72 1RT

Tel:   0121 362 1000
Fax:  0121 362 1010

## WALES

Brunel House
11th Floor
2 Fitzalan Road
Cardiff    CF2 1TT

Tel:   01222 495558
Fax:  01222 499924

* HMIP's IPC Applications Units are based at the regional offices in Bristol and Bedford. Responsibilities for different counties are divided between these units as listed below.

**Bristol Office**: Avon, Cleveland, Cornwall, Derbyshire, Devon, Dorset, Durham, Gloucestershire, Hereford and Worcester, Leicestershire, North Humberside, Northumberland, Shropshire, Somerset, Staffordshire, Tyne and Wear, Warwickshire, Wiltshire, West Midlands, Wales, Yorkshire.

**Bedford Office**: Bedfordshire, Berkshire, Buckinghamshire, Cambridgeshire, Cheshire, Cumbria, East Sussex, Essex, Greater London, Greater Manchester, Hampshire, Hertfordshire, Isle of Wight, Kent, Lancashire, Lincolnshire, Merseyside, Norfolk, Northamptonshire, Nottinghamshire, Oxfordshire, South Humberside, Suffolk, Surrey, West Sussex.

# Table of Statutes

# Table of Statutory Instruments

The Waste Management Licensing Regulations 1994 (SI 1994 No. 1056)* *157*

* as amended

## Table of Cases

Tandridge District Council v. P & S Civil Engineering Limited and Others [1994] Env L R D16 (Div Ct) *45*

Saunders v. United Kingdom Independent Law Reports (30 September 1994) *122*

Gateshead Metropolitan Borough Council v. Secretary of State for the Environment and Northumbrian Water Group [1995] Env LR 37-51 (CA) *164-165*

R v. Chief Inspector (HMIP), ex parte Chapman *100*

## Table of EU Legislation

Council Directive on the Disposal of Waste Oils (75/439/EEC)* *184*

Council Directive on Waste (75/442/EEC)* *173, 184*

Council Directive on Pollution caused by Certain Dangerous Substances Discharged into the Aquatic Environment of the Community (76/464/EEC)* *15, 169, 179*

Council Directive on the Major Accident Hazards of Certain Industrial Activities (82/501/EEC)* *174*

Council Directive on the Combating of Air Pollution from Industrial Plants (84/360/EEC) *15, 51, 57, 169, 179*

Council Directive on the Assessment of the Effects of Certain Public and Private Projects on the Environment (85/337/EEC)* *174, 175*

Council Directive on the Limitation of Emissions of Certain Pollutants into the Air from Large Combustion Plants (88/609/EEC)* *15, 31, 55, 171, 180*

Council Directive on the Prevention of Air Pollution from New Municipal Waste Incineration Plants (89/369/EEC) *184*

Council Directive on the Reduction of Air Pollution from Existing Municipal Waste Incineration Plants (89/429/EEC) *184*

Council Directive on the Freedom of Access to Information on the Environment (90/313/EEC) *150-151, 153*

Council Directive on Hazardous Waste (91/689/EEC)* *184*

Council Regulation Allowing Voluntary Participation by Companies in the Industrial Sector in a Community Eco-Management Auditing Scheme (1836/93) *154*

Council Decision Establishing a List of Hazardous Waste Pursuant to Article 1(4) of Council Directive 91/689/EEC on Hazardous Waste (94/904/EEC) *184*

Proposal for a Council Directive on the Landfill of Waste (COM(91)102, as amended by COM(93)275) *169, 184*

Proposal for a Council Directive on Integrated Pollution Prevention and Control (COM(93)423, as amended by COM(95)88) *15, 26, 55, 145, 149, 153, 169-187*

* as amended

| Table of Abbreviations | |
|---|---|
| APC | Air Pollution Control |
| AWRA 1906 | The Alkali Etc. Works Regulation Act 1906 |
| BAT | Best Available Techniques |
| BATNEEC | Best Available Techniques Not Entailing Excessive Cost |
| BPM | Best Practicable Means |
| BPEO | Best Practicable Environmental Option |
| COPA 1974 | The Control of Pollution Act 1974 |
| CRI | Chemical Release Inventory |
| CIGNs | Chief Inspector's Guidance Notes |
| CAA 1993 | The Clean Air Act 1993 |
| EPA 1990 | The Environmental Protection Act 1990 |
| EU | European Union |
| EA 1996 | The Environment Act 1995 |
| EMAS | Eco Management and Auditing Scheme |
| HMIP | Her Majesty's Inspectorate of Pollution |
| HSWA 1974 | The Health and Safety at Work Etc. Act 1974 |
| HSE | Health and Safety Executive |
| IPC | Integrated Pollution Control |
| IPPC | Integrated Pollution Prevention and Control |

| NRA | National Rivers Authority |
|-----|---------------------------|
| OPRA | Operator and Pollution Risk Appraisal |
| PPG 23 | Planning Policy Guidance Note No. 23 |
| RCEP | Royal Commission on Environmental Pollution |

# Index

Scottish Environment Protection Agency *15, 39*
Secretary of States' powers
        Appeals to *99-109*
        Approval of remediation work *133*
        Directions to HMIP *54, 56, 57, 85, 87, 93, 94, 96, 111,*
*124, 125, 138, 139, 141, 160*
        National plans *31*
        Prescription of processes and substances *28, 30, 57*
        Ruling on planning/pollution control interface *164-165*
        Statutory consultee (for Wales) *86*
        Transfer of functions to Environment Agency *39-40*
        Transmission of applications for authorisation *89*
Sewerage undertakers *16, 81, 86-87, 156, 159*
Sewers (see water, discharges to)
Sites of Special Scientific Interest (SSSIs) *41, 81, 86, 157*
Special waste *22, 52, 111*
Statutory consultees *82, 85-87, 95, 97, 104-105, 107, 108, 155,*
*158, 159*
Statutory nuisance controls *40, 160-161*
Statutory objectives of IPC *56-57, 92-93, 95*
Subsidiarity principle *170*
Substantial changes (see variation of authorisation)
Sustainable development *40, 169*

Technical guidance notes (see guidance)
Tradeable permits *31*
Trade effluent (see water, discharges to)
Transfer of authorisations *109*
Treaty of Rome *169*
Triviality *44-45, 111*

Variation notices *87, 88, 95-96, 100*
Variation of authorisation *94-99*
        By HMIP (see variation notices)
        By operator *76, 87, 88, 96-99*
        Relevant changes *94, 97*
        Substantial changes *54-55, 64, 74, 76, 87, 94-95, 96-99,*
*112*

Waste disposal licensing *158*
Waste management licensing *157-158*
Waste regulation authorities *15, 35, 39, 156-158*